The Liberal Mind

Kenneth Minogue

THE
LIBERAL
MIND

Kenneth Minogue

LIBERTY FUND

Indianapolis

© 1963 Liberty Fund, Inc.
Preface to the Liberty Fund Edition, © 1999 Liberty Fund, Inc.

Frontispiece courtesy of the London School of Economics

C 10 9 8 7 6 5 4 3 2 1
P 10 9 8 7 6 5 4 3 2

Library of Congress Cataloging-in-Publication Data
Minogue, Kenneth R., 1930–
The liberal mind/Kenneth Minogue.
p.   cm.
Originally published: London: Methuen, 1963.
Includes bibliographical references and index.
ISBN 0-86597-307-5 (hardcover: alk. paper)
ISBN 0-86597-308-3 (pbk.: alk. paper)
1. Liberalism.   I. Title.
JC574.M56 2000
320.51—dc21   00-035409

LIBERTY FUND, INC.
8335 Allison Pointe Trail, Suite 300
Indianapolis, Indiana 46250-1684

CONTENTS

Contents

PREFACE TO THE
LIBERTY FUND EDITION

THE LIBERAL MIND, FOUR DECADES ON

T HE FRENCH THINKER Charles Péguy tells us that everything begins in mysticism and ends as politics. This was a way of describing the corruption of power, since by *mystique* he meant something idealistic which politics vulgarizes. Looking at the evolution of the liberal mind in the twentieth century, I am inclined to turn this idea on its head, but not to challenge its pessimism. Liberalism certainly began as a political doctrine seeking reform of entrenched traditions, but then commencing with T. H. Green and others in the late nineteenth century, a "new liberalism" began to advance its claim to moral superiority over other political doctrines. By the middle of the twentieth century, this liberal mind had become a network of thoughtful people beating their breasts over the purported iniquities of capitalism and Western imperialism. Their remorse was anything but personal, however. Rather, these liberals were thinking of themselves as the innocent part of a guilty whole. The prosperity of the West, they claimed to discover, rested upon the oppression of others.

As the liberal mind came to dominate Western culture, it turned out to be marvelously fertile in discovering more and more abstract classes of people constituted by their pain, people whom "we" had treated badly. These included not only the poor, but also indigenous peoples, women, victims of child abuse, gays, the disabled—indeed, potentially just about everybody except healthy heterosexual white males. The first point I should make, then, is that in criticizing the liberal mind, I am in no way implying that suffering is unreal, nor that it is not a problem. Understanding begins with considering

vii

the generation of the basic premise of the liberal mind: that suffering can be understood wholesale, as it were, as the fixed experience of abstract classes of people.

In 1963, when *The Liberal Mind* appeared, the young and the radical in the Western world were in a restive condition. The restiveness had two sides, one cynical, the other sentimental. The cynical side was irresistibly seductive. It was immediately conspicuous in the satire boom, in which hilarious parodists such as Tom Lehrer, Mort Sahl, and Lenny Bruce mocked censorship, respectability, prudery, the rule of old men, and the burdens laid upon us by the past. In Britain, the success of *Beyond the Fringe* had made Jonathan Miller and Dudley Moore famous figures, and the journal *Private Eye* was extending the range of political consciousness by turning gossip, preferably malicious, into an art form. A kind of Bohemian swagger was spreading as the rising numbers going on to universities conceived the notion that to think was to engage in an activity called "questioning" or "criticism." A new mood was rising everywhere in the volatile Western world. In the United States John F. Kennedy was president and Betty Friedan had set herself up as the spokeswoman of bored suburban housewives with college degrees. Many liberations had previously happened—among the flappers of the 1920s, for example, and in the moral relaxations of wartime in the 1940s—but they had led less to a propensity to enjoy the freedoms acquired than to a lust for acquiring more. In 1963, you might say, the Sixties were about to begin.

Such is the background for a mea culpa: I loved all this, not wisely but too well. And in my defense, it can be said that mockery and derision have their place in political wisdom. What I did not immediately realize was that a political program which consisted simply of thumbing one's nose at the pomposities of the Establishment would devastate what we may, as a shorthand, call culture and morality. This is a realization that seldom comes young, or indeed cheap. Bertrand Russell spent most of his life exploiting—and thereby destroying—the pleasures of debunking what was coming to be sneered at as "conventional wisdom." It was only late in life that he remarked that human beings need piety and, he might have added, authority and reverence. All three attitudes are, to put the matter at its lowest, important elements in the repertoire of a fully human life. All can be destroyed when derision becomes formularized and, to compound matters, is further mechanized by the media and the entertainment industry.

Sentimentality was cynicism's other side. Both attitudes dehumanize people by turning them into caricatures, but whereas the caricatures of the cynic generate hatred and contempt, the caricatures of the sentimentalist provoke tears. Both attributes are equally distant from the real world, and both are corruptly self-conscious. The cynic is proud of his acumen in not being taken in by the world, while the sentimentalist regards his tears as proof of a compassionate sensibility. Put the two attitudes together and you have melodrama: quite a distance from reality, indeed, but better perhaps than either attitude by itself. The politics of the liberal mind is a melodrama of oppressors and victims.

It is said that Buddhist monks must learn to meditate on a skull in order to absorb fully into their souls the illusory character of human hopes and fears. Liberals engage the right mood by contemplating the experiences of those they take to be oppressed, in what I have called "suffering situations." You might think this an admirable altruism amid the selfish indifference of the mass of mankind, and there is no doubt that it has often been sincere and that it could at times mitigate some real evils. But the crucial word here is "abstract." The emotions are elicited by an image, as in the craft of advertising. The people who cultivate these feelings are usually not those who actually devote their time and energies to helping the needy around them, but rather a class of person—liberal journalists, politicians, social workers, academics, charity bureaucrats, administrators, etc.—who focus on the global picture. For some, compassion is, one might say, "all talk," while the feelings of those in the burgeoning army of so-called "non-governmental organizations" are closely related to a career path. As a cynic might say, there's money in poverty.

The liberal mind turned the actual sufferings of the human race into the materials of cliché and stereotype, but that was the least of it. The "suffering situations" invoked by the literature played down the active character of the objects of their indignation and saw in them little but pain. Terms such as "aid" or "help" logically entail the idea that the helper is seconding some independent endeavor of the person being helped. Aid to the Third World was thus often a misnomer, since it commonly took no account of what its supposed beneficiaries were actually doing or wanting, and merely *provided* materials which might help in making these people more like us. This is the main reason why much of it has been not merely futile but actually self-defeating. Corrupt dictators in the early days of withdrawal from empire by Europeans demanded aid and loans "without strings" and they often got it—a process brilliantly analyzed by Peter Bauer in *Dissent on Development* (Cambridge, Mass.: Harvard University Press, 1976). Today, the successors of those generous souls who agitated for giving money to the Third World are agitating for the "forgiveness" of the resulting debts that now hang heavily around the necks of the peoples of those countries. This is a campaign which suggests one more possible definition of the liberal mind—as a boundless enthusiasm for spending other people's money. But the logical point comes back to the basic unreality of the liberal mind: namely, a refusal to think in terms of real human beings. Instead, the generic man of liberal thought is like a window dresser's dummy—merely a vehicle for provoking hatred or tears.

As the liberal mind has diffused itself through modern society, our understanding of real people engaged in real politics has weakened. Whole classes of people have been lost to an image of martyrdom. Yet the reality is that no societies in the history of the world have been as generous and compassionate, both to their own poor and to the unfortunate abroad, as those of the modern West. In order to sustain liberal sentiments, the poor had to be understood as merely fortune's playthings. Misfortune does indeed play a part in the complex thing we call "poverty." So, too, do the acts and omissions of the people themselves. In order to lock this partial account into place, poverty has had to undergo a variety of redefinitions. For one thing, it has been transmogrified into "relative deprivation," which assumes that happiness and well-being depend on having most of the things other people have. For another, it has been defined as living on half the average national income. This might be regarded as an a priori guarantee of the Christian contention that the poor are always with us, yet the object of liberal endeavor is to do something called "abolish" poverty, which on this definition would require something indeed miraculous: namely a complete equalization of incomes. This remarkable definition has the perverse effect of showing poverty on the increase in times of prosperity and on the decrease in times of depression when the average goes down. The sentiment of compassion for the poor has become an undercover device for equalizing social conditions, and millions have been taught that self-pity is a way of extracting wealth from other people.

Sentimentality and cynicism are not only logically similar distortions of reality, but they also feed off each other. The sentimental response to the death of Diana, Princess of Wales, in 1998 found its cynical counterpart in the denigration of the rest of the Windsor family. Again, it has been one of the virtues of liberalism to defend what we might call its ideological clients against prejudice and denigration. Unfortunately, this virtue has not been a concern with good manners which deplore causing hurt to others as individuals. It has, rather, been an ideological program for saving some from prejudice by setting up a new class of abstract hate objects, such as racists, sexists, homophobes, and the like. It is strange that liberals who deplore the punishment of criminals coming from the "victim classes" will advocate specially enhanced punishment for those who commit "hate crimes," forgetting that a crime is an act, not a thought. One problem is thus that every advance by the liberal mind tends to leave us back where we started.

Part of the explanation of this phenomenon is, no doubt, that the liberalism that has crystallized into the liberal mind exhibited a massive misunderstanding of the conditions of human happiness. It assumed that happiness depends on distributing benefits. The overprivileged have too many, the underprivileged too few. In the twentieth century, benefits have multiplied vastly for all, and no doubt removing them would cause great misery, but it is also true that this rise in prosperity has failed to deliver a proportional increase in happiness. Perhaps abundance resembles addiction: increase is needed just to sustain the level of pleasure.

The idea that happiness depends on benefits is among the more influential illusions of the liberal mind. It can generate the further illusion that a better life is in the gift of the civil power. In the late twentieth century, a vocabulary of rights facilitated a ceaseless raid by democracy on the economy. Political philosophers have always recognized that human beings are creatures of desire, and that life was the pursuit of happiness. The desires they theorized led to choices, but the choices carried responsibility along with them; they were not mere "choices." Philosophers took for granted a conception of the point of human life which the liberal mind may well be destroying. The pursuit of happiness is not, on this view, the search for a shower of benefits. Rather, it involves the recognition that life itself is a mixed blessing, that its point is not the satisfaction of desire so much as an adventure in testing wherein what we most fear is sinking below our best, that truth comes by blows, and that failure and disappointment are as necessary to us as exhilaration and success.

In the modern world, we know better how to control than how to endure. Technology increasingly takes the place of fortitude, and the liberal mind distances us from those from whom we have inherited our tamed pushbutton world. Worse yet, liberalism replaces history itself by a saga of oppression, a saga that makes its own sentimentalities even more mysterious than they are already. How could such a sensibility as the liberal mind have come out of such brutishness? Countries sometimes become disoriented and mistake their own real identity—as Italy did in the 1920s and 1930s when persuaded by Mussolini that it was a conquering imperialist power. National disorientation can be a fatal affliction, but with the liberal mind, we encounter something even more portentous: namely, a civilization busy cutting its links with the past and falling into a sentimental daydream.

To revisit *The Liberal Mind* turns out to be something that provokes me to pessimism. In those optimistic days of yore I had confidence in the broad commonsense of my world. I wrote that the ideas of the liberal mind could never really dominate the thinking of any society, because "such institutions as armed services, universities, churches and cultural academies . . . have nonetheless a powerful impulse to generate non-liberal ways of thought" (pp. 43–44). So far as the armed services are concerned, it has been said, not entirely facetiously, that we shall soon need wheelchair access to tanks. In universities, the fact that the academic life requires active ability in students has been strongly qualified by a concern for irrelevancies such as sex or race. It is no longer just a matter of being intelligent. And the churches have largely given up any decent dogma in favor of finding a new role counseling and communalizing their diminishing flocks. What future then for saints, soldiers, and scholars? They have all been boiled down into the soup of "generic man."

Fortunately, there is an awful lot of ruin in a nation, and the West is nothing if not a resilient civilization. So far we have been lucky, and our declinists wrong. I hope we shall be lucky again.

Kenneth Minogue
Indianapolis, October 1999

PREFACE

POLITICAL ISSUES ARE like discarded loves; once out of love with them we can hardly understand what made us so excited. Not so long ago, we were arguing over the issue of a planned economy or free enterprise, and liberals confronted socialists with identities fixed. But the life has gone out of such issues, and political parties find themselves nestling together around the same set of political principles. Some have greeted this development with joy. Some have accepted it as the "end of ideology." Others have responded with boredom.

The aim of this book is to analyze the long tradition of liberalism. It regards the current fluidity of political boundaries as due to the fact that an enlarged and somewhat refurbished liberalism has now succeeded the ideologies of the past. It maintains that this liberalism provides a moral and political consensus which unites virtually all of us, excepting only a few palpable eccentrics on the right and communists on the left. Liberalism is a vague term. One of its difficulties has been crisply stated by Professor Knight: "It used to signify individual liberty, and now means rather state paternalism." But this is not quite accurate. It now means both. It is an intellectual compromise so extensive that it includes most of the guiding beliefs of modern western opinion. It has even, in the form of Humanism, begun to work out an appropriate set of religious beliefs. *The Liberal Mind* is an attempt to state and analyze it.

I should like to acknowledge here the enormous debt I owe to my educators, both in Sydney and in London. My colleagues Hedley Bull and Bernard Crick both read parts of an early draft of the book and made many critical and helpful suggestions. I am sure no one will wish to saddle them with the prejudices expressed in it. Some of this material has earlier appeared in the *American Scholar* and the *Twentieth Century*. My greatest debt is to my wife, whose constant help, encouragement and criticism have profoundly affected both the style and the argument of the book.

London School of Economics and Political Science *September* 1962

K. R. Minogue

The Liberal Mind

CHAPTER ONE

Introduction

I. SUFFERING SITUATIONS

THE STORY OF LIBERALISM, as liberals tell it, is rather like the legend of St. George and the dragon. After many centuries of hopelesssness and superstition, St. George, in the guise of Rationality, appeared in the world somewhere about the sixteenth century. The first dragons upon whom he turned his lance were those of despotic kingship and religious intolerance. These battles won, he rested a time, until such questions as slavery, or prison conditions, or the state of the poor, began to command his attention. During the nineteenth century, his lance was never still, prodding this way and that against the inert scaliness of privilege, vested interest, or patrician insolence. But, unlike St. George, he did not know when to retire. The more he succeeded, the more he became bewitched with the thought of a world free of dragons, and the less capable he became of ever returning to private life. He *needed* his dragons. He could only live by fighting for causes— the people, the poor, the exploited, the colonially oppressed, the underprivileged and the underdeveloped. As an ageing warrior, he grew breathless in his pursuit of smaller and smaller dragons—for the big dragons were now harder to come by.

Liberalism is a political theory closely linked these days with such democratic machinery as checks and balances in government, an uncontrolled press, responsible opposition parties, and a population which does not live in fear of arbitrary arrest by the government. A liberal state is one where most actions of the government are taken with the consent of at least a majority of the population. A liberal political philosophy is a description of this kind of state, combined with the attempt to work out the general principles which can best rationalize it. A fair case could be made for John Locke as its founding father, even though the actual term "liberalism" was only imported from Spain early in the nineteenth century. In their early formulations, liberal philosophers built an edifice of doctrine upon the natural rights of man. Their successors, blooded by idealist criticism and Marxist social theory, admitted that the "individual" was an abstract and implausible hero for a political doctrine. Men, liberals came to agree, were largely moulded by the social environment in which they grew, and to talk of "natural rights" bordered on metaphysical dogmatism. Indeed, as time went on, they did not merely admit their error; they positively rushed to embrace the corrections which Marxists and Idealists forced upon them—for reasons which should become clear. Out of this intellectual foray emerged modern liberal doctrine, representing political life as the struggle by which men make their society rational, just, and capable of affording opportunities for everyone to develop his own potentialities.

Liberals sustain not only a political movement, and a political philosophy, but also a moral character. Liberals are tolerant. They dislike recourse to violent solutions. They deplore stern penal methods for keeping a population in order, and they disapprove strongly of the death penalty. They have rejected the patriarchal order which Europe has inherited, and they are critical of puritanism in sexual matters. They also deplore the heritage which has organized men into competing gangs called nation states which periodically rupture human brotherhood by savagely falling upon each other in warfare. Liberals are prepared to sacrifice much for a peaceful and co-operative world order, which can only come about by the exercise of great self-control and a talent for compromise. These are moral characteristics recommended to all men. Liberal social theory is frequently an attempt to discover the social arrangements which most encourage this kind of behavior.

We have still not exhausted the content of liberalism. For it is not only the habit of campaigning for reforms, nor a political doctrine and a moral character, it is also a special kind of hope. It not only recommends to us a political system of democratic liberty; it also tells us what will result from such a system. One result will be prosperity, for the energies of the people will be released from the varied oppressions of the past. Another result will be political stability, for when a responsible opposition is allowed, discontent is not forced underground, where it may turn nasty and foment rebellion. Parliamentary government based on popular consent will, by definition, produce what the people want, and people are happy who get what they want. Many of these fruits have indeed been plucked in the centers where liberalism originated— in the English-speaking world and parts of the continent of Europe. To others, however, liberalism seems to represent both the aspiration and the promise of these things—and one thing more: that industrialized prosperity and power which has now enchanted most of the world.

This side of liberalism can be seen in its keen sensitivity to time, the character which disposes it to serious use of such political terms as reactionary and progressive. Even sophisticated liberals, who are aware of the crippling arguments against historicism, are nonetheless prone to believe in progress, because they have domesticated Victorian optimism into a general belief that progress means getting more of what one wants. Thus for liberals "the present" means not only everything that is happening now; it also carries a further meaning that the present is only what *ought* to be happening now. On the basis of this ambiguity, traditional societies like the Yemen are described as "advancing headlong into the thirteenth century." Time, like everything else in this social world, is simultaneously a fact and an aspiration.

Liberalism depends upon a consciousness of being modern, and such a consciousness began to gain ground as the controversialists of the seventeenth century worked out their rejection of Scholasticism. They began to construct a picture of the middle ages which has held its ground ever since. At the center of this picture was a static and intricately structured society. Individual men held merely a subordinate place in this medieval scheme; each was but a minor participant in a drama of propitiation. The middle ages were seen as a time of mysteries. God's will and the nature of the cosmos were mysteries whose character men could only dimly penetrate; so too was skill, as preserved in ritual-ridden guilds. In a similar way, ruling was a mystery whose success depended upon the birth of its practitioners. Men of the seventeenth century thought of their medieval ancestors as victims of superstition and ignorance. For truth, in the middle ages, was thought to have been at the mercy of feudal intermediaries: the nobility, which mediated between Subjects and King, and the Church, which mediated between Man and God. Such inter-

3

mediaries were regarded as parasitic middlemen extracting a vast and illicit profit of privilege.

The decline of the middle ages had come about because men had thrown off their chains. A long series of social and political struggles had overthrown feudal privilege and led to the establishment of sovereign monarchs. Religious dissension had culminated in Protestantism, which rejected or at least diminished the power of spiritual intermediaries, just as it simultaneously rejected one of the more prominent mysteries—the clerical mystery of priestly power. Aristocratic birth, which had been the basis of so much social and political power, had also come under criticism. Intelligent men of the seventeenth century had the sense that a great structure had, like Humpty Dumpty, had a great fall. They experienced two dominant emotions. One was exhilaration as they glimpsed the new possibilities which lay before them; the other was fear and confusion, due to the apprehension that society itself might gradually be involved in the fall, and that all the benefits of social cohesion, of settled law and order, might be lost.

What is distinctive of modern liberalism, in which the visionary and hopeful element has in this century grown stronger, is a new understanding of politics. We may contrast this new understanding with politics in earlier centuries when rulers did little more than maintain a traditional structure. Occasionally some blinding vision, such as the recapture of Jerusalem from the infidel, might captivate rulers and even provoke widespread enthusiasm. But no ruler could commit his state to any long-term objective, and the possibilities of social mobilization, even for war, were severely limited by the independence and varied preoccupations of a most unservile nobility.

Politics was seen as something apart from particular visions, but constantly bombarded by them—pressed by those who envisaged a tidy hierarchical system, or by those who dreamed of a population contentedly obedient to the Church; for all important social activities generate visions of a society most suited to their demands. The general features of medieval society were determined by the relations between the activities of worshipping, fighting and food-producing; within a complex system, poets and craftsmen, shoemakers and beggars, could all find some room to work. As time went on, more and more people were drawn into the cities; here they produced goods and exchanged them. Some men became more interested in explaining the physical world, whilst others began thinking independently and heretically about religion and morals. A new range of activities grew up, and this led to different laws and social relations resulting from struggles between activities. One cannot pursue scientific enquiry if one is hampered by a dogmatic theological orthodoxy. One cannot follow a commercial life and grow rich if social life is constantly in ferment because of quarrels between teams of nobles. In this way, activities came into conflict with one another, and as some weakened and others grew stronger, so politics changed; and as politics changed, so also did people.

Liberalism, however, has come more and more to see politics simply as a technical activity like any other. We first decide what it is that we want, how we think our society ought to be organized, and then we seek the means to our end. The politician must be an expert skilled in political means, and his ends must be democratically supplied to him by popular demand. This view of politics introduces a novel inflexibility both into the actual work of politicians and into hopes we have of it. It means, for example, that all widespread problems turn into political problems, inviting a solution by state activity. It follows logically that people commit themselves to long-term planned objectives roughly as individuals commit themselves to new year resolutions. But while individuals may break their resolutions if they change their minds, peoples cannot be flexible in this way. Faced with backsliding, governments must coerce. They must control the climate of thought in which people live, and if necessary engage in large-scale and protracted repression in order to keep a populace consistent with what it seemed to want some time in the past.

These consequences of considering politics as a technical activity are, of course, mostly fanciful if we consider Britain and America, where liberalism is prevalent in all its fullness. But they are fanciful simply because the political traditions of those countries remain stronger than the prescriptions of liberal ideology, and because what the British and Americans declare politically that they want to do represents with some accuracy what they are in fact disposed to do. The consequences of a technical view of politics can only be actually seen in non-liberal countries with a totalitarian system of government. Here only force and propaganda can whip a reluctant or unenthusiastic populace into conforming to what is taken as the popular will.

A technique of politics, like any other technique, may be seen as the servant of desires. In the case of *modern* liberalism, these desires arise from the growth of a standardized sensibility, one which also provides the commonest justification of liberal policies. Liberalism develops from a sensibility which is dissatisfied with the world, not because the world is monotonous, nor because it lacks heroism or beauty, nor because all things are transient, nor for any other of the myriad reasons people find for despair, but because it contains suffering. The theme that progress in civilization is bound up with a growing distaste for suffering in all its forms is a common one in liberal histories of modern Europe, and we find it succinctly stated by Bentham: "The French have already discovered that the blackness of the skin is no reason why a human being should be abandoned without redress to the caprice of a tormentor." He is discussing—a theme dear to an English heart—the sufferings of animals, and hopes that the "day may come when the rest of the animal creation may acquire those rights which never could have been withholden from them but by the hand of tyranny . . . the question is not, Can they *reason?* nor, Can they *talk?* but, Can they *suffer?*"[1]

Compassion may seem an odd emotion to attribute to liberalism. It was not conspicuous in the operations of the Whig lords who largely engineered the 1688 revolution, nor in the early economists who contributed so much to liberal attitudes. Certainly also there was little that was compassionate about the *laissez-faire* system whose advocacy was long associated with liberalism. If for the moment we crudely consider liberalism as the amalgam of a sensibility and a technique, it is clear that the technique came first, and was first developed for other purposes. Yet even before the end of the nineteenth century, liberal politics began to involve the state in welfare programs, converting government from a threat to freedom into an agent of individual happiness. In the last half-century, this development has gone far to reunite liberals previously divided over whether political solutions should be individualist or collectivist. The sufferings of any class of individuals is for liberals a *political* problem, and politics has been taken as an activity not so much for maximizing happiness as for minimizing suffering.

Yet compassion and a disposition to relieve the sufferings of others can hardly serve to distinguish liberalism, for these emotions may be found among men and women everywhere. There is, however, an important difference between goodwill and compassion in the ordinary concrete situations of everyday life, and these emotions erected into a principle of politics. For lib-

---

1. Bentham, *An Introduction to the Principles of Morals and Legislation*, Ch. XVII.

eralism is goodwill turned doctrinaire; it is philanthropy organized to be efficient. If one seeks guarantees against suffering, then one is ill advised to look to the spontaneous sympathy of men and women. A mechanism must be created to relieve suffering impartially and comprehensively: a ministry to pay the unemployed, a medical service to care for the sick, and so on. Suffering is a subjective thing depending on individual susceptibility; politically, it can only be standardized. And it has been standardized, over a long period of time, by an intellectual device which interpreted events in terms of what we may perhaps call a suffering situation.

A good example, because morally unambiguous, of a suffering situation would be the condition of child labor in nineteenth-century Britain, or that of slaves in the United States. In the case of child labor, a powerful group of employers was ruthlessly using for its own purposes children who could neither understand what was happening to them nor do very much about it. Here was what everyone agrees was a wrong, and one which could only be changed by the disinterested goodwill and active intervention of a third party. Negro slaves were a similarly helpless group of people; though here the criterion of suffering was less conclusive. It was easy enough to produce vicious cases after the manner of Harriet Beecher Stowe. But it was also possible to produce cases where the slaves were kindly treated and seemed content. Here the criterion of suffering had to be supplemented by arguments about the immorality of being born and growing up dependent upon the arbitrary and unchecked will of a slave owner.

The point of suffering situations is that they convert politics into a crudely conceived moral battleground. On one side we find oppressors, and on the other, a class of victims. Once the emotional disposition to see politics in this way is established, then we find people groping around trying to make the evidence fit. Of course people living in slums are miserable about it and want (the only alternative possible in modern societies) a clean, well-equipped household! Of course colonialism is an evil; look at what King Leopold did to the Congolese; look at all the African parties claiming independence. Those who do not claim immediate independence must be puppets of the colonial rulers, for we all know that colonialism is an evil! And so on. Politics proceeds by stereotypes, and intellectually is a matter of hunting down the victims and the oppressors.

Suffering situations may be extended even further. In most cases they are produced by generalizing from particular instances of suffering to the proposition that the institution is evil and must be reformed. But this line of approach is elastic enough to allow the development of what we can only call the theory of implied suffering. This may be illustrated by the case of parents with delinquent children. Here the fact of delinquent behavior is taken to imply a history of suffering, and delinquency is explained in terms of unstable family circumstances and lack of love. Parents appear as potential oppressors. This use of the suffering situation makes a number of assumptions we need not discuss here, the most important being that virtues are natural (since man is spontaneously good) whilst vices are the result of some part of the environment.

Environmentalism is an essential element in all suffering situations. Victims are, by definition, the products of their environment, and sometimes put to the test the purity of our rational concern by exhibiting unsavory characteristics. This complicates liberal moral reactions, for the ideal suffering situation is one in which the victims can be painted as virtuous and preferably heroic—noble savages, innocent children, uncorrupted proletarians, freedom-loving strugglers for national independence. But where caricatures of this kind break down, as they often have in the past, then environmentalism supplies a means of conserving liberal sympathy for the victims. The delinquency, or even the downright nastiness, of victims is an index of the extent of their suffering.

Those who fit into the stereotype as oppressors, however, are not seen as the products of their environment, for that would incapacitate the indignation which partly fuels the impulse of reform. Parents, for example, are taken as free in a sense in which children are not. Yet a logically consistent environmentalism (as far as that is possible) would invalidate this distinction: either we are all the products of our environment or we are not. Similarly, the rich are free to mend their ways, whilst the poor are driven by the pressures of the society around them. This kind of illogicality is, of course, typical of ideologies and results from the attempt to explain and to persuade, all in the same breath.

So far, we have treated suffering situations as being composed of two elements, oppressors and victims. But there is also the third element, those whose interests are not directly involved. Many of these people might agree with a liberal diagnosis of a social evil, but remain passive on the ground that it was none of their business. Against this attitude, liberals were able to assert the duties of democratic participation. This could be, and was, broadened into a general indictment of neutrals on the ground that those who do not help to remedy an abuse must share the responsibility for it. Child labor was not merely the responsibility of avaricious employers; it was a blot upon the whole community, especially those who, knowing about it, did nothing to stop it. This third element, led by the liberals themselves, was taken as entirely free of environmental pressures, and upon it rested the unrelievedly moral burden of choosing to act or not.

Two other features of suffering situations are worth noting. One is that the liberal attitude is entirely secular. It will not countenance theological arguments that suffering in this life is a better passage to heaven than worldly prosperity. The entire game is played out on earth—a feature which is important, though seldom explicit, in discussions of capital punishment. It is partly this feature of liberalism which incurs theological disapproval. The Roman Catholic Church, for example, has regarded liberalism as a product of "That fatal and deplorable passion for innovation which was aroused in the sixteenth century, first threw the Christian religion into confusion, and then, by natural sequence, passed on to philosophy, and thence pervaded all ranks of society."[2] This Catholic position must, however, be seen as an attack primarily upon continental liberalism, a more dogmatic version of rationalism than is usually found in English-speaking countries. For English liberals, theology is simply a different territory, on which they do not really have to pronounce.

Secondly, liberals choose to rely upon peaceful persuasion rather than upon violent means for the reform of the abuses that cause suffering. Liberalism is impossible without the assumption that all men are reasonable and will, in the end, come to agree upon the best social arrangements. There are, of course, some liberals who become impatient and advocate unconstitutional remedies. To this extent, however, they move outside the tradition of liberalism towards more messianic faiths. In general, liberals disapprove of violence, on the ground that it creates more problems than it solves. But their disapproval of the violence of others varies according to who carries it out. All left-wing revolutions are carried out by groups who make out their own credentials as victims, and liberals are likely to dismiss such violence with gentle

2. *Immortale Dei* (1885).

regret. The violence of a Mao Tse-Tung is more acceptable than that of a Chiang Kai-Shek, that of a Castro more than that of a Batista. The violence of left-wing revolutionaries is excused partly by the past and partly by the future—the past because violence is taken as an inevitable response to past oppressions, the future because revolutionary violence is conducted under the banner of hope: hope for the end of suffering, and the initiation of a new order.

Interpreting their behavior through the stereotype of the suffering situation, liberals see themselves correctly enough as a middle party. They have often found themselves uncomfortably sandwiched between the derisively indifferent oppressors, deaf to appeals for reform, and on the other side men eager to solve the problem by means of violent revolution. If political situations did polarize in this way—as classically they did in Russia up to 1917—then liberals were reduced to political ineffectiveness. But in more sympathetic surroundings, their influence has been enormous, the greater no doubt because they were able to present the dilemma: either carry out reforms voluntarily, or be overthrown and lose the opportunity to do so.

Liberals were also a middle group according to their moral interpretation of political life; for while most of society appeared as a complex of groups each struggling for its own interests, liberals alone were a disinterested force for good, seeking merely to correct what all reasonable men recognized as evils.

Liberalism cannot be understood unless it is seen to possess an emotional unity of something like this kind. And on this question, it is extremely hard to maintain objectivity. For it is difficult to analyze the dogmatism and crudity of the stereotype, without simultaneously seeming to imply that liberals were misguided in attacking suffering wherever they thought they saw it. Clearly they were not. The same problem recurs if we attempt to discuss the motives which led liberalism in this direction. All human behavior stems from a complex of motives, and it is a simple propagandist device to justify or discredit a movement by pointing to "good" or "bad" motives. Yet we cannot understand either the political role of liberalism, or its consequences, unless we do consider its motives. For motives in men are movements in society. We cannot therefore simply accept the view that liberalism arises out of an uncomplicated passion for good.

All we need keep in mind at this point is the testimony of the foes of liberalism. Its conservative enemies often like to attribute its power to the fact that it organizes the sleeping envy ever latent in the bosom of the masses. From the Marxist side, the attack on motives takes the form of attributing liberalism to middle-class guilt. Marxists see liberalism as the desperate attempt of the more intelligent among the privileged classes to paper over the gaping contradictions of capitalism in order to preserve that system. Both agree, for example, in deploring the condition of the proletariat. But while Marxists argue for the complete overthrow of the system which has produced proletarian degradation, liberals can only offer steady doses of welfare, insufficient to cure the sickness but enough to discourage the proletariat from drastic remedies.

Neither of these views would affect the intellectual validity of liberal doctrine. But the Marxist view is interesting in explaining some features of the liberal attempt to involve everyone in the campaign for reforms, along with its insistence that all citizens share responsibility for any evil which exists in the community.

People at any given time are likely to adopt liberal opinions, or liberal habits of thought, for a great variety of reasons. But we may at least distinguish between those who, like the French intellectuals of the eighteenth century, believed that all men are born free and equal out of a consciousness that *they* were not being freely and equally treated; and those modern liberals who adhere to the same belief simply because they consider others are not being so treated. The former group is very likely to change the moment they attain power, and their analogues will be found today in the leaders of various colonial liberation movements. The latter group consists of those who consider themselves morally bound to become involved in any suffering situation of which they are aware. These people are the product of secure societies in which notions like decency and fair play are deeply rooted; and in them, liberalism takes on something like the heroic stature of a frequently defiant moral integrity.

It is precisely these people who are most clearly aware of what we may call the liberal paradox of freedom. It may be stated thus: victims are not free, and in a hierarchical social system those at the bottom of the hierarchy will be victimized by those above. The road to freedom therefore lies in the destruction of all hierarchies and the arrival of a society which is, in a certain sense, equal. Yet in the modern world, the steady erosion of traditional hierarchies has not produced States which are noticeably freer than those of the past. On the contrary, it has produced a "dehumanized mass" subject to manipulation and control by commercial and political interests. This paradox has provoked only a half-realization from liberals themselves. They have evaded it by the use of two propositions. The first is that we live in an era of transition—in other words, that we cannot yet judge what are the consequences of the disappearance of feudal and class hierarchies. And the other proposition is that the modern world has opened up a vast potential, whose use depends upon us. The modern world is not, of course, the sole product of liberal policies and attitudes; the growths of industrial techniques and modern nationalism are both at least as important as liberalism. But liberalism has, of all movements, opened its arms widest and most promiscuously to modern developments, going so far as to regard whatever it dislikes in the modern world as being atavistic or unmodern. The domestic dragons have now almost become superannuated; and if we have not yet freed the princess, we are held back by barriers of a different kind—ones which cannot be understood in terms of suffering situations.

II. IS LIBERALISM AN IDEOLOGY?

In discussing liberalism, we must at least initially assume that it is a single entity. This is not to suggest that there is a pure essence of liberalism, nor need it impel us towards the fruitless pastime of seeking to isolate "true liberalism" from a collection of counterparts.

In many respects, we may immediately say that liberalism is not a single entity. We are accustomed at present to referring to both the Liberal and the Labor Party in Britain, to the Democratic Party in the United States, and to similar parties elsewhere as being "liberal." Each of these parties has legislated policies which can also be described as welfarist and socialist, and each would repudiate large areas of what was understood as liberal doctrine in earlier centuries. In order to talk at all of liberalism as one movement we must relegate socialism to the technical area of means and devices, and include it within liberalism as part of a continuing debate about the utilitarian political objectives of improving society and maximizing the happiness of individuals. There are indeed some people for whom socialism is itself a dogma, held with a tenacity that no political event or moral experience could possibly shake; but this kind of feeling is not common among English and American socialists, most of whom would support a more experimental attitude to social reform. There was a time not so long ago when political debate was polarized in terms of "free enterprise or a planned economy," but this polarization has now virtually disappeared from the political scene; the main battlegrounds of propaganda now lie elsewhere.

Nevertheless, it is important to distinguish between "classical liberalism" and "modern liberalism" since the former was far more radically individualist than the latter. Part of the fascination exerted by the political philosophy of John Stuart Mill arises from the fact that the tension between these two positions is unusually explicit in his work. Since his time, classical liberalism, distinguished by its uncompromising hostility to governmental regulation, has steadily declined. But it remains wherever such questions as freedom of speech or bureaucratic iniquity arise, and also in a lingering suspicion of governments aroused whenever the State is called into new areas of regulations.

The unity which allows us to discuss liberalism over the last few centuries as a single and continuing entity is intellectual; we are confronted with a single tradition of thought, whose method is intermittently empirical, whose reality is found in the concept of the individual, and whose ethics are consistently utilitarian. This tradition of thought has its own vocabulary and can generate its own enthusiasm. In dealing with such a tradition of thought, we are dealing with an abstraction; there is no single person of whom it can be said: he was a liberal pure and simple, though perhaps John Stuart Mill would be a guide to what such a person might be like. Liberal intellectuals draw upon other traditions; and liberal politicians, simply because they are politicians, cannot be consistently liberal. This necessary inconsistency results from the fact that liberalism is an ideology, and all ideologies are incoherent.

The term "ideology" is vague and often abusive. Its main usefulness as an alternative to "doctrine" is that it usually incorporates a reference to a social location which is thought either to have originated or at least to sustain the set of ideas composing the doctrine. The description of a set of interrelated ideas as an ideology consequently carries the aggressive implication that the ideology is a rationalization of various political interests; for which reason there is a strong *prima facie* suggestion that many of the assertions of an ideology are false.

The conception was first extensively developed by Marx and Engels. "Every ideology," Engels wrote, "once it has arisen, develops in connection with the given concept-material, and develops this material further; otherwise it would not be an ideology, that is, occupation with thoughts as with independent entities, developing independently and subject only to their own laws."[3] Here the source of error in ideologies is seen in the original concept formation, when distinctions arose in accordance with the distorting activity of social conditions.

Of what intellectual use is the theory? The value it had for Marx and Engels is perfectly clear. It was a superb debunking tactic. A long and impressive line of moralists, philosophers, theologians, legal theorists, thinkers of all kinds, were summarily dragged from their pedestals and attached to the ideological *lanterne.* Their subtle arguments were revealed as elaborate rationalizations of the social forms in which they lived. The majestic pronouncements of abstract reason turned out to be the flowery rhetoric which concealed the demands of the exploiting class.

If liberalism is an ideology in this sense, then we ought to be able to supply it with a social location. What then is its social base? One common solution would be to nominate "the bourgeoisie" as the promoters of liberalism; but, though plausible, this answer presents many difficulties. It might mean either that all liberals are bourgeois, or that all bourgeois are liberals, or that liberalism consistently supports the interests of the bourgeois social class. Yet each of these propositions, however much one may try to reduce its vagueness, is false. One of the difficulties lies in trying to discover exactly who constitute the middle class. Rentiers? Share owners? People with inherited wealth? Those whose earnings are within a certain income range? Professional people? Many definitions are possible, but none will pull off the trick of demonstrating an empirical connection between liberalism and the bourgeoisie, for liberalism has, over the centuries, provoked both support and opposition from a great variety of kinds of people—aristocrats, country gentry, merchants, radicals, intellectuals, trade unionists and so on.

Given that there is no consistent relation between social class and the holding of liberal (or any other) doctrine, the sociological concept of ideology may be salvaged in one of two ways, neither very satisfactory. One way is a retreat into metaphysics: the bourgeoisie (or any other chosen social entity) *as such* has produced liberal doctrine to support its interests, but given the complex-

3. Marx and Engels, *Selected Works,* Vol. II, p. 360.

ities of real situations, this does not alone allow us to argue that if X is a bourgeois, then he is also a liberal. Alternatively, one may have recourse to the democratic technique of statistics, and attempt to discover the correlation between being a bourgeois and holding liberal opinions. Those who reject these alternatives may go scurrying off in the other direction and create a sociology of knowledge. Having firmly grasped the principle that all doctrines have social circumstances and must rub shoulders with economic conditions, they may conclude that all thinking is ideological. This refurbished pragmatism, resting upon the concept of ideology, manages only to destroy the usefulness of the concept.

So far as the social relations of doctrines are concerned, it is the notion of activity rather than that of class which may help to explain some of the features of an ideology. For the idea of social class never quite manages to purge itself of reliance upon the relationship of possession; and knowing how much individuals possess tells us very little about their feelings and opinions. A few commonsense maxims—the rich are conservative, the poor radical—are sometimes serviceable, but they have been known to bring disaster even where they are most at home—that is, in politics. Intellectually, they are next to valueless. What can, however, be said of an ideology such as liberalism is that it has grown up within a particular cultural tradition, and that it has borrowed characteristics from some of the activities carried on within that tradition. It has been especially associated with the development of science, and with the politics of reform which have grown in the Anglo-Saxon world. But as far as political and economic interests are concerned, we may think of liberalism as a train, likely to transpose its carriages at any moment, and stopping periodically to allow people to get on and get off.

An ideology may therefore be defined as a set of ideas whose primary coherence results not from their truth and consistency, as in science and philosophy, but from some external cause; most immediately, this external cause will be some mood, vision, or emotion. The psychological mark of ideological entrapment is the feeling of despair which accompanies the prospect of defeat in argument. Ideologies seek to avoid such painful experiences by framing their key utterances in a vague or tautological form, in order to make these propositions impregnable. The intellectual mark of ideology is the presence of dogma, beliefs which have been dug deep into the ground and surrounded by semantic barbed wire. In addition, ideologies incorporate some kind of general instructions about behavior—ideals or value-judgments, as they would commonly be called.

In this sense, liberalism is clearly an ideology, and one whose examination might be expected to be particularly useful. For at the present time most of us are, in some degree or other, liberal. It is only the very cynical, the unassailably religious, or the consistently nostalgic who have remained unaffected. Many liberal opinions therefore seem so obvious as to be unquestionable: liberalism invites argument and appears, with some justice, to be more open to reason than other ideologies. Nevertheless, its ideological roots are buried very deep, in an understanding of the world of whose bias we are hardly aware. Our concern, then, is to investigate liberalism as an ideology. It is neither to praise nor bury it, but to consider what might be called its intellectual and emotional dynamics.

CHAPTER TWO

The Anatomy of Liberalism

I. A PHILOSOPHY OF DESIRING

POLITICS MAY be explained in many ways, and an important philosophical problem arises from the attempt to relate them. If we wish to explain Hitlerism in Germany, do we look to the childhood and psychological character of those who participated in the movement? To the megalomania of Hitler, the inferiority feelings of Goebbels, the insecurities of the people who lost their savings in the German inflations of the twenties? Or do we consider the ideas of German nationalism, or the class relations obtaining in Germany at the time? To take another example, do we explain Napoleon as an ambitious army officer who seized his opportunities and developed a passion to rule all of Europe? Or do we see him as a product of French nationalism, a man who represents forces of which he was hardly aware?

In a generalized form, this problem is at the center of any kind of political philosophy. It has many formulations. Do men make society? Or does society make men? Aristotle asserted that the state was prior to the individual, while Bentham believed that society was an abstract fiction standing for nothing else but a collection of individuals. Both were engaged in the philosophical exercise of seeking the nature of political reality. But even if we cast aside terms which now have an unfashionably metaphysical ring, the same problem pursues us. For we cannot explain the character of John Smith without talking of the institutions of the society in which he lives; and we cannot explain that society without referring to the acts of a multitude of John Smiths.

In understanding the development of liberalism, we may change the formulation of the question. We may begin with the obvious-seeming statement that politics is about people standing in certain relationships with each other; it is about king, ministers and subjects, rulers and ruled. There are two general terms to this definition: the people and the relations. Now if we are philosophically minded, we will soon be tempted to reduce this duality to a single conception. We might, for example, come to believe that the relationships are more real or significant than the people. For people are born and die, but the relationships continue. States survive the death of their kings, and regiments retain a single identity despite incessant changes of personnel. Further, the office of kingship retains a certain identity in spite of the idiosyncrasies of individual kings. Men of very different individual characters will yet as kings act in very similar ways.

Now this view of political life seemed especially obvious in the middle ages, when neither the generic character of Man, nor the particular foibles of individual men seemed of much political importance beside the political roles which birth determined. Nothing seemed more clear than that politics was about the functions of officials and of classes of people: Emperor and Pope, lord and serf, bishop and priest. And each of these classes of people could be ranked in a fairly precise hierarchical order. Political reality lay in the relationships, not in the individuals related.

But this view of affairs is only plausible if a political order has existed long enough for political relationships to seem just as natural as the stars in their courses. Without the solid backing of habit, they will lose their claim on reality. For no one can see them, or measure them; they are as insubstantial as the air. All the world may be a stage, but it need not continue to perform the same play; everything depends upon the decisions of individual men and women. For it is only individual men and women, after all, who can think and feel, and enter into political relationships. If one is looking for a political certainty, what could be more certain than that?

Liberalism developed out of a shift of interest, away from medieval relationships towards the character of the men who were related. The idea of a natural and theologically supported hierarchy gradually came to be less impressive than the power of a sovereign ruler holding together a great number of individual men, the social and political ranking of whom was less significant than their character as subjects. Such a change of attention was not entirely comfortable; it brought with it fears of political breakdown. For when the social structure and the movements that men participate in are unstable, they become obsessively self-conscious about their individuality. They begin to lament because each man seems locked up, incommunicably, inside his own skull. Speech and emotion may no doubt pass between people, but all are subject to distortion and misunderstanding. Reality begins to seem no more than the cooperative fantasies of discrete individuals.

If politics depends upon the behavior of men, then political philosophy must begin, deductively or inductively, from an account of the nature of man. This account must exclude all social relationships as derivative, and it will therefore be cast in psychological terms. Early thinkers whom we may regard as contributing to liberalism created for the purposes of this kind of thinking a social laboratory in which the pure nature of man might be studied independently of social influence. They called this laboratory the state of nature. In this political vacuum, the conception of man could be studied in such a way as to explain past evils, and point the way towards the future construction of a more satisfactory political dwelling.

This conception of political man, together with the allied notions of humanity, human nature and the individual, is a rationalist idea with a strong attraction for the empirically minded. It arises from the notion that behind the acts and follies of living men there is a single essence or model capable of explaining all human variety. In terms of Aristotelian classification, Man is the genus of which Frenchman, Protestant, rogue, or serf might be the species. It is an abstract essence with general defining characteristics. For Aristotelians, rationality is the crucial defining characteristic. For theological purposes, man must include an immortal soul, and the consequences of original sin. And in order to give an individualist account of social life, the definition of Man must include the preceding activity of self-preservation.

What then was this conception of man upon which all political explanation rested? There was considerable agreement on the broad outline to be followed. Man was a creature capable of feeling, thought, and action, but the greatest of these was action. Sensibility was left to poets. It appears in the system primarily as passion, impelling men to action. And reason, in the English empirical tradition, is similarly instrumental. "For the thoughts are to the desires, as scouts, and spies, to range abroad, and find the way to the things de-sired."[1] There was widespread agreement that Natural Man was composed of reason and passion, and the political problem was how to construct a state out of these materials. Man is simply a desiring creature. Whenever he wills an act, then we must assume that the act is produced by the push of a motion or mo-tive in the mind; and these motives can only be described and classified ac-cording to the goals or ends at which they are directed.

This is a simple scheme and, if it explains anything, it will explain every-thing. Yet commonsense explanations of human behavior consist largely of opposed pairs of moral and psychological characteristics: goodness and bad-ness, pride and humility, pleasure and pain, and so on. Commonsense enters into the matter because, in this kind of philosophizing, the aim is to account for all complex experiences in terms of their simple components. And besides, political philosophers generally seek to persuade us into following some par-ticular course of action. Liberal thinkers, therefore, had good reason to build what we may call a preference duality into their systems right at the beginning. And they attempted to do so by distinguishing between desire and aversion. "Pleasure and pain and that which causes them, good and evil, are the hinges on which our passions turn."[2] We are thus presented with the view that the *di-rection* of our desires is just as fundamental as the desires themselves. This is extremely difficult to sustain, and Hobbes particularly shows signs of hesita-tion about it. "Of appetites and aversions, some are born with men; as appetite of food, appetite of excretion and exoneration, which may also and more properly be called aversions, from somewhat they feel in their bodies";[3] is ex-cretion, then, to be explained as a desire to rid the body of something, or an aversion to the presence of something in the body? Clearly, it does not matter; as indeed it never does matter whether we choose the "negative" or "positive" formulation of the matter. The distinction depends upon the attitude of the observer to the material; but this manner of intruding preferences into the formulation of questions has remained a standing liberal habit.

1. Hobbes, *Leviathan*, Ch. VIII.

2. Locke, *Essay concerning Human Understanding*, Bk. II, Ch. XX, Sec. 3.

3. Hobbes, *op. cit.*, Ch. VI. Hobbes was acutely conscious of the habit of mind which cre-ates preference dualities. Cf. "There be other names of government, in the histories, and books of policy; as *tyranny* and *oligarchy*, but they are not the names of other forms of gov-ernment, but of the same forms misliked." *Leviathan*, Ch. XIX.

Man is seen as a creature of desires. And each desire creates a policy, which has its own logical structure and characteristic vocabulary. A policy is determined by its *end,* whether we seek to attain or avoid that end. Reason, working with our past experience of the world, supplies us with *means* by which the end may be realized. The discovery of means may be a difficult matter, requiring judgment and the sifting of evidence; it therefore poses *problems* to which we seek the *solution.* But the solving of problems, indeed, the very posing of them, requires that we should have a selective understanding of the world, discarding what is irrelevant to our policies, and concentrating upon what is *basic, essential,* or *real.* Our understanding of the world in terms of desires creates *wholes* which we may understand by breaking them down into *parts* or *aspects.* All of the italicized words are commonly used in describing the formal structure of any policy; indeed outside the context of a policy they are meaningless. The point of liberal individualism was the belief that wherever a policy existed, there must also be the desire of an individual to sustain it. We might indeed talk of the policies of states and of many kinds of institutions; but these descriptions were regarded as metaphorical, always reducible to the desires of one or more individuals.

Each individual man is thus the proprietor of a great number of policies. The particular acts of one day may be described in policy terms; but these short-term policies may themselves fit into other larger structures. Thus it is from the logic of policies itself that we get the distinction between short-term particular policies and long-term guiding ones. I desire to eat and drink this day; and some of my acts will be means to this end. But this particular policy can also be viewed as a component in a larger general policy of preserving myself; alternatively, it might be seen as no more than a means towards doing things in which I am more interested—painting a picture, or conversing with friends. Each man will have his own particular and unique structure of desires—at any given moment. But this structure is likely to change over any period of time.

It is not the logic of policies but our experience of men and the world which tells us that policies come into conflict with each other. I am hungry and wish to eat; but at the same time, I am too lazy to go and cook something. Or I wish to win the hand of the prettiest girl in my village; but so, too, do most of my contemporaries. Sometimes our desires lead us to co-operate with other men; sometimes they lead to quarrels. The early liberal philosophers thought it their business to discover the general kinds of policy which tend to harmony, and those which tend to conflict. Men desire the support and co-operation of their fellows in order to preserve themselves and enjoy the comforts of civilization. Such desires dispose them to co-operate with each other, for one of the principles which arises from the logic of policies is that ends and means are linked by necessity; we cannot have the end without also willing the means. Therefore if we seek the co-operation of others, we must also renounce those desires which lead to conflict. The latter are both powerful and varied. They include the desire to be superior in dignity or possessions to other men, and the desire to enjoy things quickly and effortlessly. If all men are equal, and if they have no political organization to preserve order and facilitate co-operation, then no man can be secure and all men will distrust and fear each other. All philosophers agreed that order and harmony were essential to any kind of human life; and they therefore sought to establish some harmony-producing agency.

The problem as they saw it was both political and psychological. The political problem arose from conflicts of desire *between* men, and it was to be solved by the establishment of a harmonizing agency usually called the Sovereign. The psychological problem was intimately related to the political; it arose from conflict *within* men between the various desires they experienced. The outcome of these internal conflicts would clearly affect the work of the Sovereign. Psychological order would solve many political problems. The internal harmonizer was therefore just as important as the external one. It was called reason.

II. THE COMMANDS OF REASON

Reason is one of the totems of the liberal movement. Yet the difficulty is to discover just what reason is and stands for. Reason must, for example, be something other than the abstract statement of all those cases in which people behave "reasonably," for reasonableness is like commonsense, and depends very much upon time and circumstance. Nor can reason stand for that style of philosophizing from *a priori* ideas which is found in Plato and Descartes among many others; for Plato, at least on Professor Popper's view, is marked down as highly irrationalist. Nor again can it stand for the presiding faculty of that critical tradition of intellectual curiosity which has produced science, philosophy, universities and intellectual culture generally. For many people who are attacked as rejecting reason undoubtedly belong to this tradition, carry on arguments and seek to discover truths. In that sense, all who argue are using the power of reason, but they are not doing so to the satisfaction of liberals, because they do not all come to the conclusions which appear to constitute rationality.

The reason with which we are concerned is by definition an agency or power in the mind, one which asks and answers questions like: What do I want? By which kind of behavior can I attain the greatest number of my ends? How can I attain them most efficiently, that is, with least danger to other ends which I also pursue? Reason explores the logic of policies, and supplies knowledge derived from experience relevant to attaining the ends desired. Rational behavior excludes habitual action, impulsive action, or acts done in slavish imitation of ossified traditions. Rational individualism assumes that all behavior can be explained in terms of desiring policies, and that we are in a position to discover and rationalize the ends which arise in our striving.

But reason has a more ambitious role to play than this would suggest. For, as it occurs in liberal thinking, reason appears capable not only of exploring the logic of policies, but also of supplying us with guiding policies which act as criteria to discriminate between our ends. It tells us, for example, that the life-preservation policy which we all at times follow is to be preferred to the murderous policy arising out of hatred. And it yields us this judgment on the strictly limited ground that our satisfaction will not be maximized if we follow the murderous policy. Reason thus appears to solve the insoluble but much assaulted philosophical problem of discovering a source of prescriptions which cannot be exposed as simply a disguise for someone's special interest—the sort of enterprise Aristotle undertook in arguing for the existence of natural slavery, or Locke attempted in asserting that private property was a right of nature. The problem is strictly insoluble, and there is no consistent course of behavior which does not benefit, and harm, various groups of people. Therefore such bundles of prescriptions may be regarded as ideologies—outgrowths of some way of life in the society from which they spring. In so far as it is expected to produce general rules of behavior, reason can only produce an ideology. What is the ideology of reason?

Reason primarily commands respect for other individuals as selves whose desires are as legitimate as one's own. Therefore it places a very high value on individual life. The Hobbesian first law of nature, by which one should seek to maintain peace in so far as the behavior of others makes this sensible, is a good example of this concern for one's own life which makes the prescription rational. The seeking of peace, though it is for Hobbes the supreme command, is logically dependent upon the general rationale of the laws of nature—"*Do not that to another which thou wouldest not have done to thyself.*"[4] Here the communal bias of the Sermon on the Mount has been, by a negative formulation, transformed into a kind of right of privacy, a freedom from the invasion of others.

The formulation approved by Locke softens the rigors of the Hobbesian version. Locke quotes with approval "the judicious Hooker": ". . . how should I look to have any part of my desire herein satisfied, unless myself be careful to satisfy the like desire, which is undoubtedly in other men, being of one and the same nature. To have anything offered them repugnant to this desire must needs in all respects grieve them as much as me, so that, if I do harm, I must look to suffer, there being no reason that others should show greater measures of love to me than they have by me showed unto them."[5] Although Hooker (and Locke) regard this as creating "a natural duty" of bearing reciprocal affection to one's equals, what has been established is simply a rule fitting into a technology which we might call the Art of Liberal Living. In order to get X, it says, I must do (and as the rule develops, feel) X towards others. The rule is in fact psychological but it is claimed as ethical to the extent that it derives from a moral recognition of other individuals.

It is significant that in Locke's Treatise this argument comes in the context of a discussion of natural equality; for it is only where equality reigns that people will treat you as you treat them. The serf's deference to the squire carries no guarantee that the squire will respect the serf. Nor would so charming a rule of reciprocity have the same effects in a despotic society. Here, as so often in abstract rules of behavior, a society is being assumed to underwrite and fill up the gaps in the abstractions. Partly, Locke is relying on English society as he knows it—a society long composed of free men who will tend to have a civil respect for each other—and partly he is jumping ahead to the kind of society for which he solicits our support.

---

4. *Leviathan*, Ch. XV.
5. *Second Treatise on Civil Government*, Ch. II, Sec. 5.

Respect for human life is thus at the center of liberal thinking even in these early formulations. Partly this is a Christian respect for each individual as the possessor of a soul; but whereas in medieval times (and in modern non-liberal formulations) the care of the soul is of far greater importance than the actual life of the individual, the liberal view is more "naturalistic." The soul exists, but that is another department. "Life" is valuable because it is a condition of any desiring; death is the end of all desiring and therefore the worst possible evil. On liberal premises, it is irrational to die for one's country, unless perhaps the self-sacrifice is interpreted as an attempt to minimize the extinction of similarly desiring selves. Heroism can only be admitted through the rational back door. Of course, any nation involved in war does value heroism—but that is only to say that liberal countries, in a crisis, forsake parts of their liberalism. There are moods, and there are doctrines, in which human life is regarded as simply serving some higher cause—the nation, the race, the creed. There is the circumstance of martyrdom, in which the continuation of desiring is subordinated to spiritual integrity. But such circumstances have no place in the way of life which, liberalism asserts, is recommended to us by reason.

Reason is thus pacifist in its conclusions. War is only justifiable in the clear extremity where national survival is at stake, though limited or colonial wars—the kind which widely prevailed in the eighteenth century—may serve as outlets for surviving irrationalities. The nature of military life also changes; the element of honor, so prominent where defense is the task of an aristocratic class, is put aside as irrational, and military virtues are only admitted into the rational way of life in so far as they can be explained as serving individual desires. This is the strictest effect of liberal attitudes in the field of international relations. Projects for peace, the establishment of peaceful leagues of nations—these are by-products of liberal sentiment, and have seldom been taken seriously by governments when the national interest is imperilled.

The rational man is, further, a moderate man. Excess as a general principle can only lead to disaster—too much food to ill-health, too much drinking to cyrrhosis and a muddled head, too much . . . one need not go on. The rational mood is a mood of caution and moderation, one in which the traps of the short run and the safety of the long run are vividly before the mind. Habits of moderation arise from calculation and give rise to further calculation—and calculation is obviously the presiding activity of the man who, conscious of many and often conflicting or tangential desires, wishes to maximize his satisfaction. Part of the calculation is how to increase the goodwill of others, and this leads the rational man to appreciate gratitude, accommodation to others, and a refusal to grab at benefits from which others are excluded. Whatever acts arouse the resentment of others endanger the performer materially or morally.

The policy of the rational individualist bent on preserving himself carries the rational ethic to its limits. Pressed in this direction, rational behavior is determined by fear, and amounts to the search for a policy which can infallibly keep the individual alive. No such policy exists, and the man who consistently attempts to follow it is an impossibility. Yet this is at least the direction in which a self-consciously individualist ethic would lead. As with any abstract moral principle, it can lead to various kinds of behavior. In a despotic social system, being the apotheosis of self-preservation, it would lead to a kind of servility. Indeed, in most social situations, men are unequal—that is to say, there are always some who may be treated with indifference, and some whom it pays to placate. Subservience is the obvious policy which a rationally desiring man will follow in a society of unequals. He will wish to *please* those who can harm or benefit him. Again, this policy of self-preservation may lead to the self-righteousness of one who knows he has conscientiously refrained from giving offense to others. A similar moral mechanism at times operates in international relations, for liberal states, confronted with the aggressive demands of dictatorships, have a disposition to find moral ambiguities, and to retreat rather than fight, since fighting always presents moral problems requiring rationalization. The self-sacrifice involved in such personal and national situations is of an empty kind, implying no love for or involvement with the beneficiaries of the sacrifice.

Perhaps the core of rational behavior is the idea of flexibility or resilience. The rational man, seeing his world collapse, will never turn his face to the wall (like a tragic hero) if there is the slightest possibility of accommodation with the force which has overwhelmed him. Hobbes, the uncompromising rationalist, deals with this possibility without attempting to disguise it. Overwhelming force determines the will of the rational man whose primary aim is to stay alive; there is no place for honor or heroism. The importance of flexibility also comes out in the hostility of rational thinkers to the social institution of the oath. One cannot rationally make a promise binding beyond the point where one gains from it, a point which Spinoza, for example, brings out clearly. The oath, in fact, is a feudal institution which seemed to liberal thinkers an attempt to impose more on the human flux than it could bear.

Rational flexibility involves an overriding concern with what will happen in the future. Such a concern is far from universal. For clansmen, priests, aristocrats, scholars, the past is seen as the source of a heritage which must be conserved and continued. For the artist, the past is a spiritual backdrop which deepens our apprehension of the immediate. But for the rational man, the world begins anew each moment. As the patterns of present environment change, so the rational man must adjust himself to what happens and to what, on the basis of his knowledge, seems about to happen. The single criterion of this adjustment is the satisfaction of desires and the conservation of a desiring self. Thus for Hobbes it is a law of nature that "in revenges, men respect only the future good." It is also for this reason that oaths are a restriction upon the perfectly rational man. Contracts and promises—where clear benefits are exchanged—are the only instruments by which a rational man can consider himself bound.

This then is a general and simplified account of the ideology of reason as it developed during the seventeenth century. It is an indispensable component of liberalism. It has about it the look of a philosophy of old men—the kind of advice that gout-ridden fathers write off to their bibulous sons. It stands as a solemn check on everything that is spontaneous, wild, enthusiastic, uncaring, disinterested, honorable or heroic—in a word, irrational. Early in the eighteenth century these romantic phenomena were referred to derogatorily as "enthusiasm" and appropriately scorned. One of the early presentations of this kind of rational man, softened by a romantic situation, is Robinson Crusoe. And rational man soon turned into economic man, a suitably dismal hero for a dismal science. We begin to enter a world of functions in which religion is *for* consolation, art *for* decoration and distraction, and armies *for* defense.

We have already noted that abstract formulations of the rational way of life recommended as laws of nature rely upon the details and circumstances of a society that actually exists. Or, to put this in a manner to which Professor Oakeshott[6] has given currency, they are "abridgments" of that way of life. But rational man is a curious plant to have grown in any soil. Whence, then, does the rational ideology derive?

6. *Rationalism in Politics*, London, 1962.

One might perhaps derive rational ideology not from the behavior of any particular man or groups of men but from the moods of self-conscious deliberation which we all experience. Our actions are sometimes deliberate, sometimes impulsive. As a matter of experience, it appears that disaster follows more frequently from the impulsive than from the prudently calculated act. If prudent forethought cannot help us avoid disaster, then success is entirely beyond our control. Machiavelli, who also constructed a technology of success, admitted freely that his rules might be effective in perhaps half of the situations they dealt with; beyond the controllable half of men's life lay another half over which fortune presided. The laws of nature would thus arise out of linking together these moods and constructing an ideal man behaving in an ideal way. In other words, what they really recommend to us is less a collection of rules than a mood, an emotion, a way of looking at things.

The Marxist answer is clear and unequivocal. The seventeenth-century philosophers are said to be expressing the outlook and defending the privileges of the rising bourgeois class whose advance had already broken the shell of medieval society and was now in the process of constructing one more fitted to its demands. This in fact is a double answer. It might mean simply that the "laws of nature" express the demands for rights of a certain group of people; or it might mean that rational prescriptions describe the kinds of procedure and attitude needed for success in such "bourgeois" activities as buying and selling, bargaining, double-entry bookkeeping and entrepreneurship. The emphasis on calculation would be appropriate to these activities. The interest that, say, Locke has in proving a natural right to property would support an interpretation of rational behavior in terms of bourgeois class privileges. The Marxist explanation might at least explain why the rational ethic crystallized at one particular point of time.

The mention of Machiavelli highlights a point which might even give us a third answer to this question. Machiavelli created a technology appropriate to the requirements of politicians working within a certain system. Now inspection makes it clear that the laws of nature are useful to politicians in two ways. Firstly, in so far as the citizens behave in accordance with them, the work of the politician will be made easier. And secondly, they describe a highly politic manner of behavior. The rational preference for peace, and the reasons for it, is one which any ruler will be foolish to disregard. Rational man has the single fixed objective of his own preservation; how much more true this is of states, which can command the sacrifice of their parts in order that the whole should survive intact in its given structure. States equally are unwise to cultivate enemies and irritate other states. Nor should revenge ever be a motive of their behavior. And pacts and alliances are of small value in the field of international relations, where no state can possibly pursue any loyalty or obligation in a direction which leads to its own ruin.

Pursuing this line of thought, a logical similarity forces itself upon us. The state, on this rational view, is an artificial whole composed of a multitude of individuals; but then, so also is a human being. He is a whole—also perhaps artificial and certainly unstable—whose art of living must consist in the accommodation of a multitude of desires. Rational living is a prescription for the governance of desires. The form of government, furthermore, is democratic; each legitimate desire may have its day, but no more than its day. Impulsive desires are despots whom reason must control, and a democratic majority of desires can best facilitate the long-term interests of the whole.

This analysis, which deliberately echoes Plato's treatment of democracy, might seem no more than a facile exercise in analogy were it not for one thing. And that is, that throughout the modern history of political thought, the mind of man and the field of society have been the two competing structures in terms of which human behavior has been explained. Given a convincing and effective social structure, such as medieval Christendom or the modern nation state, philosophers will explain man in terms of social conceptions. A man has such and such a character because he is serf or aristocrat, French or German, proletarian or bourgeois. But if for any reason there is scepticism about or rejection of these larger structures, philosophers will turn to psychological explanation as being the only "real" understanding of human behavior. A man will be described as rational or passionate, enlightened or ill-instructed, sane or neurotic, mature or immature.

The seventeenth and eighteenth centuries were times when this retreat into psychology took place, and all social arrangements were regarded as utilitarian and artificial. The progress of knowledge, instead of being a co-operative social activity, was regarded as the work of the faculty of reason. The theories of tolerance which became current in the decades after the end of the Thirty Years' War all admitted the right of the civil power to coerce the outward behavior and control the speech and assembly of citizens; freedom was found in what then seemed the most secure bastion of all—inside the human skull.

Here alone was an area into which magistrates could not effectively pry, and attempts to do so, such as the Inquisition, were regarded as in the highest degree despotic and illiberal. All of this finds its most general formulation in the philosophical distinction between subject and object, between the inner and the external world.

Description of social activities, by a process of abstraction, as arrangements entered into between independent and rational minds was an altogether typical seventeenth-century manoeuvre. It has been widely observed.[7] Religious and moral authorities turned up as Protestant conceptions like conscience and the "inner light." Knowledge cultivated in such social institutions as the university became the search for the indubitable propositions of reason. There was indeed a good deal of intellectual co-operation in seventeenth-century philosophy and science; but it was a thin era for the universities. The best men worked on their own. It is as though, in fright, men had gathered all their possessions inside the house and pulled down the shutters. Then they peered out through the slats and turned to the epistemological question of how accurate a view of the countryside the slats gave them.

But, while many forms of authority gave way to some sort of psychological conception, nothing was found to replace government. There were of course reasons for political obedience, and in Spinoza we find the view that a society of rational men would have no need of a political authority: such men would co-operate naturally and without the need of coercion. But while other social institutions decayed, government, strong, centralizing, sovereign government, prospered. The seventeenth century is the century in which the theory of sovereignty, the heavy weight of political order holding together a mass of centrifugal individuals, came into its own. The political intricacies of the medieval order were stripped down to the dualism of Sovereign and subjects, of State and individuals. Philosophers reacted to this in different ways. Hobbes clearly gave most to the Sovereign power, a compound of king, judge, high priest, university rector, censor and father. For Hobbes, all authority is political and can have only one source. The people are never allowed any real existence; at the very moment they emerge from the state of nature, their common identity resides in the sovereign and thenceforth he acts in their name. Locke,

---

7. David Riesmann, to take a recent example, sees part of it as a movement of social character from tradition direction to inner direction. See *The Lonely Crowd*.

on the other hand, sets up the State and Society as distinct entities. And while everything he says about the State purports to show its utter dependence on the wishes of the people, the very fact that it is a separate and complicated institution is a recognition of the importance of authority—and the starting point for many liberal developments.

The laws of nature as prescriptions of reason may be seen not as the uniquely wise way of life which they purport to be, but as a set of abstractions arising out of the intellectual and social milieu of the seventeenth century. They provide not so much an ethic as a set of prudent manners, and were to be extensively developed as time went on. But they remain the core of liberal thinking.

III. THE USES OF CALCULATION

If man be taken as fundamentally a desiring animal, morality is likely to be a criterion which distinguishes those desires which may be pursued from those which may not. The moralist may direct his attention either to human actions or to the desires which are their presumed causes; but in each case, the problem of choice will be his primary concern. His main difficulty will be to reach any point which is recognizably moral at all. His first problem will be to free himself from the notion that all men are consistently selfish, for in one sense at least this is built into his assumptions. Every act which any human being performs must, on the assumption of rational individualism, be an act which he *desires* to perform. A number of thinkers have been tempted to conclude from this definition that every act is a selfish act. The martyr going to the stake, the warrior plunging into the thick of the fray, the patriarch defending his clan—all alike are deflated by this theoretical pinprick; the good and the shabby are both following their own desires. The only difference is that the desires of the one happen to be admired whilst those of the other are not.

Our rational moralist has little trouble here, or so it seems. This kind of cynical argument can be refuted by attending to the various meanings of the term "selfish"; by pointing out that "a selfish act" is not any human act, but one of the special and more or less definable kind; and by insisting that when someone says "I didn't want to do it" he is not just talking nonsense. The view that all men are selfish can be exhibited as a facile tautology. But it points to a risk that the individualist moral thinker has to face: the difficulty of using the distinction between "self" and "others."

The main problem involved in creating a morality out of the conception of man as a desiring animal is that of showing that anything distinctively moral can emerge from desires. If I want various of my desires satisfied, then no doubt I must live in society; and social life collapses unless most people follow the rules. But the restraints which a desiring individual accepts in society can only be shown as the *means* whereby he attains the satisfaction of *his* desires. Restraints are part of a technology of desire-satisfaction; there is nothing that can be called moral about them.

The usual solution to this problem is to present morality as the conquest of solipsism. Morality is the recognition of the autonomous existence of other selves. The individual is not a cunning desirer locked up inside a body from which there is no escape; he is (and must see himself as) part of a field of desires. He must be concerned in the outcome of all of the desires within the field that he inhabits. Such a concern will not come to him merely as the result of rational calculation; he must be equipped with special desires which make it natural to him. In the early stages of liberal morality, these desires were seen as arising from a feeling called sympathy. Sympathy is a composite conception. It is one of the concessions that individualism makes to ordinary experience, for we all experience sympathetic involvement in the affairs of others. But sympathy, as it functions in individualist moral philosophers, is generally used to do the same work as reason does; the main difference is that sympathy *moralizes* the acts it inspires, whereas reason remains no more than a technological calculation.[8] Reason, however, must still remain part of this kind of psychology, for otherwise sympathetic impulsive acts may lead to disastrous consequences. It is sympathy's crutch in the real world. Further, reason is still necessary if we are in pursuit of a science of morals. Charmed as people were by the idea of sympathy, few were prepared to rely upon it as the sole foundation of civil harmony. They preferred to show that social life was to the advantage of each individual. Reason appealed to each man's self-interest,

---

8. Some defenders of reason would not entirely agree. Thus Professor Ginsberg: "It seems to me that the essential point in the theory of progress remains true, namely, that in the course of historical development man is slowly rationalized and that man is moralized as he becomes more rational." *A Humanist View of Progress,* in Huxley (Ed.), *The Humanist Frame,* London, 1961, p. 113.

demonstrating the long-term advantages of political obedience; and sympathy was on call, as a parallel agency, to moralize and soften these calculations.

If, then, legitimate desiring is taken as the beginning of ethics, then duties (which are, after all, the practical core of this kind of moral philosophy) admit of a more precise determination. I legitimately desire to live healthily and without undue restraint, and sympathetically admit this as a legitimate desire of my neighbors. Very well, I must treat their legitimate desires as I would have them treat mine. I have a duty not to threaten the lives of others, not to impair their health, not to obstruct their use of their own property. Duties may be logically deduced from the policies constituting any given situation, and the dream of a determinate solution to moral problems becomes, as Locke thought, a possibility. If the entities with which we calculate are precise enough, then we indeed have a kind of mathematics, something which might attain the two objectives of a moral science: objectivity and precision.

A duty is in these terms a compulsory desire, rationally generated from the desires we naturally have. It has to be a desire, or the implication of a desire, because in terms of this kind of psychology, only a desire can provide a spring of action. Further, in so far as we are rational, we will want to do everything we ought to do, for our duties have been shown to be in our interest. And again, here, we have the familiar process of internalization: a duty no longer arises from participation in a social relationship: it is internal and psychological.

The seventeenth-century individualists laid the groundwork of later liberal ethical, political and social thinking. Hobbes had demonstrated, in the times of greatest doubt, that society was viable even on the most extreme hypothesis of individual selfishness, so long as the selfishness were rational. Yet consistent egocentricity seemed to later thinkers a less and less necessary assumption. One might not be able to rely upon human gregariousness and co-operativeness, but experience suggested that it existed. To the extent that it existed, political authority might diminish in importance. Indeed—dizziest dream of all—political authority might even, with the help of reason, be made to disappear.

This may be explained in terms of a road transport system. Everyone driving a car knows he must obey certain rules and drivers mostly do. Over long stretches of road, no policemen are needed to maintain the system; but at peak traffic times they are needed to direct drivers and enforce rules. If individuals behave selfishly and irrationally, policemen are needed every few yards if there is to be any system at all. "Traffic education" consists in inculcating into the minds of the driver exactly the principles which the policeman enforces. The driver must become his own policeman. A truly virtuous man will be one who follows the rule: If in doubt, give way to others. Also, he will always understand the long-term objectives of the system—keeping himself and his car undamaged and moving—and will resist those moments when he might be carried away by impulse into showing off, getting there a little quicker or flaunting the speed of his engine.

A community of perfectly rational drivers would have no need of policemen. There might be times when the drivers would have to have a rally and decide to agree on new rules to meet a new situation. But being rational men, and understanding that the good working of the system is far more important than any individual advantage, they would have no difficulty about this. A natural harmony would reign, for the best communal policy would also be the best one for each individual driver. But, one might say, men are not rational all the time. That, however, need not matter, for in this system, a driver might well get off the road, and in the freedom of privacy amuse himself just as he liked. So long as he never mixed up his private indulgences with his public conduct, all would work smoothly. What is more, it would work smoothly (and democratically) without any need of political authority.

We must abandon this metaphor, which although cherished by those who believe in a common good, obviously cannot be pressed too far. All that it might show is the possibility that political authority also might be internalized; and further, that the more "morally" people behave, the less need there is for strong authority. The dream of a post-political condition, a "withering away of the state," has a strong appeal for liberals, though few have dallied long with it. Government, said Paine, is a badge of our lost innocence, and at the moment before the French Revolution and Romanticism came to complicate matters, the idea of self-regulation was in many minds.

Most liberal thinkers cultivated some part of this idea. It is clearly an individualist picture of social life. Each individual is essentially complete, and social relations cannot change his nature; they can merely determine the satisfactions he may experience. But this picture of the human individual offers a number of divergent possibilities. These possibilities can be seen clearly in Locke. In the *Second Treatise,* individuals are found complete in nature; they can establish the laws of society by their reason, and the satisfaction of their desires by labor and enterprise. Society and the State are created by them in the full knowledge of what each institution will involve. No fundamental change can occur in such individuals, though they can be taught to reason better and to be less impulsive. In the *Essay*, however, we find a different picture of the individual. Beginning with a blank mind, he is determined by the impressions he receives. If the evils of society arise from the receipt of bad impressions, the road to a good society is opened up by way of education.

Liberalism arises from combining these two accounts of the individual. The contradiction is resolved by dividing society into two groups of people, the enlightened and the unenlightened. The enlightened are the rational who have understood the truth. Their goodness, their command of truth, comes from within; it is not dependent upon any social agency. These are the liberals themselves. And the liberals are the reformers. They seek to reform the unenlightened, both the very rich and the very poor—that non-liberal majority whose development has been stunted by the impact of false impressions, and the weight of superstition and prejudice.

The liberal concern with liberty is the fight for the conditions of a certain way of life. Certainly all manner of moral virtues are associated with liberty—happiness, strength, independence—but the place of liberty is often instrumental to something else. It is usually the means to an end arising out of the liberal conception of man as a desiring, a satisfaction-seeking animal. In Hobbes, there are three terms of this relationship. The *desire* in man moves towards the *object* (or away from the aversion) and on attaining it, experiences pleasure or *satisfaction*. In a reductionist atmosphere, it will not be long before the object is relegated to an inferior level of reality, and human behavior seen simply as the pursuit of satisfactions. This is a very significant step. It is also attractively obvious. Thus Pascal, who is some distance from the liberal tradition to say the least of it, writes: "All men, without exception, seek happiness. Whatever different *means* they employ, they all aim at this goal. What causes some men to go to the wars and others not, is this same desire, which is common to both though the *point of view* varies. The will never makes the least move that is not towards this goal. It is the motive of every man's every action, even of the man who contemplates suicide."[9] I have italicized here the

9. *Pensées*, 370.

35

terms which have replaced the "object of desire." "Means" is a significant substitution, for while an object of desire is a value determined by that desire, a means is simply a technical thing which can, in principle, be calculated on the basis of a science of satisfactions. Problems of choice may then be solved by a process of satisfaction-measurement. "Point of view" is significant because it demotes the object of desire to something which can be affected by persuasion or "education." We can be "educated" to desire socially approved objects; the only possible dispute will concern the amounts of satisfaction. Further, although this utilitarian statement is in fact totally uninformative about behavior (as are many such general statements in the rationalist tradition), it is not just nonsense. It performs two functions. One is to build up a formal system, of great plausibility, which accustoms us to explaining human social behavior in psychological terms—desire, pleasure, pain, satisfaction, interest, and tautological uses of good and evil. The other is to convince us that in spite of the variety of men and pursuits they engage in, nonetheless in reality everyone is doing the same thing—pursuing satisfaction. The fact that some men are sybarites, some mystics, some philanderers, some warriors, some grasping and mean, no longer stands in the way of achieving one society which fits them all. For the only ethical problem remaining is the efficiency with which men pursue their single objective. Modes of behavior which do not fit in with the society which the liberal is building may in principle be discarded or modified as being inefficient and anti-social.

The most ambitious attempt to work out this system in detail was Benthamism. Here the sovereign mastery of pleasure and pain is explicitly asserted, and what appealed greatly to many people was the irrelevance of the object of desire, a point epitomized by Bentham's assertion that "pushpin is as good as poetry." Whatever the mood in which Bentham made this assertion, it was clearly the crux of the matter. Here we are at the furthest remove from a notion of "the good life" as being constituted by a hierarchy of objects of desire. Ignoring human variety, Bentham went on to develop his calculus of pleasures and pains—the whole apparatus of proximity, fecundity, extent, etc. The association of goodness with pleasure results in the virtuous man being presented as a clever calculator of the consequences.

Bentham's science of happiness began as a doctrine of politics to be placed at the service of an intelligent Legislator—a figure who hovers around many eighteenth-century prescriptions for a reformed society. Governing then became first a process of creating equilibrium. If the Gadarene populace began rushing towards the cliff, the Legislator placed pains in their way to divert them. If people would not do the required things, pleasures were annexed thereto to encourage them. The required things? The only criterion of what was required lay in the greatest happiness principle. The Legislator was a man without interests of his own, an agent of total rationality. This attachment to benevolent despotism comes partly from the eighteenth-century atmosphere, and partly from Bentham's debt to Hobbes. It is well known that Bentham, disillusioned with sinister interests standing in the way of reform, was influenced by James Mill in a democratic direction. But this simply changed the location of the harmonizing agency. A democracy would carry out the task of ruling: men in their rational mood would protect themselves against their own inefficient impulses.

The step from rule by a rational Legislator to rule by a rational people was a move in the direction of self-government. But there, for the utilitarians, the matter rested. The dream of each individual completely ruling himself, without the need of coercive political authority, was left either to dreamers and enthusiasts, like Paine and Godwin, or to the arrival of new techniques. Yet the germ of the idea is to be found in the Benthamite notion that government, properly interpreted, is a branch of education. The matter may crudely be seen as quantitative. The more individuals can be educated to rule themselves, the less need there will be of political authority. The utilitarian state might not ever wither away; but it would move a long way towards vanishing point.

Benthamism is a typical liberal doctrine, in many ways it is typical of modern thinking.[10] For it has more than its share of that iconoclastic, reductionist spirit which has delighted modern moral philosophers. Like Hobbes, Bentham delighted in showing up the absurd pretensions of moral obligation—natural rights, or loyalty to divinely appointed kings. The sentiments and ideas which propped up throne and bishop, father and magistrate, were shown to have no grounding in reason, to be, in other words, mere imposture—"contrivances for avoiding the obligation of appealing to any external

---

10. As an example of a neo-Benthamite exercise in political reasoning one might take *In Defence of Public Order* by Richard Arens and Harold D. Lasswell, New York, 1961. Thus: "Any community can be viewed as a social process in which everyone is seeking, consciously or unconsciously, to maximize his value position."

standard, and for prevailing upon the reader to accept the author's sentiment or opinion as a reason for itself."[11] Bentham sweeps them all away, and substitutes his principle of utility on the ground that it is realistic and objective. Alas! The iconoclast has his own icons. Utility is no more than a masked puppet dancing on the string of such conventional notions as order, property and rectitude.

It is peculiarly empty. Happiness by definition is simply what everybody wants. But by distinguishing between what people want on impulse (in the short term) and what they might be likely to want in the future (long term), one can import a normative element into the idea. Happiness is what everyone wants in so far as he is rational: i.e. what he *ought* to want. Depending on how much force we allow to the assumption that each man is best judge of his own wants, we can justify any kind of system from the repressive to the liberal, or any combination of policies a government may choose.

The moral emptiness of Benthamism arises from its dependence on prevailing standards on the one hand, and the bogus "object of everyone's desire," happiness, on the other. The individual, faced with some sort of moral choice, must simply decide what he and others want; but the utility of competing courses of action does not *determine* our choice, for the simple reason that it *depends* on our choice. Yet all manner of fascinating possibilities arise. Why not establish sado-masochistic co-operatives, in which those whose greatest happiness lies in inflicting pain meet up with those whose greatest happiness consists in enduring it? Why not co-operation between those afflicted with blood lust and those about to commit suicide? Why should not the poor steal a loaf of bread from rich shopkeepers? Such disruptive possibilities could be plausibly defended in utilitarian terms. But it is clear that Bentham would not accept them. The reason is that his moral standards are those arising from the way of life found among the English middle classes. He would object that their moral ideas are unreflective and inefficient. But his attempt to put morals upon a rational basis clearly evades the issue, subsiding into prudential advice upon the irrationality of preferring the immediate impulse to the long term. Since the *certainty* of the future pleasure or pain is one of the dimensions of his calculus, it is possible that even this defense of the conventional is not open to him.

Again, while Benthamism purports to explain everyone's way of life, it ob-

---

11. *Principles of Morals and Legislation*, Ch. II, 14.

viously reflects some activities more plausibly than others. A cool and calcu-
lating merchant can easily be presented as a natural utilitarian. But it is unlikely that a general watching his cavalry charging the enemy lines will be mut-
tering to himself: "Nature has placed mankind under the governance of two
sovereign masters, *pain* and *pleasure*. . . ."[12] Nor is religion explicable in these
terms. The most doctrinaire of utilitarians is, of course, quite likely to argue
that religious martyrs, as they go to the stake, are nonetheless maximizing
their pleasure in a highly peculiar manner. But it is precisely the peculiar manner people have of behaving which is the point; variety is not a regrettable detail, it is exactly what has to be explained.

It is a simple matter to establish that the utilitarian principle that all men
seek happiness is tautological, that it reveals to us none of the mysteries of human behavior. But while utilitarianism fails in the grandiose project of un-
ravelling the nature of man, it yet covertly influences us to believe that human
behavior must be explained in terms of individual desires. The doctrine may
not win any intellectual battles; but its greatest achievement (and the great
achievement of all tautologies) is to determine the battlefield and accustom us
to the weapons and tactics which it recommends.

As a formulation of the principles of a liberal utopia, utilitarianism clearly
failed to live up to all that it claimed. Bentham did not place ethics on a scientific basis; all his vagueness and generality were constantly underwritten by
the society he and his followers lived in. Yet the importance of philosophies
does not reside exclusively in their truth. Bentham tried to make the commonplace idea of happiness the core of a liberal politics and ethics. In that he
failed. But he laid down the program. Subsequent generations have seen a
proliferation of notions which have been intended to play the same logical
role as happiness does in Bentham's system—welfare, maturity, harmony,
mental health, "society," to mention a few which we shall have to consider.
Benthamism reinforced our individualist habits of looking at human behavior; it impressed us with the idea that a virtuous man is a rational, sober, cal-
culating man distrustful of his impulses; and it enhanced our appreciation of
the view that the role of government is not simply to keep the peace, but also
to guide or "educate" the wants of individuals in such directions as will tend
to facilitate social peace and co-operation.

12. *Principles of Morals and Legislation,* Ch. I, 1.

IV. THE PURITAN CONTRIBUTION

One of the common paradoxes of regarding human beings as creatures of desire is that such a philosophy frequently issues in the most profound distrust of desire. This possible outcome was clear in the Epicureans, whose policy of maximum satisfaction of desires led them to advocate the minimization of desires. The fewer desires one permitted oneself, the less likely one was to be disappointed. All philosophies of desire include some element of this feeling. The Epicureans were a group without any great hopes of the world; they did not look forward to controlling it. But in the modern world, the advance of scientific knowledge and technical control has kept alive the possibility of manipulation in any field. It has not encouraged the prudential abandonment of hope.

Again, if man is regarded as a creature of desire, then his desires may be seen as primarily "good" or primarily "bad." "Good" and "bad" in this case are used to describe social consequences. One extreme possibility was the Hobbesian state of nature; the other extreme was the anarchist utopia where government was unnecessary because human beings spontaneously respected each other's interests. Most conservative views, with their emphasis on coercion, restraint and tradition, leaned towards Hobbes, and hoped for little from government. Most radical and natural right thinkers leaned in the anarchist direction, and somewhere around the center of this possible spectrum we find the eighteenth-century writers who had placed sympathy, an emotional faculty which did the socializing work usually attributed to reason, at the center of their system. Few followed Mandeville into a theory of the pre-established harmony of selfishness. Now clearly, the less "faith" we have in the good nature of human beings, the more we will be inclined to distrust desire profoundly. Not merely will we be impressed by the disastrous fruits of impulsive desiring—the hangover that follows the drunken evening, the enraged husband in pursuit of the adulterer—but our whole outlook will be colored by a deep pessimism about the possibilities of social life. This will be especially true if (as was the case with the Puritans) Heaven is our destination.

The Puritans added a further reason for distrusting desire. Wedded to a distinction between the elect and the damned, they became acutely aware of any sign which might indicate the states of election and damnation. A character of flabby self-indulgence, an absorption in the pleasures of the flesh, quickly came for the Puritans to be one sign of a damned soul. An important strand of thinking among the English Puritans was that success in worldly endeavors indicated God's favor to His Elect. Further, those who denied their indulgent desires, particularly laziness, and the spending of money on idle distractions, were generally the most successful. Assuming, as some have done, that the commercial life has affluent ease for its end, and thrift and hard work for its means, then the Puritans averted their eyes from the end and made a religion out of the means. They regarded the moral life as a ceaseless conscious struggle between worldly pursuits on the one hand and holy restraint on the other.

Such an account of Puritanism is selective and therefore a caricature. It is not what was most important in Puritanism, nor is it in any sense at all the "real significance" of the movement. But it isolates those characteristics of Puritanism—in particular the Puritan love for austerity—which contributed to the development of liberalism. For in this Puritan climate, the doctrine of needs grew up with great plausibility.

The doctrine of needs is probably the most obvious form of social explanation, and it has always been prominent in social contract philosophies. A need is an imperative form of desire. "I desire bread" imposes no serious demand on anyone. "I need bread" does impose such a demand. We may be justified in denying children, for example, what they desire, but we are not justified in denying them what they need. A need, therefore, is a legitimate or morally sanctioned demand. Now the conservative use of the propaganda of need is to argue that any detail of social organization exists because there is a human need for it; and, at its crudest, this argument is simply proved by the fact of existence. Whatever is, is right. Social inequality exists; therefore it must have satisfied some deep human need. In more sophisticated forms, this argument can become: people have grown up within a given social system and developed needs, satisfaction of which would be denied to them by revolutionary social change.

It is, however, the liberal use of need propaganda which is significant for us here, and which we will have to examine in more detail in a later section. The Puritan distrust of desire made the pursuit of any objects of desire a morally ambiguous operation. Needs, on the other hand, were morally sanctioned: by definition it was legitimate to satisfy needs—just so long as we do not extend the conception of need too far. A more or less frugal life can be seen as the legitimate satisfaction of the need for food or shelter. On the other hand, the aristocratic way of life, involving the development of a fashionable style of luxurious living, the wasteful consumption of food and services, is impossible to defend in these terms. Aristocratic life seemed from this point of view to be merely the wilful indulgence of desires.

The aristocratic and Puritan ways of life are thus in direct conflict. They can exist together in the same society so long as there is reasonable political stability; but the conflict is always there. When tension arises, it will bloom forth into a direct moral attack upon luxury. Those who lived luxuriously could be attacked in moral terms as selfishly indulgent; and this attack was sharpened by the contrasts of poverty. Doctrines of equality were quick to spring to men's thoughts. And since the whole tenor of seventeenth-century and subsequent thought was to emphasize man as man, in his original and natural equality of endowment, defense of social inequality became logically a secondary matter. It had to be seen as something socially imposed upon the "real" equality of human beings.

Seventeenth-century individualism based society on human needs. A defense of society therefore had to show that government uniquely satisfied some human needs. Some were clearly more important than others. The need to eat, drink, procreate, be sheltered and save one's immortal soul, were at the top of the needs hierarchy. They were necessities, or "basic needs." As time went on, a whole comedy of emphasis grew up around the term "need" so that people would talk about "absolute needs" or "basic essentials," even though the word "need" says it all. This urgency of emphasis constituted a liberal battering-ram against defense of any inequality which depended on birth. The one general lesson which liberals, and eventually liberal governments, accepted from this encounter was that wealth and privilege were insecure in a society in which many people suffered privation in their "needs."

The Puritans were, of course, a curious and in many ways an isolated group. Though hostile to the aristocracy, whose levity and indulgence they despised, they could not afford to press the attack too far. One reason was that their own way of life, the gentility of manners, the rejection of the uncouth, was largely based upon a caricature of aristocratic manners. What for aristocrats had been manners became morals for their selective Puritan imitators. Cleanliness came to be next to Godliness. The second reason was that the Puritans were a middle group, and an all-out political assault upon the aristocracy might involve them too closely with the lower classes who were sometimes ready to grasp them in the unwelcome embrace of alliance. To be a Puritan was to cut oneself off from the lower classes, but not to enter the upper classes. The Puritans could get very rich and live very respectable lives, but until well into the nineteenth century most of the important avenues of social priority in England remained closed to them. Caught in a situation in which inertia was intolerable and revolution hazardous, they evolved and elaborated the usages of the most characteristic of all liberal ideas: reform.

The English social structure, then as now dominated by an alliance of traditional and commercial interests, was thus under attack in several powerful ways. The utilitarian idea of happiness was admittedly so vague as to be capable of defense of any system; but this logical point did not prevent its being taken up by many whose ideas strayed in a democratic direction. And one of the advantages of utilitarian theory was that it would operate as the servant of expectations. Once large numbers of people developed a powerful discontent with the existing system, then the principle of utility put no barriers in the way of change. A second line of attack on the English social system came from the ordinary agrarian and industrial discontent which arose from economic changes—and manifested itself in unsettling riots, hayrick burning and machine smashing. This provided a background against which those who governed might be impelled to make either stubborn resistance or steady concessions. The prevalence of reformist theory was conducive to making concessions. And further, the Puritan notion of needs was generating a new idea which in the long run was capable of carrying on from "happiness"; namely, the idea of welfare.

The advantage of welfare over happiness is simply that it is more precisely calculable. Bentham had tried with the felicific calculus to make utility into a science of reform, but no one was ever very much impressed with this part of his achievement. But welfare could be broken down into a hierarchy of human needs. Here was a criterion of social reform: a society in which the needs of some remained unsatisfied whilst others idled in the lap of luxury was a society which failed the primary test of "social adequacy."

As we have observed before, liberal ideas have never monopolized, and almost certainly will never monopolize, the thinking of any given society. The main reason for this is that such institutions as armed services, universities, churches and cultural academies, while they can be run on liberal lines and according to liberal slogans, have nonetheless a powerful impulse to generate non-liberal ways of thought. But around the turn of the nineteenth century, liberal reformers ran into a less inevitable barrier to their aspirations—and one which ironically was an illegitimate offspring of liberal thought itself. This barrier to reform was the belief in the natural idleness of mankind. It was well-entrenched in respectable circles and was crudely implied by the rational explanation of human behavior: for unless men had some good *reason* to get to work they would remain idle. What better reason was there than starvation and the fear of unemployment? The conditions which struck the more compassionate among the liberals as the scandal of the age, seemed to many other people the motive force upon which the whole engine of civilization was run. Privation, as Dr. Johnson remarked of hanging, cleared the head wonderfully. It encouraged the worker to see—what a full stomach might dispose him to miss—the real identity of interests between the rich and the poor.

The advance of reform therefore depended partly upon the slow and steady recession of this idea into the background. Many considerations contributed to its weakening. The compassionate moral feelings encouraged by liberalism grew stronger; perhaps their most important location was in the minds of the younger sons of the middle class who, eager to indict their fathers and display their own independence, often turned to liberal and radical ideas. A proportion was never re-absorbed into conservative ways. The general circulation of ideas of progress, and especially moral progress, was at times a good vehicle for social philanthropy. And, of course, it was an era of expansion which could afford to spread its benefits widely; as time went on the economic benefits of such a spread also became clearer.

Welfare, then, was seen in terms of need. As such, it is a bare and abstract criterion, but then, it was being applied in a society with definite social standards. The need for shelter might be said to achieve satisfaction in a cave or a hovel; yet dismal as were most of the lower-class houses built in the nineteenth century, they incorporated, for example, a division into different rooms, the precondition of privacy. Human beings were no longer expected to live in one room (though overcrowding might, of course, fill each of the rooms with many individuals). Again, the need for food might be thought to be satisfied by the bowl of rice or piece of bread which can keep body and soul together under oriental conditions; but it was not. Existing standards, though not part of the actual philosophy of the movement, played a vital part in its development.

The absence of welfare came to be seen as a social problem. This might arise from the conviction that it is unfair and immoral for some to starve while others gorge themselves. This formulation appeals to people with the direct voice of compassion. There are, however, other arguments calculated to appeal to the most hardheaded. Poverty, it might be said, supplies in all our cities the ignitable material of revolutions. For so long as you allow it to exist, you will not be safe from the inflammatory incident or from the agitator. Therefore the course of safety lies in steadily removing the poverty. This general argument remains a staple of liberal thinking. In its up-to-date version, it asserts that unless the poor of the world are helped to industrialize they will turn to communism.

The argument can be, and has been, refined further. Society has always included criminals, prostitutes, delinquents, sadists, neurotics, etc.—various classes of undesirable and often unco-operative people. Whether they are regarded as social problems or not is largely a matter of taste. Prostitutes may be licensed, criminals punished in traditional ways, neurotics ignored. In modern liberalism, they are all, for various reasons, social problems. In one sense, they might be described as resisters or objectors to happiness. More generally, in utilitarian terms, they are following irrational modes of behavior, and are thus inefficient producers of happiness for themselves and others.

Fairly early in the evolution of the idea of liberalism, poverty came to be seen as the major evil, and the source of most other evils. It was the poor girl who turned to prostitution; it was the poor who cracked safes and burgled houses; it was the poor who were stubborn and irrational. Eliminate poverty, the doctrine continued, and you eliminate also these other unpleasant pimples on the otherwise smooth face of society. What began as a movement of social philanthropy made by the rich in voluntary organizations came in time to merge with socialist ideas. If the job were too big for private enterprise, then clearly the state must take over; an institutionalized Robin Hood, taxing the rich and giving to the poor. Socialism in England has been predominantly of this nature—seldom seriously concerned with the working class as having a character of its own; only with that class as being *bourgeois manqués.*

By now, of course, everyone is very well aware that it is not poverty, or at least not poverty alone, which causes crime, delinquency, prostitution and war. This has not, however, in any way affected the general theory. For the theory states simply that social problems arise because the needs of the human being have not been satisfied. Therefore, the modern liberal goes on, it is naïve to believe, as some did in the past, that the provision of adequate food and shelter would solve all our problems. Man, we must remember, does not live by bread alone. He is an emotional creature who needs to be loved, to feel that he belongs to something. Out of this strand of thinking comes a wide assortment of modern liberal shibboleths. Such propositions as that society is really the criminal, and that it is really the parents who are to blame for the sins of the children primarily depend on it. Modern psychology has grown up in this environment, and much of it has now become a technology which teaches how to discover and then satisfy more and more subtle and refined needs.

V. THE STRUCTURE OF GENERIC MAN

The liberal conception of man has all the beauties of a child's meccano set; from the basic device of man as a desiring creature, any kind of human being, from a Leonardo da Vinci to a Lizzie Borden, can be constructed. The generic account of natural man presents him as a creature of detachable parts, and there is no obvious limit to the number of parts which can be evolved.

For a desire, being a vague and ambiguous conception, permits of endless modifications. The movement from the desired to the desirable launches an ethics of improvement in terms of which any moral term can be reinterpreted. A need is a legitimate desire to whose satisfaction there can be no justifiable moral or political barriers. A duty is an act (or omission) which recognizes the desires of others, and in so doing also serves to promote the long-term interests of the bearer of the duty. A right describes an individual's status in the desiring policies of other individuals. My right to life indicates a relation between me and the policies of those I encounter, especially those entrusted with the conduct of affairs of State.

This technique of analysis can move on to deal with all social phenomena, for each particular man can be analyzed down into generic man *plus* certain environmental peculiarities. In some moral description for example we encounter different moral types—criminals, saints, traitors, heroes. In liberal terms, each of these types is essentially the same, and they are distinguished by the values they pursue. A saint or a criminal thus ceases to be a particular kind of man; he is everyman, but with different values.

Or it might seem that if we are to give any reasonable account of a duke or a banker, we must describe an aristocracy or a particular economic structure. But, even here, the movement away from individualism can be averted by the use of another detachable component called privilege. A privilege is a standing satisfaction of desires and is peculiar only in its limited availability. From this individualist conception we may go on to reconstruct a sociology of a peculiar kind, by distinguishing between privileged or underprivileged social classes. And—a further boon—the difference between a duke and a dustman can now be measured off on a scale of privileges.

The liberal ideology casts a long intellectual shadow on each of us, and the shadow is natural or generic man, a creature composed of a great number of components. But if one strips off from this abstract figure each of the components—the privileges, desires, rights, duties, values, moods, impulses, and the rest of the paraphernalia which liberalism has borrowed from commonsense individualism and made into a system, what then remains? Only the creature who was born free and yet everywhere is in chains, a faceless and characterless abstraction, a set of dangling desires with nothing to dangle from. The individual self, stripped of its components, is nothing. But how is it related to these components? There appear to be two primary relationships—that of possession and that of pursuit. The individual self is an empty function of proprietorship and pursuit; and it can only be made plausible by a species of intellectual trickery.

The trick consists of switching the components to whichever side of the relationship happens to be convenient. Such an abstract figure could not possibly choose between different objects of desire; therefore the values are for the moment seen as constituting the man and thus determining the objects of desire; or vice versa. At any given point in a liberal argument, an individual will be taken as constituted by a set of values; or by rights and duties, or by privileges, or by a given set of objects of desire, but at the same time some of these detachable parts will be under examination at the other side of the relationship. Without this device, the whole structure would collapse. An individual is thus seen as a *self* in relationship with a number of concepts which intermittently constitute that self. And if one strips away all of these detachable parts, one is left with a phantom, a chooser without a criterion of choice, a desirer incapable of movement.

Yet this residual self has at least one important role to play, for it is the bearer of human identity. The rights, duties, desires, needs, values, etc. of any man will all change in the course of a lifetime; they are possessions or pursuits which may be acquired, or shed like snakeskin. But John Smith remains John Smith so long as he lives, and his identity is both legal and psychological. Legal identity, and to a lesser extent moral identity, is something demanded of people and quite consciously learned. For we must presuppose an identity between the man who committed the murder and the man who is hanged or imprisoned for it; and children must be taught that if they break a window or set the house on fire, these acts continue to be related to them as persons, and cannot be attributed to an essentially different being who existed only for the doing of the act. Identity is a matter of consequences.

Still human identity is not entirely an artificial creation produced by social demand. It also has a claim to be an entirely natural product of memory and self-consciousness. But this self-consciousness is a highly unstable thing. In range it can shrink to almost nothing, so that (as in liberal theory) it dissociates itself from any psychological experiences of which it is aware. Equally it can expand—in moments of pantheistic ecstasy—to include everything, so that one "feels" for the tree which is being chopped down, or the flower which is plucked. More usually, it can absorb—or be absorbed by—state, church, locality or any other social institution or grouping. But most important of all, it does not have a continuous existence. There are many moments when we are not self-conscious at all. Locke defines a person as "a thinking intelligent being, that has reason and reflection, and can consider itself as itself, the same thinking thing, in different times and places; which it does only by that *consciousness* which is inseparable from thinking, and, as it seems to me, essential to it." And he adds, as evidence, "it being impossible for any one to perceive without *perceiving* that he does perceive." This might perhaps be an unusual definition of perception; but the way Locke continues makes it clear that he takes it for a true psychological statement: "When we see, hear, smell, taste, feel, meditate, or will anything, we know that we do so. Thus it is always as to our present sensations and perceptions: and by this every one is to himself that which he calls *self*."[13] This view is false, for we often perceive things without being aware of it, the most obvious evidence being that we sometimes become aware of earlier perceptions at a later date. And the mistake is the result of

13. Locke, *op. cit.*, Bk. II, Ch. XXVII, Sec. 9.

Locke's view of consciousness as a relation (that of possession) between a mind and ideas.

As far as human identity over time is concerned, we may concentrate either upon what is continuous or what is discontinuous. The liberal conception of man, accepting the operative assumptions of law, morality, and everyday life, takes the view that the continuous self constitutes identity and remains the same over time, irrespective of the moods, values, impulses, thoughts, or any other of the various detachable parts. But, as we have argued, this residual self is a mysterious phantom. It is the same over long periods of time, but this sameness is purchased at the heavy cost of vapidity. It is logically objectionable because it inserts a rationalist essence (of a peculiarly empty sort) into the center of a series of situations and thus prevents us from taking the discontinuities of human character seriously. It is primarily in art, and also in some special social circumstances ("I don't feel I know you any more") that the phenomena of discontinuity are seriously explored. Because we always bring our assumptions of stable human identity to the consideration of such cases, they seemed to us strange and paradoxical.

The assumption of a continuing self over time is necessary not only in law or social life, but also for the prudential behavior which liberalism has to recommend to us; indeed, this assumption is necessary for all policy. I can only decide now that I shall make it my policy to get rich if I have some confidence that I shall still desire riches when the policy matures. If I knew nothing of my future likes and dislikes, then I could not rationally plan for them. In actual life, my assumptions are often correct; I get rich and enjoy it. But there are also occasions when the "I" does change, and I find myself repudiating a policy which I have been following for a long time—a situation recognized in the German saying which recommends caution in the things one wishes for, since one may actually get them.

The liberal view of man must be regarded not as inadequate or as unfruitful but simply as false, because of the superior logical status it accords to a grouping of interests or desires called the individual self. For in social life, we find ourselves confronted with a considerable number of these groupings of interests, and all share the characteristic of self-consciousness. We find not only individuals but families, states, nations, churches, universities and so on. Within each, many activities are carried on, but each can become self-conscious and concerned with its own comparative status, or with its own survival. The philosopher who recognizes these phenomena most unequivocally is Hobbes, and he is preoccupied with self-consciousness about comparative status between individuals; he calls it pride. It results from an individual comparing his power—defined as "his present means to obtain some future apparent good"[14]—with the power of another. The demand for this power is limitless, for an individual "cannot assure the power and means to live well, which he hath present, without the acquisition of more."[15] This preoccupation with comparative status turns up in all the Hobbesian psychological definitions, even that, for example, of laughter. "*Sudden glory* is the passion which maketh those *grimaces* called LAUGHTER; and is caused either by some sudden act of their own, that pleaseth them, or by the apprehension of some deformed thing in another, by comparison whereof they suddenly applaud themselves."[16] The general idea of comparative status is a very common one, and has a variety of names, from the urge to power to the Adlerian concept of the inferiority complex. But what is important about it in political terms is that it is a characteristic of institutions, of self-conscious groupings of interests. It is not only individual human beings who behave in this way; but also—as Hobbes recognizes—States, and, we may add, all social institutions. Concern with comparative status is a standing cause of competition and struggle in human affairs, and Hobbes argues that its consequences for individual human beings would be disastrous were there no common power or Sovereign to keep them in awe.

Now what makes liberal individualism so plausible is that the individual is the only self-conscious entity whose limits appear to correspond to a physiological creature; and also that the thoughts and feelings which constitute institutions such as states or churches must be physically located in the minds of human beings. A prime minister is undoubtedly at various times an individual self standing in competitive relation to other selves; especially, indeed, when he is struggling with political rivals. But there are other occasions when his thoughts and acts must be taken as State-thoughts and State-acts, and when they cannot be reduced to the psychological operations of an individual. In its extremer forms, liberal individualism is a fallacy which since Mill

14. *Leviathan,* Ch. X.
15. *Ibid.* Ch. XI.
16. *Ibid.* Ch. VI.

has been called Psychologism: the doctrine that each individual may be psychologically explained, and all social institutions must be explained in terms of individuals. This mistake is endemic in liberalism, though its presence has in recent decades been camouflaged by adding to the basic model of generic man various sociological components—class membership, social norms and so on. Yet if we wish to learn about the military behavior of soldiers, we must study military activities, not psychology. And similarly, if we wish to understand politicians, we must attempt to understand the activity of politics, not discover whether politicians are nice or nasty men. It is not that psychological (or sociological) knowledge is in these cases of no account; it is simply that the distinction here between psychology and military art or psychology and politics is a false one, and that the starting point for explanation must not be the rationalist essence of the individual, but the complex situation we are trying to explain.

A social institution is a self-conscious grouping of interests. But we are not always self-conscious, and the study of institutions is far from exhausting political and social life. For in philosophizing we are confronted with another kind of evidence which in liberal individualism must be explained away, but which for other philosophers is itself a starting point. As examples of this evidence we may take a philosopher absorbed in a problem, an artist in a picture, or a soldier engaged in an attack. None of these people is self-conscious, and the behavior of each can only be explained if one understands the relevant activity. None of them is in the least concerned with his own survival, or with his comparative status *vis-à-vis* others. There are a great number of circumstances of spontaneous co-operation and unself-conscious absorption in activities which provide the evidence for the Aristotelian view that man is *by nature* a political animal, and that the state (or any institution) is prior to the individual. It is, of course true that if a fire breaks out in the philosopher's house, he will usually abandon his problem and become a prudent self-preserver. And the artist may turn to thinking of the market in which he can sell his picture; perhaps he will even change some details of his picture in order to sell it. And the soldier who in attack preserves himself or not according to the requirements of victory, may find that the attack has failed and it is now a case of *sauve qui peut;* at that point he too may become a self-preserving animal. There are many circumstances in life where we become self-conscious in this manner. But what is false in liberalism is the doctrine that these moments, times of concern with self-preservation and comparative status, rather than the times of self-forgetful absorption in activity, are the yardstick of reality.

It is the rationalist doctrine that there *is* a yardstick of reality which is the main issue here, dividing philosophers on the question of which facts are basic or real. Even the supposedly empirical English liberal school of thought appears closer to the truth only because its particular yardstick happened, by a confusion, to coincide with visible and audible human beings. Spontaneously co-operative human activities, which cannot be explained as outcroppings of the desires of individuals, appear far more prominently in other traditions of thought: in Plato's discussion of justice, Rousseau's of the general will, and in Hegel and Marx. Here we find the individual explained as one of the products of social co-operation rather than the key which explains that co-operation. Indeed, all of these thinkers went further, and found a moral excellence in spontaneous co-operation which could not be found in the prudential calculations of individual desires; for it is in co-operative moments, when absorbed by an activity, that individuals perform heroic and self-sacrificing deeds, and in which they attain moral stature by—so many idealist accounts have it— merging themselves in something greater.

Yet even in these accounts of social and political life, a yardstick of reality begins to rise above the evidence and, as it develops, it often turns out to be even more intellectually oppressive and obscurantist than the generic man of liberal thought. This yardstick is usually the State; but the State is conceived, like the individual self, as the organizing center of many activities, and any institution will do. Yardsticks of political reality do not even have to be existing institutions which are already self-conscious. In the case of the nation, or the Marxian idea of the class, we find organizing categories whose self-consciousness exists over a limited area and for very limited periods of time; and "reality" here is a bastard which can only be legitimized, if at all, by strenuous political exertions.

We have suggested that those philosophies which arise from the evidence of our participation in activities, rather than those which start from self-conscious institutions like the individual self, will provide an adequate account of social and political life. Yet the reputation of idealist theories in liberal circles is poor. Plato, Rousseau, Hegel and Marx have been selected as the particular targets of attack. While much of this contemporary liberal criticism is hysterical in tone, and most of it is perpetually on the edge of a confusion between the fate of ideas and the actions of men, it is certainly true that these philosophies all end in some strange and unlikely account of political life. The logical reason, as we have noted, is that some institution presently emerges as a yardstick of reality. The political reason is that all these philosophies incorporate attempts at political persuasion, and are therefore inclined to manufacture spontaneous co-operation whenever it does not exist. Many people find great moral beauty in all instances of unself-conscious co-operation, and this kind of admiration is not even withheld from the solidarity and loyalty of criminal bands. The moral features which are pleasing to the eye can perhaps be most explicitly grasped in propaganda: in pictures of happy workers on collective farms, or a people united in indignation against its enemies, cotton pickers singing at their work, or a national army marching off joyfully to engage the enemy. Here is a solidarity often found within teams, combining joy and self-denial. In cases of this kind, acts which in other contexts must be prescribed as virtues are performed naturally. These situations support the view that society is natural, and the idea finds a general expression in the Marxian notion that production (with its implications of co-operation and solidarity in pursuit of some common good) creates society, and consumption (with its implications of selfish demands and possessive acquisition) creates the State.

There are times when we step back from some venture, or break the connection which binds us to an institution, and ask, in effect: "What's in it for me?" This is a disharmonious question, for while we may still continue doing the same series of actions, the spirit will be different. We will not like what we are actually doing so much as the advantage which we hope to derive from it, for in this mood we have become rational men and do things for reasons. If we are disappointed, as must sometimes happen, we may become angry, resentful and envious. A plausible line of argument in moral philosophy would identify this kind of self-centered withdrawal as morally evil. This line is taken by those utilitarian moralists whose key categories are selfishness and unselfishness; and it is also taken, in a much more sophisticated form by many idealists for whom self-forgetful participation in some "higher self" is the measure of good.

It is thus easy to understand why English liberals often regard idealist political thinking as a pompous fraud masking only a demand for unconditional obedience to the State; and why the idealists have regarded utilitarianism as a base and mean-spirited defense of prudent selfishness. But while utilitarianism can give no account of those occasions of self-forgetful participation, it is not hostile to them. For the idealists, individual prudence, where it conflicts with the demands of the State (or other institution nominated as the yardstick of reality), is something which must be extirpated as a moral fault; a course of action which politicians are strongly inclined to follow anyway.

What has happened here philosophically is that whilst idealist theories begin with the sophisticated notion of participation, they generally end by vulgarizing this idea into that of obedience, which is simple and easily testable. The only proof of virtuous loyalty and participation becomes uncritical obedience, and the virtue of spontaneous co-operation is thought to be generated simply by the bark of command. And this is absurd; for moods of prudent self-interest in individuals, whatever their moral character may be, are often produced by conflict within an individual between an activity he is on the point of abandoning, and one or more which he is proposing to take up. Selfish moods are often those in which an individual works out, indeed creates, his own identity. But they are highly dangerous to institutions, which therefore are often found in decline to glow with an incandescence of moral prohibition. The decline of the Puritan way of life pared it down to a barren sabbatarianism, that of Victorian England, produced a generation of ageing moralists deploring the selfish indulgence of the flapper. The prohibitions which in a vigorous institution are boundary lines lightly indicated to control a few straying members are transformed by decline into obsessions, the last clear beacons in a darkening world.

Generic man must be seen, not as the isolated folly of liberalism, but as a member of a class of essences whose conflicts have long dominated political philosophy. He is on the same logical level as the state, the class, the nation, the church and similar political concepts which tower over political philosophy. He is indeed a tame creature; there is no blood on *his* hands, for it has all been defined away. But even so agreeable a yardstick of reality belongs to a fantasy world, and obscures our view of what is actually going on.

VI. TRADITION AND THE TWO LIBERALISMS

Liberalism has emerged quite self-consciously from communities dominated by traditional ways of doing things. In this context, its key idea has been that of improvement, or, in politics, reform. Such improvement requires that we should ask ourselves what it is exactly that we are trying to do, and then search for more efficient ways of doing it. We are thus presented with a contrast between reason and tradition, and the contrast operates clearly to the disadvantage of tradition.

Yet the term tradition is one which must be used with care, for it has two quite distinct and indeed almost directly opposed meanings. The meaning it has when under criticism depends primarily upon the idea of repetition. It is doing things in a time-hallowed manner. It is the refusal to countenance any kind of innovation. It is the admixture in clearly purposive behavior of ritual and usages which do not advance the task in hand, and quite often impede it.

That is the derogatory meaning of tradition. But people will be found also to assert that nothing is possible without the development of traditions of skill and enterprise which are transmitted from generation to generation. A tradition in this sense is a knowledge of how to go about tasks, one which can only be transmitted by imitation, and which cannot be written down and summarized. In this sense of tradition, it is development rather than repetition which is the central idea.[17] And what leads such traditions into decadence is precisely the conscious operations of reason. For reason fragments a tradition into a set of policies, ends and means, and works in terms of principles, which are to traditions just what dogmas are to ideologies—distorting fixed points outside the range of criticism. We may talk, for example, of traditions of military skill, and, in this sense, the tradition *is* the capacity for innovation, and adaptation to new circumstances. The behavior of the French general staff in the 1930s in building a Maginot Line and in thinking of war in terms of trenches, artillery bombardments, and static masses of infantry may be regarded as traditional in the first sense; it was emphatically not traditional in the second sense.

The political tradition against which liberalism was primarily in revolt was one of authority and obedience. King, Pope, magistrate and patriarch were all figures of authority who claimed obedience from their subjects. The political structure in which all found a place was not, however, either tyrannical or despotic. There were two general kinds of limitation upon the power of authorities. One was the result of custom and usage, and the other was the consent of the subjects. Both these limitations were the subject of extensive discussion in medieval political thought, which, in spite of the many caricatures

17. The best modern account of political tradition is to be found in Oakeshott, *op. cit.*

prevalent in liberal writings, was far from being either uncritical or unrealistic. It is in these writings that we find the principle *vox populi vox dei;* and it was from Aquinas, through many intermediaries, that Locke derived many of the principles which in his formulation became dogmas of liberalism. Besides, the sheer plurality and localism of medieval conditions, combined with the ceaseless conflict between institutions, made a situation in which appeal to popular support was, then as now, one of the most powerful political cards that could be played. Medieval use of popular support was a legacy of great importance; for example, extensive use of Lancastrian precedents was made by the Parliamentary side in the English Civil War; the Lancastrians, a dynasty with shaky claims to legitimacy, had relied heavily on popular support.

The development of modern conditions must therefore be seen as the continuation of a long history, and one in which very little was radically novel. It was at first developments in a few limited activities which provoked rejection of particular claims of certain authorities. Thus the Pope's doctrinal hegemony came under violent attack centuries before the Reformation, and the commercial inconveniences of a multitude of petty authorities advanced the claims of the monarch long before the nation-state took on any recognizable shape. Similarly, intellectual endeavors led to friction with authorities. It was for a long time the sovereign who remained most untroubled by this anti-authoritarian feeling; and this immunity was the consequence of his remoteness.

The main exception to the popularity of kings is to be found in the field of religion, for it was here that hostile royal intervention could press most heavily. And among the first people to develop politically liberal ideas were the intellectual spokesmen for religious minorities. The arguments they used, being philosophical, were couched in highly general terms. And besides, the intellectual momentum produced by the criticism of *some* traditional authorities did not stop before it had engulfed all authority. The most popular formulation of anti-authoritarian criticism, then as now, contrasts the individual and the institution, particularly the State. But given that the conception of the individual is as incoherent as we have argued, it would seem more accurate to formulate the criticism in terms of activities: liberalism was the assertion that the conduct of authority should be determined by the activities which grew up or declined within the institution. In directly political terms, this was the demand for government by the consent of the governed.

But this principle of consent was not, as we have seen, a new one. It existed in the middle ages, where its range and implications were more limited. For this reason, the picture of liberalism emerging by the power of reason from out of a superstitious and static traditional society is a false one. And this means that the relationship between liberalism and tradition must be examined with some care. For in rejecting traditional authority, liberalism included two elements which, while they are generally found yoked together, must be clearly distinguished.

One element is a rejection of the whole structure of traditional societies. Seen in this way, liberalism is a liberating force which rejects a static and crippling security in favor of a dynamic and progressive social system, one in which all social institutions are free to develop as they wish, checked inevitably by the development of others. This is less a social program than a spirit abroad; it scrutinizes existing organization and repudiates whatever is rigid and constrictive, and it romantically embraces the unpredictable consequences of its rejection of tradition. This free spirit is, in particular, hostile to political expediency and to rationality; it is itself irrational and unpredictable. There is a good deal of this attitude in the early American rejection of European class structure; it is also invoked by democracies when at war with totalitarian States—turning then into an ideology which asserts the adaptability and self-reliance of free men in comparison with those who unquestioningly serve a leader or Führer. Yet the more this spirit is turned into an ideology, the more it becomes a dogma, a caricatured inversion of the spirit from which it derives. The area in which this element of liberalism is most at home is that of the intellect; it is here that we find the passion to follow an argument wherever it leads, trampling over dogmas and the convenient orthodoxies maintained by authority. Liberalism embraces this exploratory and experimental spirit in all fields. Yet it is irrational in both possible senses; it is uncalculating—unconcerned with security or the preservation of interests—and it is incalculable. Its consequences cannot be foreseen, and its very presence may be inimical to social and political harmony.

This disposition to subject everything to critical enquiry, and to take nothing on trust from authorities, is sometimes called rationalism, especially in the context of religious discussions. But rationalism has a number of meanings, some of them precisely antipathetic to this spirit. And to call it rationalism falsely suggests that free criticism is spun out of the presiding faculty of reason like honey from a bee. We may more suitably call it libertarianism.

The libertarian element in liberalism constitutes a direct threat to all authorities, traditional or not. But liberalism has not been consistently hostile to authority. For the other element of the doctrine is the search for a manner of social life which would dispense with the inefficiency, waste and misery which always seem to have characterized all human association. The search for harmony, the pursuit of happiness and the doctrine of progress—none of these is libertarian, and each may be directly hostile to the critical spirit. For the critical spirit disrupts harmonies, causes a good deal of direct unhappiness, and may or may not seem progressive. The only way in which libertarianism can be harmonized with these other elements of liberalism is by taking a dizzying jump into the future, and making an act of faith to the effect that in the long run the products of the critical spirit will increase the amount of happiness. But for many people, and especially in the short run, it is a dubious proposition.

We may call this the salvationist element in liberalism. It arises from a persistent belief that society is in the midst of a revolution which will no doubt last for several generations, but which will have a perfectly definite end—one in which science would have taught us all her lessons, and bequeathed us the comforts of technology and the harmonies of political agreement. History, like time, must have a stop. This feeling is stated in different terms by such disparate figures as Bacon, Bentham and Marx.

Salvationism is a heresy which periodically thins the liberal ranks. The major problem of politics, in terms of salvationism, is to know exactly when we have reached, or are about to reach, the moment of salvation; for the true liberal, it will never arrive. An early salvationist threat to liberalism was very powerful in Cromwell's Commonwealth, and took the form of a demand for a Rule of the Saints. The Saints were dedicated men who believed that all the struggles against King, Bishop and Pope were to culminate in a reign of perfection, government by the Saints themselves (though in Christ's name).

These episodes illustrate one of the curious characteristics of liberalism: that while it is itself a balanced and cautious doctrine, it is nonetheless a prolific generator of fanaticisms. These fanaticisms are partly the product of liberal salvationism, and they can introduce into political life an element of savage ferocity which is quite alien to the more or less traditional régimes which fall to them. The Reign of Terror, in pursuit of Jacobin salvation, broke over a France which had been mildly, if eccentrically, governed for over a century.

Fanaticism arises because one particular part of the liberal program, or one particular enmity, has become obsessive and over-riding. In this century, Nationalism, Industrialism, or some form of Collectivism has conspicuously generated this kind of blind allegiance. Parties absorbed by such goals remember enough of their liberal derivation to persist in the use of liberal slogans; they continue to talk of liberty and equality and the dignity and rights of man. But their behavior is far from liberal.

Can these two elements in liberalism be separated? Do they ever make an independent appearance? The libertarian spirit is a characteristic likely to be found wherever liberal doctrines are asserted; but it has no necessary relation with liberals, and it is not the product of planned or willed activity. All that liberalism can do is provide it with suitable channels for its irruptions. When libertarianism becomes a doctrine, equipped with its own moral scale and set of beliefs about the world, it turns into a romantic fantasy; it becomes fully irrationalist in the way which frightens liberal intellectuals. It has appeared as anarchism, nihilism, and the theory of the *acte gratuit;* it usually asserts the legitimacy of destruction and violence, doing for these what Rousseau tried to do for all feelings. These are doctrines which attempt to intellectualize what is spontaneous and unplanned, and thereby produce only self-conscious caricatures fit for timid men to prove their courage, and slavish ones to prove their independence.

Liberal salvationism can, as we have said, lead a life of its own; and it is the most frequent cause of liberal heresies. For it arises from the passion for order, tidiness and harmony. Liberal utopias are marked primarily by an explicit concern with happiness; and in the name of all future joys, many present sorrows must be endured. It is one of the ironic signs of the pervasiveness of moral demands that even the liberal philosophy of desiring is vulnerable to ought-desires; that is, to desires which any decent and rational man must have. In liberal utopias there is little talk of order, discipline and obedience; authority demands not only to be obeyed but to be freely obeyed. But authority makes demands all the same, and is ready to punish and kill if our feelings will not play the harmony game.

Here we are concerned with a spectrum of orderly passions which is mildly found in the early Fabians and insanely present in the Russian purges. But in making this connection, we do not thereby cast a stain on liberalism; neither people nor doctrines can free themselves from shabby and disreputable relatives. What is clear about liberalism is that both elements, the libertarian and the salvationist, must be present to constitute the movement as it has identified itself over the last few centuries. And here is one of the marks of ideology, that of internal incoherence. For liberals are simultaneously to be found praising variety and indeed eccentricity of opinion and behavior; and gnawing industriously away at the many sources of variety in an attempt to provide every man, woman, child and dog with the conditions of a good life. They are to be found deploring the tyrannical excesses of totalitarian government, and yet also watching with bird-like fascination the pattern of order and harmony which those excesses are explicitly designed to promote. Liberalism is like all ideologies, a bickering family of thoughts and emotions; and sometimes parts of the family move out and set up on their own. But liberalism describes the family, and it would therefore be not futile but simply wrong to look closer at the various members of the family in order to discover which is most truly liberal.

Whatever the nature of liberalism, it is a clear instinct of self-preservation which leads traditional societies to fight against the entry of liberal ideas by such devices as censorship and repression. For once liberalism gains a foothold, a sort of traditional innocence is lost. The political consequences of liberal ideas may be the establishment of a liberal democratic society of the western European kind. But this outcome requires the co-operation of social and economic circumstances, or perhaps simply elements of good fortune, which are far from being universally distributed.

CHAPTER THREE

Ethics and Politics

I. MORAL EXPERIENCE

L IKE MANY OTHER modern doctrines, liberalism cherishes the hope
that one day politics will fade away, and the era of "power-mad politicians" (Lord Russell's phrase) will come to an end. In Marxist doctrine, this belief is quite explicit: with the coming of communism, the State
will wither away, and power over men will give way to power over things. The
liberal view is much more oblique. Liberals are rather like ingenious accoun-
tants shuffling figures from one column to another. They have, over the years,
transferred many issues from "politics" into a variety of other columns. They
seek to find moral substitutes for war, to educate the ignorant and superstitious, to cure the criminal and delinquent, and to clarify the goals of mankind.
Given a progress of this kind, democratic politics will turn (in the dream of
Lenin) into a simple administrative matter to be handled by clerks: the
people's wishes will be ascertained and the people's wishes will be executed.

This illusion arises from one of the more indestructible fantasies of
mankind. Nor does it greatly matter whether present discontents are attributed to the presence of something—passion, or original sin—or to the absence of something—such as understanding, reason, or education. Scope always remains for a remedy. And with the arrival of the remedy, we shall find
ourselves released not only from political conflict, but from moral conflict as
well. And this is quite inevitable, for ethics and politics are inseparable.

The effect of modern liberal doctrine has been to hand over the facts of moral and political life into the maladroit hands of social and political scientists, and the results have been intellectually disastrous. For moral issues, shuffled into the logician's column, turn into formalized imperatives; transferred by the device of generic man to the sociologist, they turn into culturally determined norms. As likely as not, the psychologist will regard them as neurotic symptoms. Politics similarly loses its autonomy, dissolved into a set of reactions to supposed external causes. The criterion of a "value-free science" is no doubt scientific in excluding propaganda from intellectual investigation. But it is merely superstitious when it turns "values"—in fact the subject matter of ethics and politics—into an intellectual red light district into which no thinker may stray, on pain of losing his respectability.

The commonest kind of moral evasion found in liberalism is some variation of utilitarianism. "It is no derogation from promise-keeping as a moral principle to say that the reasons for it are ones of social convenience . . . if we could never rely on people to keep their promises social life as we know it would be rendered impossible."[1] This is similar to the Hooker-Locke argument already quoted,[2] and to Hume's view that we obey the state "because society could not otherwise subsist."[3] And the most obvious point about it is that it has nothing at all to do with ethics. Social convenience and political advantage are social convenience and political advantage; no more. These are the statements of a political technology. In order to promote "convenience" and a "comfortable society," certain modes of behavior must be established as duties. Assertions of this kind may be true or false, but they remain technological calculations. The fallacy involved is a simple and familiar one—that of undistributed middle. The argument is of this nature: promise-keeping is socially necessary. Promise-keeping is a moral principle. Therefore a moral principle is what is socially necessary.

It is not for example true that "We accept it as a duty to keep our word *because* we recognize the advantage for social relations of reliability and predictability."[4] If this is a psychological statement about our mental condition as

---

1. H. R. G. Greaves, *The Foundations of Political Theory,* London, 1958, p. 120.
2. See above, p. 24.
3. Hume, *Of the Original Contract.*
4. Greaves, *op. cit.,* p. 120 (my italics).

we keep our promises, it is untrue. And if it is a moral statement describing why promise-keeping is moral behavior, then it is also false, though it is more difficult to demonstrate why this is so. One reason, of course, is that promise keeping (like any other generalized moral category) does not have a consistent moral significance. It depends upon a complex set of circumstances, and we can invent cases where the keeping of a promise may be a brutal act of revenge. But this is a detail. The point is, I think, that in all the conventional cases, a promise-keeper has a different character from a promise-breaker, and this character can only be adequately described if we consider it in moral terms. To establish this is enormously difficult, and the temptation is to retreat, as Moore did, into intuitionism (which is dogmatic) and to the assertion that good is indefinable.

The argument that "if we could never rely on people to keep their promises social life as we know it would be rendered impossible" runs into a dilemma. If everybody except me keeps their promises then social life is not threatened; and if promise-breaking is extensive, I will only suffer fruitlessly if I keep mine. Hobbes and Spinoza understood this situation more realistically, and they had little patience with rationalist appeals of this particular kind.[5]

This utilitarian treatment of moral principles obscures the fact that it is exactly the seeking of advantages which often leads people to break promises. Quite often, furthermore, people are perfectly right in their calculations, and they do reap an advantage from betraying a trust. Indeed, one way of describing the evil in cases of promise-breaking is in pointing to the fact that it arises from a prudent concern with advantages, whereas goodness results from moral or spiritual integrity. Promise-breaking is a refusal to accept the consequences of one's past act; it indicates an incoherence in the character of the person who does it. The description of such acts as evil depends upon moral understanding, not upon any supposed social consequences.

What makes it difficult to give an account of moral experience is the intense practical interest we all have in the behavior of others. Even moral philosophers suffer from a deep anxiety about the possible consequences of the theories they suggest. "It is hardly necessary to add," remarks Mr. Nowell-Smith, talking about that form of objectivism in ethics which attributes ethical dis-

---

5. Cf. Hume's classic argument on this point in the *Treatise of Human Nature,* Book III, Part II, Sec. II.

agreements to perversity and insincerity, "that this theory has had the most tragic consequences in international affairs."[6] This is a headlong jump from philosophy to action; on a par with the notion that Hegel must share the blame for Hitler. The difficulty with any principle of behavior, of course, is that there will always be circumstances in which it will have undesirable results; and we may perhaps conclude that one thing determining the content of such moral principles is the wish to generalize what the philosopher considers (independently) to be desirable.

It is further true that all the terms of moral discourse turn up very frequently in an imperative use: "Don't be vain!" "Be honest with me!" "You ought to be loyal." This is a common, perhaps even the most common, way in which they function. And for this reason, it is a perfectly legitimate concern to analyze the logic of imperatives, and to distinguish (as does Mr. Hare) neustics from phrastics.[7] But to consider that moral philosophy is *no more* than preoccupations of this kind is false. It is an example of what we shall later discuss as meliorism. It derives from the view that the imperative element in ethics is the only part of it which cannot be reduced to facts and thus assimilated to other fields of enquiry. This view can itself become a crude form of reductionism: "When Plato asks 'What is Justice?', it is clear that he keeps his eye continually on the question 'What ought we to do?'"[8] But whatever biaxial distortions of vision philosophers may manage in compounding the two questions, the questions themselves are perfectly distinct, particularly, indeed, in Plato. When he asks "What is Justice?" he means exactly that, and the answer that he gives is in the indicative, not the imperative, mood.

We might perhaps begin by suggesting that there are two parallel kinds of moral philosophy distinguished by their vocabularies. One vocabulary is a functional one, indicating abstractly a direction of behavior: it includes such terms as ought, right, wrong, duty, obligation and end. There is another vocabulary which is descriptive and includes terms like vain, loyal, heroic, deceitful and honest. The functional set of terms is imperative; the latter, because it sometimes functions prescriptively, may also—though falsely—be thought of as essentially imperative, but as containing a psychological ad-

---

6. P. H. Nowell-Smith, *Ethics,* London, 1954, p. 23.

7. R. M. Hare, *The Language of Morals,* Oxford, 1952, p. 1.

8. Nowell-Smith, *op. cit.*

mixture. The result of this view of moral philosophy is, rather curiously, to establish a practice for which there can be no uniquely appropriate theory. Whatever looks like ethical theory must forthwith be handed over to the stewardship of another type of enquirer.

Against this view, I am suggesting that there exists something which we may call the moral life, some kind of moral experience which is to some extent shared by all. This moral experience is certainly not identical with "being good." It is something of which we are all only intermittently conscious, but it is not to be identified with conscious moral choices, since we often discover afterwards that some act which we did unreflectingly was far more ethically significant than those choices which kept us awake at nights. All manner of apparently casual acts are incidents of the moral life, at least on a par with those thorny questions, such as the nature of our obligation to return borrowed books, which have captured the attention of professional moralists. For most moralists are concerned either to discover or to analyze reasons why we ought to do the right thing; they are partly concerned with the practical—in fact the political—issue of how we ought to act. Whereas the moral significance of such situations is found in the discoveries we make about ourselves in the course of our deliberations, the kind of temptations we encounter, and the moral character which is implied by the act when it is done.

For this reason, a concern with the moral life in this sense is inescapably part of the materials of the novelist. As far as, for example, Flaubert is concerned, the choices made by his characters are of interest as evidence of the character they have, while for the moralist the interest lies not in the act itself and what the act reveals, but in the reasons which may be given for it. Flaubert is dealing with moral issues in *Madame Bovary*. He is, among other things, examining an intricate moral network of relations between his characters, as they act and develop, as they gain one kind of understanding and lose another. Yet this moral interest is certainly not an interest in guides to conduct or imperatives or prescriptions of any kind. Flaubert is not circuitously telling us that adultery is wrong and that we ought not to engage in it. He is not a moral propagandist.

A character in literature—and often in life—is conceived as vivid, concrete, and particular. It is *partly* understood as a disposition to make particular kinds of choices, and each choice made both contributes further evidence about the character and at the same time changes the character. But the regularities of character are no more than dispositions. People are not reliably predictable. Worms will turn and heroes quake. As moral characters, our own privileged introspections give us little more advantage in understanding ourselves than we have in understanding other people. For part of the drama of the moral life is that, while we struggle to understand, we also struggle to maintain our self-deceptions. There are many things which we are determined *not* to understand. Our knowledge is therefore incomplete and, in any case, the thing we are trying to understand is unstable and changing—

> Because one has only learnt to get the better of words
> For the thing one no longer has to say, or the way in which
> One is no longer disposed to say it.

Perhaps the most spectacular exemplars of the conscious cultivation of the moral life were the Puritans—those relentless moral athletes minutely examining each performance with the stop-watch of dogma. They imported into everyday life a type of moral cultivation normally found only in monastic circumstances. Their entire religious organization was calculated to facilitate the spontaneous operations of conscience, and some of their more searing scorn was reserved for those whose moral life was either abandoned to others, or merely mechanical. For Milton it was not only Papists who thus disembarrassed themselves of conscience; he railed against many a Protestant as being too ready "to give over toiling, and to find himself out some factor, to whose care and credit he may commit the whole managing of his religious affairs."[9]

Many attempts have been made to describe the general structure of moral experience, but all describe some varieties of moral life better than others. The cause of this lies partly in the practical concerns of the philosophers. Liberalism, for example, is antipathetic to the unreflective adherence to traditional moral rules, and has therefore attempted to rationalize these rules by constructing a generalized policy adapted to the character of natural man. In this policy, most of the conventional moral rules reappear as items of technical advice. This teleological view of the moral life appears only to affect the structure of morality; in fact, it also affects the content. For it turns moral agents into calculators of consequences, opening up possibilities of individual variation which cannot appear where morality is taken to be conformity to a code.

9. *Areopagitica.*

Alternatively moral experience may be explained in terms of law and will. There exist moral rules—duties, laws, obligations—which are independently valid. The moral problem faced by individuals is partly cognitive, mostly conative. The cognitive element comes first. It is to discover, in any particular situation, which of the rules or duties is appropriate. Once this is done, the only problem remaining is to will the act enjoined by the rule, the difficulty being that impulse, pleasure, or evil may all be pulling in some other direction. This description of the moral life gives us such notions as the "loosening of moral standards" and "the hard path of virtue."

The teleological and the legislative views of moral experience are those most commonly found, both in philosophy and in ordinary life. But they are far from exhausting all possibilities. The moral life may be understood as the maintenance of an internal coherence or harmony; the good man, as his life proceeds, is one who maintains this harmony, the evil one being divided within himself. Goodness here is something which permits a constant understanding of one's surroundings. The good man has no illusions because he lives in the present and his mind is unblinkered by emotions like avarice or ambition.[10] This view is found in Plato's doctrine about the goodness of the philosophical life, and appears in literature especially in criticism of conventional bourgeois ways of living. Related to it is the theological notion that goodness is a matter of imitating a divine model, of being Christlike in one's behavior. And a similar view is to be found in such advice as: "You must do what you must do." Any of these views are likely to turn up in any extended moral discussion, and either pure or in combination they may be put forward as explanations of the moral life.

The difficulty, of course, is that each account is certain to generate commands and imperatives.[11] Each view can be used, like any other piece of knowledge, in the actual conduct of life. Further, the moral life is something which imperatively must be controlled, especially from a political point of view. It is spontaneous; it is unpredictable; and it can often be disruptive of social and political arrangements. In so far as people act rationally, they are cal-

10. A popular version of this view of moral experience, one which has had great currency, is the character of Larry in Somerset Maugham's novel *The Razor's Edge*.

11. We should note, however, that on some ethical views (in Plato, for example) goodness *cannot* be an object of striving. Commands and imperatives would therefore be an illicit use of moral knowledge.

culable; one can appeal to their interests and their fears. But what is most characteristic of the moral life is that within it neither interests nor fears are decisive. It can produce martyrs, crusaders, heroes, megalomaniacs, and a variety of socially indigestible (though often in some terms valuable) phenomena.

In all the issues of moral experience, moral character is the crucial thing, for it is only character which determines the existence of a moral problem. There is no such thing as a moral problem (or any other kind of problem) outside the context of a human situation; and in talking of particular problems we always imply the kind of human being who could have that particular problem. There are some people in the world who are virtually immobilized because every decision they have to make turns into a moral problem; and there are also others, called psychopaths, for whom nothing at all presents a moral problem. Moral philosophers concern themselves with a vague concept of ordinary men, whose moral problems are assumed capable of some approximate standardization. But even ordinary people vary enormously; and what is at one stage of life no problem at all may become morally significant at a later date. Those who associate moral philosophy with the study of imperatives take no interest in such variations; for them, that is psychology. But psychologists are hardly equipped to give such intractable questions much attention, and the whole area goes by default[12] because it happens to be included in no one's disciplinary boundaries.

I take it, then, that moral experience is found everywhere in human behavior, and that it is not something which can be ignored without serious misunderstanding of social and political life. The term "duty" for example is one that turns up in ethics, politics, sociology, and law. But the way in which it must be understood depends upon variations both in the bearer of the duty and in the environing situation. To an eager young military volunteer, an account of his duties as a soldier has a purely descriptive force; it tells him what is involved in an activity for which he already has a great deal of enthusiasm. Should this enthusiasm wane with experience, then tasks like cleaning his rifle and polishing his buttons will become duties in a far more prescriptive sense; they become things which he has to do as a condition of being some-

---

12. Not entirely. Part of the attraction of Existentialism is that it does at least recognize this field, and the issues are also discussed in novels and literary criticism.

thing else. Here the prescriptive element, as in many other cases, arises only with the coming of internal conflict, a conflict which may be induced by laziness, boredom, or perhaps some more philosophical criticism of military life. It also appears to be a common experience that duties begin as things which "ought" to be done, and end by becoming part of the structure of a person's life, so that he feels lost without the doing of them. "Doing the right thing" is very frequently less the product of imperative rules, calculations of ends and means, or awareness of internal coherence, than a kind of itch; a person can get no peace of mind till it is done.

Moral knowledge is sometimes a thing we seek; more often it is something we have forced upon us. A Nazi bureaucrat receiving orders to arrest and execute a Jewish friend, has, in the classic textbook sense, a moral problem. Does he obey the State, to which he owes allegiance? Does he resign? Does he help his friend to get out of the country to safety? He may formulate his question as: what ought I to do? He may rank the various appropriate rules (help friends, obey the law, keep promises, etc.). He may calculate the utils of pain involved for everybody concerned. He may ask what Christ or Luther would have done. He is in fact unlikely to do any of these things with much resolution. It is far more likely that a set of incidents—watching his children, the remark of a superior, or an obsessive memory—will give him some vision of things in which his decision will emerge. But whatever he does, his choice will be evidence about his character. It may indicate weakness or strength, vanity, self-sacrifice, honesty or self-deception. The conflict may be seen in quite other terms than "what ought he to do?" as, for example, whether he *is* a loyal friend or an obedient supporter of the régime. If our Nazi functionary were singlemindedly dedicated to the régime, he would not be aware of a moral dilemma at all. He would simply do his "duty." And if, later, after executing his Jewish friend, he began to suffer remorse, he would be criticizing not only his act or choice; he would be implicitly criticizing the narrowly obedient way of life which, unchosen, had led up to the decision.

This, then, is a brief sketch of what I take to be moral experience, a field of human concerns which liberalism, for reasons we shall indicate, has ignored. It may be that some stubborn meliorist will insist that what I have been describing is a matter of fact, and *therefore* belongs in the intellectual province called psychology rather than to that called ethics. I have no wish to quarrel over labels; someone who starts from the premise that ethics is concerned with imperatives and obligations will no doubt be led to the conclusion that what I have taken to be moral facts must be facts of a different kind. But *if* we must regard the empirical study of moral experience as part of psychology, then I can only observe that it is psychology of a highly peculiar kind. It has no relation at all to those textbooks called *Psychology* which have chapter headings like "Drives," "Memory," "Learning," "Maturation," etc. and which report in statistical detail the behavior of mice and control groups of all kinds. Nor is it to be identified with psychoanalysis, though indeed part of the greater subtlety which we may find in Freud, and some of those who have constructed similar kinds of depth-analysis, results from the fact that some psychoanalytic concepts are close to moral ones. One might, for example, give a tolerable account of vanity in terms of narcissism. There are further analogues of the moral struggle in the conflict between the analyst and the subtle evasions of the subject. But while psychoanalysis can tell us much about moral experience, there can be no comprehensive theory of ethics which does not arise from ethics itself.

II. THE ILLUSION OF ULTIMATE AGREEMENT

We may either attend to those forms of moral life like loyalty, treachery, avarice, cruelty, saintliness, etc., which have long been observed and, in a haphazard way, documented; or concern ourselves with the intellectual justifications and exhortations which in one way or another emerge out of them. There is no form of moral life which is incapable of some sort of justification, but each justification necessarily distorts what it tries to justify. For justification is a support-gathering device, which assimilates all moral acts as closely as possible to contemporary moral beliefs. The situation is analogous to those political situations in which political parties are driven towards the "center" where the mass of public support lies. But what is in politics a "center" is in ethics a kind of logical elevation; it lies upwards, in the clouds of generality, at whose top are to be found those ultimate values which concern philosophers, or the most basic rules of any system of natural law. Here we all conspire in a meaningless agreement upon what are incorrectly thought to be fundamentals. Here also are to be found the generalized justifications ("Anyone would have done it," "I mean well," etc.) which turn up in ordinary life, slowly changing with each generation. And also residing here is the fantasy of an omnipotent and merciful judge, who will understand that only the good in people is real, and the bad merely the result of things they couldn't help.

Now while it is clear that between Protestant and Catholic, Arab and Jew, Monarchist and Republican, there is at certain times nothing but unyielding and irreducible hostility, it is also clear that if we look not at their behavior but at their justifications, we begin to move upwards towards this moral center. And we begin to participate in a philosopher's dream; the dream that the dispute is really over intellectual questions, and that, as in deductive argument, or in the formulation of policies, once the major questions have been agreed, the minor questions are matters of detail which will yield to technical skill and goodwill.

We may perhaps illustrate some of the issues arising here by considering the workings of a typical moral criterion. "In times such as this," remarked Richard Nixon recently, "I say it is wrong and dangerous for any American to keep silent about our future if he is not satisfied with what is being done to preserve that future. . . . The test in each instance is whether criticism is going to help or hurt America. We certainly do not help America by running her down in the eyes of the world." The patriotic policy, which Nixon advocates, supplies the criterion of "helping or hurting America." The journalistic policy finds its most extreme formulation in the slogan "publish and be damned." Some compromise is possible between the two policies: politicians admit a qualified right of press freedom, whilst journalists allow a qualified right to States of withholding strategic information. Somewhere on the borderlines, these formulae break down. Is scathing criticism of the blunders of politicians within the area of press freedom or State security? Assuming that a journalist accepts both policies (the patriotic and the journalistic), then the question of whether he *ought* or *ought not* to publish critical material depends on the *factual* question of how that material is related to agreed definitions of the rights of each institution.

Assuming that the government insists that the journalist's material endangers the State, but that he goes ahead and publishes, how does he defend his act?

"I agree," he may choose to say, "that the test is whether we help or hurt America. But America can only be helped by free and open criticism, which will prevent the multiplication of political blunders. The government's disapproval is misdirected; if it understood its own policy (or best interests) properly, then it would have no objection to my criticism." This places the act *within* the policy from which the attack derives, but reinterprets the criterion. If successful, it cuts the ground away from under the feet of the attacker. In any actual controversy, of course, the debate is endless, and expires from exhaustion rather than illumination. In historical discussion, subsequent fashions often give a tendentious answer to the question. Did the *Dreyfusards* weaken or strengthen "France"? Later liberal opinion, if forced to pronounce on the question as formulated in this way, would probably answer that they strengthened France. The opposite conclusion could also be argued. Both arguments would take the form of selecting later events and attributing them to the Dreyfus scandal.

In this kind of justification, our journalist refuses to enter into a "conflict of values." He insists on placing his act within the same "value-system" as that of his opponents. But alternatively, he might choose to take a more aggressive line.

"My allegiance," he might say, "is to Truth, not to the details of national conflicts. Because I am a journalist, I have a duty to speak out as my allegiance to truth directs. If I accept political direction as to what I say, then I am betraying myself." Here the policy of journalistic freedom has been converted into an impregnable metaphysic. Our journalist, in this mood, has become what is popularly known as an idealist. He will still be beating out his copy as the last trumpet sounds. If he attacks an unsympathetic government, he will either be shot or exiled. His political opponents can only, in fact, use the same tactic we have already observed. They can start by agreeing that Truth is indeed an ultimate value, and then argue that the maintenance of democratic government is a necessary condition of the continuance of devotion to truth. Small compromises must be made for the main object. This kind of argument, in the twentieth century, has a sophistical ring; but there is no other.

Now this "conflict of values"—National Security versus Truth—must not be seen as a matter of irreducible personal preferences. Those who do see it in this way proceed to conclude that there is an unbridgeable gulf between "facts and values." In that case, our journalist is commonly supposed to be making up his mind "what he ought to do," "what is the right thing to do," "where his duty lies," "what values he adheres to." These formulations pose the question for generic man, a neutral calculator outside a social context. If, however, we see his choice in the context of possible policies to be followed, then it is clear that the question is not: "What ought I to do?" nor even "what policy ought I to follow?" but simply: "What am I?" Our journalist is in fact deciding on the question of whether he is more a "patriotic American" or a "fearless journalist."

The actual situation is clearly far more complicated than that—and not merely because I have used crude stereotypes to identify adherence to these two policies. The journalist's act in publishing his critical copy is the result of a whole range of policies arising out of his past, his social and personal relations, his intellectual background, and his physical composition. The events which happen from moment to moment ceaselessly strengthen some policies and weaken or submerge others. There is no explicable "he" who rationally takes a decision on this question; that "he" is simply a mysterious substance, the phantom of individualism. As far as he can be studied, he is *constituted* by these policies, and they "choose" him just as much as he chooses them.

"Conflict of values" is not a matter of conflict between the preferences of individuals; it is a matter of conflict between irreducibly different things which exist, as a matter of fact, in the world. Nor can social conflict be explained away as a matter of ignorance and confusion about which means lead to which ends. It is a fact of life, resulting from the existence of a social thing like a journalist (or some kind of truth seeker) and another kind of social thing (in our example, a patriotic politician); and the conflict between them is not a conflict of "opinions" or "beliefs" but one between different characters, complicated by the fact that this conflict goes on *within* individuals, as well as between them. Social characters in this sense are no doubt highly unstable, just as States are often unstable. Nonetheless, advocacy, persuasion, propaganda, are political activities concerned to change not merely people's opinions, but people.

Changing people and dominating their behavior does not depend upon prescribing courses of action to them. It often depends only in purveying information, true or false. The man who shouts "Fire!" in a crowded theater has no need to add any prescription. The audience is way ahead of him. On such occasions, they know exactly how to "maximize their goal values."

The effects on behavior of social and political doctrines—that politics is an outcome of pressures, that capitalists live off surplus value, that a person's character is formed by childhood experiences—are less dramatic but equally clear. Each proposition is like a stone dropped into a pool; it sends ripples

73

across the moral face of the community. The values do not have to be supplied, the prescriptions spelled out; they are built into the character of those who acquire the information.

Intellectually, we seem to have the alternative of either concentrating upon the policies, aims, justifications, exhortations and prescriptions—the legal tender of moral characteristics—or upon those characteristics as they appear in people, complexes of thought and feeling by which people react upon each other. If we choose the former possibility, we will create something like modern moral philosophy, formalistic and concerned with logic and language. Working in this isolated field, we shall signalize the separation by distinguishing values from facts. Thus Professor Popper: "Perhaps the simplest and most important point about ethics is purely logical. I mean the impossibility to derive non-tautological ethical rules . . . from statements of facts." And having separated the two spheres, we are immediately faced by the difficulties of reuniting them. Professor Popper continues: "As one of the most central problems of the theory of ethics, I consider the following: If ethical rules (aims, principles of policy, etc.) cannot be derived from facts—then how can we explain that we can learn about these matters from experience?"[13]

We can explain the matter simply enough if we refuse to make the separation in the first place, and recognize that moral knowledge is knowledge of facts; not of aims, ends, policies or values, but of what in social and political situations sustains them: ambition, enthusiasm, ignorance, avarice, loyalty, and so on. It is, of course, true that no statement of non-moral facts can generate a decision; the decision depends on us. In particular, it depends upon what we are, what moral constitution we have at the time. And if there is conflict within us, the problem which we have to work out in making the decision is exactly the problem of what we are. Nor is any particular decision final; we go on changing, and may begin to regret the choice we made from the very moment we made it. All of these are features of moral experience, and they may be studied politically, socially, psychologically, morally, logically, or indeed linguistically. The intellectual difficulty is that each way of studying human behavior tends to expand in an attempt to explain everything in its own terms.

Moral discussion (like, indeed, any other kind of discussion) has to begin

13. K. R. Popper, *What Can Logic Do for Philosophy?* Aristotelian Society Supplementary Volume XXII, 1948, p. 154.

with agreement somewhere. Now since I have argued that moral disagreement is conflict between different social characters, there can in fact be no significant change of values which is not also a change of character. Those people whose dominating concern is to search for what unites rather than divides us nonetheless search for some kind of agreement. Their quest is as relentless as that of the alchemist, and it is for moral principles which are so devastatingly obvious that no individual can rationally reject them. Nor, indeed, do they search in vain. They have produced a string of abstractions and tautologies upon which most men will agree. Happiness, satisfaction, truth, beauty and goodness—these things are generally agreed to be "intrinsic goods."

The real strength of the illusion of ultimate agreement, the emotion which reconstitutes it intact after every critical onslaught, is to be found in its more down-to-earth formulations. Assuming that people are "basically" rational, can they not be taught that violence and selfishness are self-defeating? Happiness, which we all by definition seek, is not to be found in injuring and destroying the happiness of others. Is not the cause of racialism and fascism to be found in fear and neurosis, which can be cured by education, understanding and therapy? Are not the other evils of the world caused by poverty and illness, which modern technology is in the process of conquering? Have we not here the prescription for a better world on which we can all agree?

We met this program before when we considered the ethic of rationality. And the simple answer to its feasibility would be to say that men are not rational; or, more exactly, that they are only intermittently rational. A rational world is only possible assuming flexibility in most people most of the time. In economic terms, the demand for everything must be elastic. If one cannot have what one wants, one must be prepared to accept substitutes. Now this kind of flexibility does not depend upon intellectual agreement; it depends on social character. And given that all societies result from the interlocking of varied ways of life, it is strictly impossible that everyone can be consistently flexible. To put the matter another way, men are prolific generators of absolute principles. Manifest Destiny, *Algérie Française,* There is no God but God, Britons never will be slaves, *Nemo me impune lacessit,* Publish and be damned, A woman's place is in the home—principles of this sort, in all fields, constitute rocks upon which the rational ship will be constantly bruising its side. And the difficulty does not reside in the principles; intellectually speaking, argument might in some cases lead to their being qualified. It resides in the ways of life, the social characters, which generate the principles, and which are not amenable to argument. And these ways of life result from different environments, from religions, from languages and the obscure dreams which constantly flicker about the lives of men and which are occasionally capable of seizing direction of whole societies. Liberalism itself partly floats along on a dream of warmth and harmony of this very kind.

In any case, the things which are most valued in any society are not the result of rational flexibility. They result from the quite irrational attachment of men to the ways of life in which they are involved. What could be more irrational than Socrates preferring death to silence? Science, philosophy, art, capitalism, nations—all have been built up by men passionately and inflexibly attached to what they were doing. So indeed has liberalism itself, proud, like any movement, to lay claim to its martyrs. Compromise, flexibility, rationality in this sense, are important political virtues. They are indispensable to the maintenance of some peace and security. But it would hardly be a high civilization which would result from their unquestioned dominance. And it would certainly be an authoritarian one.

Nonetheless, liberalism pursues a political policy of chipping away at all pretexts for conflict. For, if conflict disappears, then so does the main business of politics. In the past, men have fought ferociously over religious creeds. The liberal responds to this by preaching the virtue of toleration and asserting the privacy of self-regarding actions. Intellectually, the liberal response is an attempt to deny the importance of differences. All the creeds, it has been argued, contain a common core of reverence, worship and sociability: that is what is most important in religion. The rest is merely local variation. Why come to blows about transubstantiation or the immaculate conception? Doctrines of the Trinity are matters for theologians, not for ordinary men. In the seventeenth century, Spinoza argued that the essence of religion was in good works and good behavior. Teaching a man religion was thus teaching him good behavior: in other words, no more than a way of manipulating him.

Men have fought over issues of honor. That too is irrational—dangerous to the welfare and happiness of the people who get involved. Men have fought in social riots because they were hungry, or feared to be hungry. This political problem can be solved by feeding them. Races have fought each other. The liberal teaches that racialism is evil, that all races are equal and should be free and respected; beliefs about the inferiority of some races can be shown to conflict with scientific investigations. Scientific findings are real; they indicate that "potentially" all races are "fundamentally" (i.e. in the respects which interest liberals) the same.[14]

Men have fought each other in nations. Liberals look to international organizations and, more distantly, forwards to the prospect of world government, a super-society in which their ideals will find fulfillment free from any earthy threat. There has been economic competition between workers and between firms. The economy must become more co-operative. If economic failure cannot be rendered impossible, then its consequences must be circumscribed by welfare services. Men have envied each other wealth and the advantages of birth; these must also be eliminated, by progressive taxation and a uniform system of school education. Private schools, in Britain public schools, are a threat to this program, and therefore ought to be abolished. And, of course, men have simply disliked each other and fallen out. The original liberal ethic therefore made social accommodation one of its major virtues. More modern doctrine scientifically sees friction between individuals as the result of neurosis, aggression, and frustration. In the form of adjustment, it has found a cure for those, too.

The politics of modern liberalism is thus centered on the attempt at a permanent removal of all pretexts for conflict. It seeks agreement not merely by argument, but (quite sensibly) by undermining the economic circumstances and ways of life which sustain disagreement. The end result is a utopia, an association of individuals living according to the same principles and in the same manner. The only test of discrimination is the test of ability.

It might be objected that this is a caricature of liberalism, which has of all doctrines been far the most hospitable to variety and eccentricity. And this objection is perfectly correct. Liberalism has, in particular, never ceased to maintain a distinction between the private and the public spheres, a distinction which is the doctrinal ground of any kind of individuality. The distinction is formulated both in natural rights theories, and in John Stuart Mill's often derided distinction between self-regarding and other-regarding actions. Liberals have also attacked the notion of adjustment. They have worried

---

14. This view is nicer than the opposing view that some races are "fundamentally" superior to others. Intellectually speaking, both views are meaningless. But both have a political point.

about the dull uniformity and the limited range of obsessions found in what they themselves call mass culture. They have never ceased to attack authoritarian attempts to impose uniformity in the name of pure doctrine or the national interest.

All this is true, but it states only a part of the liberal position. For, as we have already argued, liberalism is like all ideologies in that it attempts to hold together in one single viewpoint elements which are hostile to each other. The hatred of suffering and the love of freedom are equally characteristic of liberalism, and each is indispensable to it. If we seek, rather pointlessly, for some essential liberal position, then we might find it in the belief that happiness and individual freedom are always in harmony. Just as liberals believe that the good of the people may always be identified with what the people want, so they also believe that we can have variety without suffering. There is little historical evidence to support this view, and much to contradict it. Harmony obviously does not exist. It may, however, be imagined in some future; and the test by which we shall know when that future is nearly upon us is a world-wide moral agreement upon fundamentals.

It is also a clear mark of ideological thinking that certain things are viewed in a fixed policy context. This device is sometimes called functionalism; it attributes an essential role or function to things. (In more expansive versions of the doctrine, *everything* has a single function.) This doctrine yields us such propositions as that sex is *essentially* for procreation, full employment is a means not an end, books are *for* reading, and so on. This device is the basis of what we shall later discuss as scientific moralism. It is relevant here because it also implies that an ideal is *essentially* an ideal, and this happens to be false. To put it another way, the same program may fit into a number of policies, and an act which is a means in one policy is an end in another. Social harmony, for example, features in liberalism as an ideal; it is desirable for its own sake. But for the people who exercise authority over the great corporations of the modern world, social harmony is also a means. Such people are often fascinated by the possibilities of social manipulation turned up by liberal social scientists. Like liberals, they dislike wasteful and threatening social phenomena like strikes, crime, delinquency, and irresponsibility. They are kindly people who only want everyone to be happy—but on their own terms. They constitute a rally of conservative forces, entrenched in powerful and rich institutions, who are ever ready to promote the cry: "Our society is now perfect and just; only the second task, the rationalizing of the individual, remains to us." These people have no powerful attachment to such things as rigid patriarchal sexual codes, already a casualty of liberalism. Nor do they have any love for such institutions as inheritance by birth. Quite the contrary, for the independently wealthy and the aristocratically privileged are far more difficult to break into the corporation system than eager young men with nothing to sell but their "ability," and no standards with which to criticize except those they have picked up in the course of vocational training.

The notion that ideals and values are *essentially* ideals and values is so prevalent a version of functionalism that we might call it the idealists' trap. It is often found in propaganda, but it may also arise in intellectually respectable fields like social and political philosophy. Thus the notion that political philosophy is concerned with the study of political ideals is an instance of the idealists' trap, for it isolates ideals in the fantasy world of the desirable. One cannot effectively study liberalism, for example, by concerning oneself only with its ideals—liberty, equality, democracy, social justice, harmony, peace, rights and so on—for this would be to treat these things as essentially ends. It has the effect of turning political analysis into the higher justification.

To guard against the idealists' trap, we would be well advised to establish as a guiding principle the view that *everything* in social and political life is both a means and an end, depending upon the policy context in which it appears. Indeed the policy characterization of social events is an important clue to the policy which is at work. We must remember that ideals need not be loved because they are ideals. If we wish to study a political movement, we must observe the social changes which it promotes, not those ideals to which it purports to be dedicated. The most naïve and dangerous individual in politics is the idealist who imagines that he is using others and moving towards his ideals and values. The first step to political wisdom is to realize that one is not only using others, but being used by them, and to try to understand how one is being used, and by what.

III. POLITICS AND TECHNIQUE

Politics obviously arises when there is conflict, and often seems to cause or at least to heighten conflict. The ambition of those who seek harmony thus involves the elimination of political activity. But just as the solution of ultimate agreement is an illusion, so the attempt to eliminate politics from human affairs can only result in disguising it.

Everyone seems agreed that politics is an activity of some kind. But it is an activity whose characteristics are extraordinarily hard to pin down. For while there are many general descriptions of politics, most of them have an unconvincing flavor of prescription about them. When we define activities, we normally assume that they are rational: that is to say, we assign to them a general end, and perhaps make one or two remarks about the kinds of means appropriate to that end. This is what Locke does, for example, when he suggests that the end of the State is the protection of the natural rights of individuals, and that a certain organization of the executive and legislature is most appropriate to that end. The difficulty here is obvious: Locke is not, as he purports to be doing, *describing* politics, but making demands upon it. The end he suggests (it is, for Locke, one among a number of ends) is an external criterion intended to guide our approval or disapproval of any particular political act. Many such ends have been suggested: that politics should maintain peace, maximize happiness, enforce virtue, hinder the hindrances to self-realization, purify the race or unite the nation. Now some of these formulae have attained a considerable currency, and some of them have been accepted by politicians themselves. All of them imply an intellectual system in terms of which political decisions might be worked out. But all of them suffer from the crucial difficulty of describing one brand of politics far better than other kinds of which we have some knowledge. Clement Attlee and Gladstone may perhaps have had some interest in maximizing happiness (assuming that such a phrase means anything) but Genghis Khan and Bismarck are more difficult to fit within this formula.

Descriptions of politics in terms of the ends it must serve have long been current in political thinking. Such descriptions are ideological. Each formula supplies us with a general criterion by which we may estimate political policies. But the only possible criterion by which we may judge a policy is simply another, more general, policy.[15]

15. The fact that politicians are at all times and in all places to be found betraying any given policy suggested to them must make us suspicious of this whole mode of thinking. It is puerile to explain such betrayals in terms of the peculiar wickedness of politicians. Such explanations can only be the sour fruit of disappointment and disillusion. It seems more likely that political thinkers have brought unrealistic expectations to their study of politics, and then saved their expectations by distorting their account of the world.

One sophisticated avenue out of this impasse is worthy of attention. It arises from distinguishing politics from government or administration. The description "politics" is denied to unconstitutional States and to revolutionary situations, each of which indicates that political skill has lapsed in favor of some cruder governing devices. This view of politics derives from Aristotle and has a more or less continuous history up to the present day. "Politics, then, can be simply defined as the activity by which differing interests within a given unit of rule are conciliated by giving them a share in power in proportion to their importance to the welfare and the survival of the whole community."[16] Politics thus entails considerable skill of a special kind, a readiness to negotiate rather than impose a rule by force, an acceptance of the diversity and plurality of things within the State, and in more conservative formulations, a suspicion of far-reaching political plans of change.

I take it that the point of this selective meaning of "politics" is to distinguish the manner in which free States such as Athens, Great Britain in modern times, and the American Commonwealth have been governed from such régimes as Imperial Rome, Tsarist Russia and Nazi Germany. Certainly most examples of "politics" are taken from these free States, and it never seems to make much of an appearance elsewhere. Now we need not doubt that what is isolated by this tradition of political thinking is both real and important; it is clearly possible to mark off a tyranny from a polity. But the distinction itself is always on the verge of being sustained by a preference, always struggling free from the notion of politics-as-a-good-thing. We may reject it on the ground that the facts it refers to are not political, but moral and social. For there are some interests which cannot be conciliated by giving them a share of power, some social incoherences which cannot be negotiated without force; and in these cases it is in the moral character of the interests rather than the absence of political skill, that the explanation is usually to be found. In spite of its sophistication, this view also treats politics as an activity having a certain general end—that of conciliating interests and adjusting conflict—and it fails in the same way that any teleological account of politics must fail.

We may escape from these difficulties by simply refusing to attribute any end at all to politics. For politics is a mode of behavior common to many kinds of social entities, and the ends which are found in politics are supplied by the

16. B. R. Crick, *In Defence of Politics,* London, 1962, p. 16.

social entity on whose behalf the politics is conducted. We never in fact encounter "pure politics"—and for this reason, any theory which takes power as the central conception of politics has merely entered a world of realistic-sounding fantasy. All that we ever do encounter is the politics *of* something. How we describe the various "somethings" which generate politics has always caused intellectual difficulties, but in ordinary discussion we normally find some way of expressing it. We talk of British politics, the politics of the Labor Party, of Arab nationalism, of the Presbyterian Church, or of capitalist societies. In highly general terms, we may say that politics is a mode of acting found in certain self-conscious complexes of thought and feeling which we may call movements; and the result of the emergence of politics is the creation and maintenance of institutions.

A politician may thus be regarded as a man who conducts the political business of some institution. But any actual politician is a complex human being with responsibilities[17] to a number of institutions, some of them traditional and highly articulated, others mere shadows of possibility or nostalgia. The leader of a constitutional opposition, for example, is a politician *of* his country; simultaneously, he is responsible to his party, and in a vaguer way to a vision of what his country ought to be, the details of which are partly stated by the ideological beliefs to which he gives adherence. His political relationship to these various institutions may be seen in terms of interests and demands made upon him; and quite obviously they are likely to conflict. He may find forced upon him a choice between country or party, or between office or integrity.

This situation is further complicated by the fact that in political life we cannot always know the character of the acts (what the politics is *of*) before they have happened. Further, the politician himself does not always know; whatever policy he adopts will, in combination with events, go on revealing to

---

17. The term "responsibility" in this section is used in a purely descriptive sense to indicate a relationship of involvement between a person's acts and an institution. The term has strong prescriptive overtones, and is crucial in moral and political arguments where allegiance is at stake. In moral discussions, people are said to be "irresponsible" or "forgetting their responsibilities." But these uses suppress (sometimes because it is obvious from the context) what the responsibility is *to*. If we refuse to look at the matter from a restricted point of view, people are never irresponsible; they simply cease to be responsible to some things, and become responsible to others.

him new facts about the social entity on whose behalf he acts. He may fall in or out of love with his party or his country; he may strive to change his followers at the risk of his office. All political acts have a moral character; and many may be seen as hypotheses which events may confirm or falsify. The act of a Brutus in assassinating Caesar only makes sense upon the hypothesis that the decline of the Republic could be averted by the removal of the bewitching presence of Caesar. The consequences—and probably only the consequences—revealed the presence of moral changes in the character of the Roman ruling classes such that, given those people at that time, a republic was unworkable. But it is only unworkable because of *resulting* decisions on the part of a great number of different people, who could not themselves have predicted with much certainty how they would behave in the event. Convinced believers can wobble, and those who doubt themselves have often found an unsuspected element of resolution.

On the view I am taking, then, politics is inextricably bound up with moral and social entities, and the content and issues which arise in politics cannot be explained without reference to them. In a quite empirical way, ethics and politics cannot be separated without distortion; though this certainly does not mean that there is any set of prescriptions which is uniquely appropriate to political activity. Indeed, the whole apparatus of prescription, justification and exhortation, whilst deriving its plausibility from its reference to moral characteristics, is properly one of the devices of politics, in so far as it is concerned with persuading people to act in required ways.

On this view, then, the vocabulary of politics will not include the traditional concepts of political philosophy—equality, rights, freedom, justice, nature, law, etc., for all of these notions are explicable only in terms of the social entities which generated special kinds of political activity. Politics can only be characterized in a highly general and abstract way, for it is a highly general and abstract field.

The most important political distinction is between what is external and what is internal. Each ruler is a Janus-like figure, facing both inwards to his subjects and outwards to other sovereign States. To his subjects, he is a protector; in his external relations he is a defender of his people and therefore a potential enemy. This is a point which was made most elaborately by Hobbes, and it is recognized in the liberal yearning for an institution—world government—which has nothing external to it. For this would seem to solve the problem of enmity; the world ruler would be an enemy to none. The difficulty of this dream is that what is physically internal to the institution may yet be politically external. Thus criminals, by definition, are people for whom the ruler is an enemy; and if, as in revolutions, the State is politically conceived in terms of allegiance to a set of ideas, entire classes of people may be externalized—Jews, Bantu, Kulaks, Aristocrats, oppositionists, to take only the most conspicuous examples.

In an admittedly whimsical sense, then, we may say that the distinction between internal and external may become a matter of life and death. How the distinction is actually conceived depends upon what the ruler is in fact responsible to. Stalin, for example, in becoming responsible to *Communist* Russia necessarily externalized huge classes of people—both nationalities and social groupings. The responsibility of politicians is in constant flux; they may become responsible to something very different from the institution they actually rule—as did James II in attempting to make England Catholic and absolutist; they may become responsible to something larger, as in the various national unifications which have occurred in the last two centuries. Institutions like the Holy Roman Empire may languish and decline as politicians withdraw their interest and allegiance, or they may develop and grow in the manner of the European Common Market. But the course of political activity keeps on redefining what is taken to be internal and external.

Externally, the politician seeks to maintain the security of the institution over which he presides. Internally, he generally seeks order and coherence. Politicians who accept the traditional constitution of the institution they govern are usually to be found working out kinds of accommodation between conflicting parts of the institution; between warring religious groups, struggling commercial interests, racial or linguistic elements or just people who do not like each other. This kind of activity is commonly found in European politics, and gives rise to the view of politics which we considered earlier, as the maintenance of order by adjustment of interests. Certainly this kind of activity requires considerable skill; for often there is only a limited range of formulae which will settle a dispute. Political antagonists are prone to falsify their demands, and mislead others about the nature and extent of support and opposition. The skilled politician facing a problem of this sort must discover the truth of the matter; but for much of the time he must use a kind of intuition, for the facts upon which he must base his solution will not exist until the solution has actually been attempted. Should he conciliate—and provoke a stiffening of demands? Should he use force—and provoke only desperation and disorder? He has to judge, and only his experience and understanding can help him.

But politics cannot be defined as the activity of adjusting interests. For we shall often find politicians seeking for various reasons to provoke disorder and to intensify differences. Instead of seeking to promote coherence and maintain order and security, they do just the opposite. To deny such people the description of politicians is to beg the intellectual question. We must attempt to explain their behavior; and it can, I would suggest, only be explained in terms of a shift in their political responsibilities. They have become politicians *of* something different, and in many cases, the best available definition of that something different is an idea. Thus communist politicians in Britain who often seek to intensify differences must be seen as politicians not of Britain, but of either the ideology of Communism, or of a shadowy institution called Communist Britain.

The distinction often made between practical politicians and ideological ones cannot be seriously sustained; but it does have the virtue of pointing to actual differences between say a Robespierre and a Talleyrand, a Charles II and a James II. It refers to variations in political behavior between an idealist at one end of the scale, and an opportunist at the other. We also find that opposition groups are prone to formulate political issues in ideological terms; that is, they tend to moralize these issues and present them as matters of right and of justice. Politicians in office, whilst prepared to meet moral argument with moral argument, will often reply with variations on the idea of political necessity. But the difference between politics and ideology is not one between "ideas" or the absence of ideas. A Lenin leading a proscribed political party, for example, is no doubt very much an ideologist in his relation to Russia; but in relation to his own followers, he is necessarily a politician.

We may next observe that politics is an area of force and coercion; it is rife with sanctions of various kinds. The reason for this is not that politicians are naturally disposed to force, but that human beings are complicated and often inconsistent. No institution is ever held together simply by force; there is always some element of consent, a preference for an existing situation over the costs of changing it. But equally no institution ever embodies a comprehensive common good. Britain at bay in 1940 was pretty nearly as cohesive as any such large and plural society ever has been; but even then, we find phenomena like defeatism, profiteering, grumbling, distrust of the competence of the leadership, not to mention such irrational but sometimes decisive factors as laziness or boredom. What social harmony exists is partly spontaneous; but in States it is never sufficiently so. The harmony—the common good or the national interest—must constantly be created by politicians. And where it cannot be created, it must be forced. If soldiers will not volunteer in sufficient numbers, they must be conscripted. If people will not pay their taxes, governments will force them to. And those acts which are permanently necessary to the maintenance of the institution will be described as duties.

Where a spontaneous common good exists, political activity is hardly necessary. And there are situations where we can perhaps discern what may accurately be called a common good. We find it at moments in sporting teams, or in any army with a high morale, or in a city under siege and united in a cause. But there are two major difficulties in basing a theory of politics on a common good. One is that it is virtually never exactly identical with the institution; most of the State may be united in a cause, but there are always some who are left out, or who are at least lukewarm. Or, alternatively, the common good may spill across institutions and threaten them, as often happened during the wars of religion. The second difficulty is the inconsistency of people. They may at one point be united; but it takes little—as Rousseau regretfully observed—to make them begin thinking of their own advantage, the good of their families, their comparative status, or the good of some other cause they support.

It is because anything genuinely recognizable as the common good so seldom occurs in political activity that politicians have to be calculators. They must quantify things which are qualitatively different, and terms like "better," "worse," and "on balance" turn up extensively in their discourse. They must give money to national sport and to national art; and as far as sport itself is concerned, the money given to art is lost and wasted; and vice versa. Appeals to the common good in competitive situations of this kind are appeals to the plurality of interest found in people. A sportsman may have no interest in art; but one may be able to appeal to his national feeling, his generosity, or his interest in social co-operation. In politics, nearly everything is done by some people for the wrong reasons.

Politics is an activity without values of its own, and things which are widely valued in various cultures—things like truth, or human life—are *politically* valued only for their usefulness, which is often unstable. Truth, for example, has its uses; no one can retreat too far into a fantasy world without becoming ineffective; but equally it is often highly inconvenient. The facts can alienate much needed support. When they don't, when indeed they promote a following, then the truth may emerge. It would be reckless to attribute Krushchev's revelations about Stalin to a concern for the accuracy of Russian historical ideas. The differences between régimes in the amount of lying, deceit, fraud and illusion must be attributed not to political variations, but to the moral character of the régime.[18] Certain ways of life—notably those of Western Europe—are capable of generating institutions (such as the press, an opposition, free universities) which lessen the advantages of deceit. Politicians *qua* politicians are interested not in Truth, Beauty, Sanctity or human life, but in advantages, and there is nothing in the world which is consistently advantageous.

A good deal of deceit is essential to the proper working of any kind of institution. Antipathies must be suppressed so that antagonists may work together for various purposes; the extent of support for or opposition to some measure must be falsified, for this knowledge itself will change the situation; and very frequently a politician must disguise his intentions until the time is ripe for revealing them. For timing is often essential to the success or failure of a political move. For these reasons, politicians have elaborated the usages of a mellifluous and soggy form of discourse, justly famed for its vagueness and ambiguity. The use of this discourse, and the understanding of it, require enormous skill. Thus in diplomatic communications between powers, the wording of a phrase or the omission of a claim is all that may indicate a major shift in policy. By such devices, political discussion between leaders can go on with the minimum interruption from popular clamor. Political communications must say different things to different people, and preferably can be abandoned and denied if they should cause embarrassment.

This oblique and tortuous character of politics often provokes nothing more than exasperation from the common man; and that very exasperation

---

18. For a fascinating comment on this point see "That's No Lie, Comrade" by Ronald Hingley, *Problems of Communism*, Vol. XI No. 2, March–April 1962. The strains of truth often come out in the conduct of American foreign policy, as exemplified in the U.2 incident and the Bay of Pigs Invasion.

will launch us into the illusion of ultimate agreement.[19] We all want peace, don't we? The diplomatic brouhaha can only seem like the possibly dangerous indulgence of politicians, playing for their own purposes a game that may do for us all. The liberal program which seeks to drown politics in the liberated goodwill of ordinary men has a compelling attraction. But on the argument we have presented, politics cannot be isolated in this way. For the content of political calculations is not itself political; it is moral and social. It is, in fact, the passions and desires of ordinary men—especially the things they are prepared to fight for. And men, at various times and places, have been prepared to fight for a bizarre collection of objectives; in many cases, they have been prepared to fight just for the sake of fighting.

I take it, then, that what we all recognize as politics is simply a manner of human behavior which has its own peculiar characteristics, but which can never be isolated from moral and social circumstances. Politics is always parasitic upon ends and purposes which exist independently.

Further, both in our account and also in common usage, we find politics everywhere in human affairs. We may talk not only of national politics, but of church or trade-union politics, or the politics of any institutions. The institutions which exist politically at any given time depend upon circumstances. "Italy" (having been, in Metternich's phrase, "a geographical expression") had very little in the way of politics until the end of the eighteenth century. The proletariat was not a political institution until Marx tried to make it so.

Perhaps the most interesting example of this point is to be found in the liberal invention of the individual. For liberalism has, since at least the seventeenth century, conceived of the individual as an autonomous political institution. It began by regarding him as complete in himself; fully formed without the intervention of social influences. It proceeded to work out the ways in which he might secure his external security—namely by entering into a social contract. It explored the consequences of this contract for the internal governance of his desires. It created a politics of the individual, and called it ethics—for many of its prudential principles happened to be identical with long-held ethical precepts. As the social contract theory declined, utilitarianism took up the task, associated in many cases with a terminology of rights,

19. It may also launch us into Fascism, as happened in the thirties when there was widespread impatience with parliaments as ineffectual "talking shops."

which is a common indication that new political structures are emerging. Whether the individual is at any time a self-contained autonomous institution, and whether he ought ever to act as if this were so, is one of the main issues dividing idealists and utilitarians.

Finally, we may make a few remarks upon the competing conception of politics which is found in liberalism—and which, like many things found in liberalism, is also the unreflective view of the common man. This view begins with a rational evaluation of our political situation. The rational evaluation seeks to clarify our objectives; to work out exactly what it is we want. We all want peace, happiness, security, freedom, and so on. Given agreement on these ends, only the technical problem remains of finding the means to them. For this reason we may call this competing view of politics a technical one.

We have already stated one objection to this view, namely that the ultimate agreement does not exist. It is a fake. The large words on which it is based are empty receptacles of meaning which will, in discussion, accommodate any desires or aspirations we may choose to put in them. A consistent pursuit of this line necessarily involves us in the implication that all human conflict has been the result of an unfortunate misunderstanding; if only the Carthaginians and the Romans had got together and talked things over in an atmosphere of goodwill and negotiation, those Punic wars would have been unnecessary. And this is absurd. Admittedly generic men have no fundamental conflicts to worry them, but this is only because generic men have been constructed out of what stands above the fights of ordinary men.

Secondly, technical politics inevitably makes a great play with terms like problem and solution; for this is the language of technique. In the propagandist uses of the doctrine, problems exist in a vacuum: they are simply problems, with nothing attached to them. Here we may repeat the point we made in discussing moral experience: Any given situation only presents a problem to people of a certain character. One man's problem is another man's solution, and many social problems only arise because in some way they are solutions. The problem of slavery, for example, was the solution to problems arising in a way of life notably different from ours. For liberals, apartheid is a problem; for the Afrikaner, it is a solution, and it would only cease to be so either under highly unlikely circumstances (such as the consistent docility of the Bantu) or if the Afrikaners ceased to be what they are.

The position is even more complicated than this, for it is perfectly possible to find situations which constitute both a problem and a solution to the same person at the same time. Hypochondria is one example of this, so are cases of masochism where the masochist both likes and fears the threatened pain. People do not have a single core of selfhood which steers them on a consistent course.

The question: What is it exactly that we want? is, in the circumstances of the present time, the only unassailable generator of evaluative responses. And its difficulty is that, strictly speaking, it is a question which we are not fully competent to answer for ourselves, much less for other people. This point can be exaggerated, providing only a camouflage for timidity. In actual life, we do plan years ahead, and make our dispositions with a fair confidence of success. But in a liberal atmosphere the point is far more likely to be forgotten. And it can be forgotten or ignored if we imagine that our failures are solely the result of carelessness and incompetence in the initial planning. This may be so; though even these failures are not casual; they too have a more complicated explanation than simple ignorance or incompetence. And politicians who also must plan and predict—quite unavoidably—are in an even more difficult situation, for they must be attempting to predict the responses of great numbers of people. For what in ordinary social life are slips of the tongue, casual revelations, or currents of sympathy, antipathy, fascination or impatience may become, on the grander political stage, portentous movements capable of crushing whatever gets in their path.

Technical politics, then, would only be possible on the assumption that all individuals were fixed, their characters fully known, and their society frozen in a single mould. Such characters would be incapable of development or change. If we are uncertain and afraid, security and stability have great charm. In this century, liberals have mostly been afraid, and for this reason, the salvationist current has been running more strongly than the libertarian. But quite apart from what *we want*, technical politics is an illusion—though it has been a very influential one.

CHAPTER FOUR

Moral and Political Evasions

I. THE DOCTRINE OF NEEDS

MUCH OF THE STRENGTH of liberalism as an ideology results from the manner in which it takes over ordinary words and
gently inflates them into metaphysical tenets. Sometimes
these words go in pairs. "Improvement" for example is a very ordinary
and untechnical word which can either be used in its own humble sta-
tion, or can give support to its more ambitious brother, "progress," and
"happiness," by this process of conceptual elephantiasis, can become the
unique object of human striving. But the logic of this ideological operation can perhaps best be seen if we turn from "desire" (which we assumed
to be the key term of liberalism in its earlier development) to its partner,
"need."

The ordinary uses of "need" are familiar enough. "I need brushes," a
painter might say ("otherwise I can't finish my picture"). This is little different from saying "I want brushes," except that "need" implies that the
things wanted are *for* something, in other words, are means to some important end. Desire may be capricious; need always claims to be taken seriously.
It is for this reason that "need" is a vehicle of pleading, often of sentimental
pleading. "I need brushes," the painter may say with desperation in his tone
if he is talking to a patron, from whom he wishes to extract money. A need

is imperative; it is something which, by definition, has a right to satisfaction.[1]

Such a term is likely to attract both propagandists and philosophers (and
especially those political thinkers who combine both roles). Its emotional
overtones are beautifully persuasive. Further, in a puritan environment, a
need is free from even the most austere kinds of objection to human desires.
Thus we find that the writers of advertisements are eager to show that the
product they wish to puff is not a luxury; it is a necessity—something which
everyone *must* have. (There are times when the implausibility of this is evident; and the intelligent advertiser takes the bull by the horns and insists that,
once in a while, everyone *needs* a little luxury in his life.) On the other hand,
"need" as a term of propaganda has one serious disadvantage compared with
"desire"; it always refers to an end, and thus invites enquiry as to what the
thing needed is *for*. It therefore conflicts with a general rule of sophisticated
propaganda, by which the terms used must seem to be absolute; they must be
purged of all embarrassing relationships.

Philosophers are attracted to the term "need" because it opens up interesting variations of utilitarianism. The needs doctrine may be stated as follows:
If our needs have been satisfied, we shall be happy. This is not a particularly
interesting statement, but it becomes rather more so if it is converted: If we are
not happy, then one or more of our needs has not been satisfied. This too is
vapid. It simply inserts the term "need" into the assertion that if we aren't
happy, there must be some reason for it. But the insertion of emotionally
loaded terms into a rather empty doctrine, a favorite device of utilitarianism,
is never a casual matter. In this case it suggests a program for social scientists:
if we find unhappiness (and therefore a social problem), then search for the
need which is being, or once was, frustrated.

At this point the requirements of liberal philosopher and social propagandist coalesce. Both wish to establish the term "need" as something whose relationships do not require serious examination. This can be achieved by first
establishing "need" in contexts where its imperative character is unlikely to be
denied. Here we find the bedrock case. Food and drink are "basic human

---

1. Compare one of the later dicta of Simone Weil: "Where there is a need, there is an
obligation." This is a good example of the analytic statement with the synthetic overtones.

needs." What are they basic to? To survival. At the present time, one can get no more fundamental.

It is formulation, not fact, which is here at issue. No one denies that any particular man will starve to death after a certain number of weeks if he has no food. No one denies that he is likely to be miserable while it is happening. Although these statements are perfectly general propositions about human beings, there are very considerable variations. A well-fed bourgeois is likely to be hysterically hungry after a day or so without food, whereas an Asian peasant will go about his business for a considerable time on very little. Hunger is partly a matter of habit.

Now if the issue is life or death (or survival, as the liberal ideologist prefers to put it) then people will agree that death ought to be prevented where possible. One might parenthetically observe that there have been some cultures in which the imperative did not operate so strongly. But the important thing here is the belief that life—"life itself," sundered from any activity at all—is the most important thing for every individual. The issue may actually arise in a number of ways. We may imagine an isolated and starving community whose only available food happens to be the subject of a religious taboo. Is life then more important than a religious injunction? The liberal would say yes. Here is one of the functions of his criterion of rationality; here is one of the reasons why liberals regard rites and taboos as mere prejudices and prefer the generalized deity of natural religion. Here is one of the points where talk about survival and "life itself" involves the suppression of vital facts in a situation.

The issue arises again where the inhabitants of a richer country are faced with a choice: should money be spent on organizing a new symphony orchestra, or sent to buy food for famine relief? In welfarist terms, there is no doubt of the answer. Life is more important than music. But to whom? And in what mood? The situation also arises today as a result of a popular argument: In order to "conquer world poverty," the educational system of the richer countries must produce more technicians, and this involves withdrawing resources from the teaching of the classics. Assuming for a moment that all the welfarist assertions about the nature, extent, and means of eliminating world poverty are true, is the dedicated teacher of Latin and Greek exhibiting a cold indifference to the needs of others?

The formulation of such questions in terms of "basic human needs" is thus a device which serves to obscure the conflicts and social changes which will result from following a welfarist policy. Every social policy requires sacrifices—which is why all political movements include one clause on the beauties of sacrifice. And sacrifice is good because it is self-sacrifice, the conquest of self-indulgence. Even the classics teacher resisting the encroachments of science can be presented as self-interested. So can the painter who thinks of painting but not of how much white bread for Red China his Chinese white would buy. Not to accept a welfarist policy can come to seem a moral defect, a lack of compassion, pity, sympathy for one's fellow creatures.

The logical fallacy of this way of thinking is not far to seek. It consists of jumping from:

> x is a necessary condition of y.
> to:
> x is more important than y.

Examples of this would be: food is a necessary condition of maintaining a symphony orchestra. Therefore food (and especially the provision of food) is more important than music. The form this often takes (as in Spencer, for example) is to suggest a list of priorities from the rational (or welfarist) point of view. First one must make sure that people are properly fed, clothed and housed. *Then* there will be time for us to be cultured. This was one of the assumptions of nineteenth-century socialism, which believed that it was only poverty which prevented the working class from entering into its cultural heritage. There are two related mistakes in this argument. The first is to assume that culture is what the bourgeoisie thinks it is, an assumption which exhibits the bourgeois presuppositions of virtually all socialist movements. Thinking in this way has led to the vice of negative definition. The proletariat was defined (even by Marx, who in some moods was perfectly aware of this trap) as the poor, the deprived, the suffering class—defined in other words in terms of non-possession. The bourgeois insistence on personal possession is so powerful as to create entire definitions which leave the subject a complete mystery. Who are the poor? They are those who do not possess what others have. This is rather like defining a horse and cart as a thing that lacks an engine. It is equally a matter of ideology to talk about the "underdeveloped countries" and it reveals the political direction of liberalism. The liberal has little interest in the way of life of the peoples who live in these countries; in so far as he has, it is usually the sentimental interest of pity and compassion. He is simply concerned with the fact that in the "underdeveloped countries" people do not live as he does. And they ought to.

The other point in the slogan of "first security and then culture" is a mistake of fact. It is the assumption that affluence and security are both necessary *and* sufficient conditions of a cultured existence. And this assuredly is not true. There may be some relation between the leisure and resources of the upper classes of Western Europe who have produced so much of what we now revere as culture. But it is certainly a very complex relationship, and it has little to do with security. To a large extent, people who become interested in affluence move on to pursue more affluence: bigger and better things to buy.

The bedrock case of survival establishes the emotional tone of the doctrine of needs, and this tone can be carried over into its many other uses. For the important point about a need is that it is a way of discriminating between conflicting desires. Each man, as Bentham insisted, must be his own expert upon what he desires; no one else can try to overrule him on that point. With needs, the case is different. People may need things without knowing that they need them, and their needs may even directly contradict their desires. There is an element of truth in this view. The desires that people express vary from day to day, and they are often contradictory. There are also cases where, for complicated reasons, people insist that they desire something very different from what they in fact want. Our judgment in such situations must always depend upon our knowledge of the people involved; but even with the best knowledge of those close to us, we may miscalculate. Now just as the doctrine of needs requires a validating case where no one seriously contests its absoluteness, so also it requires a validating class of people where the discriminatory use of needs, contradicting expressed desires, is most plausible. And the conspicuous class of people who satisfy this requirement is children.

Exactly to the extent that they are inarticulate, and their actual desires need not be taken seriously, children are an ideal field for the use of the doctrine of needs. Children need understanding, security, love, discipline, punishment, and so on; given the absence of these factors (and any others yet to be dreamed of), then the troubles of later life stand explained. The doctrine of needs in the hands of psychologists and social workers is somewhat modified: if we are unhappy (and especially if we constitute a social problem), then the cause must lie in the frustration of some need whilst we were children.

This kind of explanation—it is highly elastic and often inscrutable—is simultaneously moral, and also morally evasive. It evades ethics by ignoring the moral experience of the relevant human beings to be explained, and seeking a chain of inevitable causes in human affairs. But it is also moral (in the conventional sense) because it prescribes behavior for us. It tells us what we ought to do, and we may accept Hume's advice to look carefully at such terms.

It is of course immediately evident that no statement involving the term "need" can claim to be scientific unless the relevant consequence is specified. The proposition "children need love" may be passed off as expert advice, but it is clearly elliptical. The expert can only supply us with a set of possible consequences. If a child is not loved, then x will happen; if it is loved, then y will happen. But no expert is in a position to recommend either x or y to us;[2] nor indeed are many such actual relationships any more than highly tenuous connections.

The authority of the needs expert is buttressed in a number of oblique ways. Political writings, for example, contain large numbers of references to needs, basic needs, human needs, or social needs, where no particular need is involved. These statements appear to say something, and accustom us to the idea. Next there is the bedrock case, where the need is validated by the fact that death may follow frustration of the need. Here our preferences can usually be taken for granted, and any uneasiness about the actual concept of "need" looks like pedantry. Further, by formulating the question as "such and such a class of people need x" (to achieve y implied), the needs expert may persuade people to fight on the ground: Is x really a need? And on this question, shaky statistical correlations look more convincing than they do when the question is directly faced: does x lead to y, and if so, under what circumstances? For these reasons, the elliptical use of "need" is a virtual index of the propaganda content of social science.

The relation between the concept of need and the fact of inarticulateness reveals part of the political significance of needs. Classical liberalism concerned itself primarily with desires, and a need was simply an auxiliary component more or less clearly related to the policy of which it was a necessary condition. Modern liberalism has reversed this order, playing down desire to elevate need.

---

2. The overall coverage of the expert is sometimes upheld at this point by casting the moral philosopher in the role of ends expert. V. 1, p. 133.

The cause of this reversal would seem to be the successive and rapid enfranchisements of large and inarticulate masses of people with little experience of political life. In democratic theory, all government acts must emerge from the popular will; but if the popular will is confused, immoral, inconvenient or otherwise defective, then some oracular device must be found by which it can speak with clarity and decision. The political theory of modern times has been singularly fertile in such devices. The notion of the general will, and that of the class-consciousness of the proletariat, are examples of this kind of device; for in each case, a small set of people may establish themselves as experts in the pronouncements of these oracles. Actual popular support is unnecessary; it can be rigged up after the event, if necessary. The concept of need is a less dramatic example of the same kind of device. Like most liberal conceptions, it looks innocuous, and it has never been saddled with atrocities like the reign of terror or the dictatorship of the proletariat. Most of its practitioners are mild social scientists, or benevolent welfarists, rather than wild-eyed fanatics like Robespierre or Lenin. Yet the logical and political identity remains.

Just as the conception of necessities was, for the Puritans, a moral battering-ram against the aristocratic style of living, so the attraction of "needs" is that they appear to exclude anything frivolous, eccentric, subjective or capricious. A need is a demand which has passed into the world of absolute moral acceptance, a thing not to be denied. The furniture of a rich minority in the past satisfied no needs: it was part of a way of life, and its aesthetic and its "functional" attributes were held together within that way of life. The mode of mass production of furniture is strikingly different from individual craft production. The concept of need breaks up a way of life and inevitably changes it. Not indeed always for the worse. The eccentricities of aristocratic taste may be at times as disastrous as the fashions of a mass market. Restricted aristocratic education may become a dogma for dilettantes, the learning of a few tags in a classical language which will serve as marks of social distinction. This is merely to say that there are corrupt pressures invading the exercise of every skill.

The political advantage of "needs" is that, because of their lack of discrimination, they permit of substitutes. A human need does not discriminate: it is for food, not for chop suey or goulash. It is for shelter, not for a brick bungalow in Brighton with two garages and all mod. cons. People can be encouraged or taught to satisfy—indeed to develop—needs in a required manner. A certain quantity of calories or of vitamins is needed to satisfy the need for food, and calculations of floor space and the existence of facilities like bathrooms can serve as precise criteria marking off the slum area from the new town. The satisfaction of medical needs can be calculated in terms of a ratio of doctors to patients. All this is welfare and, in a world of statistics, is far more useful than attempting to enquire into the purity, fecundity, etc., of pleasures and pains as Bentham suggested. In the conception of needs, utilitarianism has at last succeeded in becoming more or less "scientific"—that is to say, measurable.

The final task in any criticism of propaganda is to remake the social connections which propaganda severs by making its terms absolute. If a social need is a necessary condition of something, the question we must next consider is what that something is. It is a question which admits of no easy answer. To satisfy the basic needs of a population presumably involves allowing them the conditions of an austere way of life. There was undoubtedly an element of this in early formulations of need thinking, because the upper classes considered that too much prosperity for the lower would lead to lazy self-indulgence. This element of vicarious puritanism also enters into liberal approval of Soviet communism where it is precisely the sacrifices, the austere way of life, which commands admiration.

Yet by now, the idea of welfare depends so completely upon the variable standards of a rising industrial society that any question of austerity falls into the background. The concept of need is validated by reference to malnutrition in the underdeveloped areas of the world; its imperativeness depends upon its association with suffering. But with that imperative tone guaranteed, needs doctrine may move in any direction.

For social needs are those conditions which must be satisfied if social life is to be organized *in a certain way*. The propaganda function of needs doctrine is to confuse the issues which would arise out of a direct confrontation of competing political policies. Consider the argument that we must accept a high degree of central planning if the need for full employment is to be satisfied. The need for full employment is an end, indeed an imperative, likely to appeal to all who deplore poverty and enforced idleness. Economic planning features as a means; whether we support it or not appears to depend only on the technical question: does it promote full employment?

But this subordinate role is deceptive, for central planning can lead to a life of its own. It appeals by its rationality to all who have a passion for order and tidiness in political life. Remembering our principle that in politics everything is both an end *and* a means, we may formulate the argument in a less fa-miliar way. In order to get a centrally planned society, full employment must become a need. Or, to take a related example, in order to organize society for the satisfaction of human needs, the political influence of unfettered capital-ism must be replaced by governmental control. And again, we may reverse this neat arrangement of means to ends: in order to destroy capitalism, needs doc-trine must be developed into a moral imperative.

It is thus a mistake—and not merely a liberal mistake—to imagine that the ends of policies arise in a moral field, and that political policies have only the subordinate role of means. All of these policies—full employment, economic planning, developing a welfare state, and destroying capitalism—are simulta-neously moral and political; each leads a life of its own. How they are con-nected—whether cast for the role of ends or means—depends entirely upon the persuasive climate of the time, and it is that which is crucially moral. Pol-itics is strongly influenced by changes in moral sensibility, and advocacy of such changes is therefore a political act.

Misunderstanding on this issue is virtually inevitable. Needs conceptions have, for many people, a vise-like grip which nothing will shake. Each attack on the conception of needs will be met by a baffled reformulation: *Surely* it is obvious that people do have certain fundamental needs if they are to live. And each reformulation will miss the point. There is no factual issue at stake, but the semantic issue has large philosophical implications. "Need" belongs to a particular language of political and moral thought arising from the concep-tion of generic men. Once we have entered into that language, we can only say individualist things. It is a language which has grown out of the liberal move-ment (and some associated movements) and it has, like all languages, its par-ticular blind spots, the things which it cannot say. Once inside, no matter how much we thresh about, we shall be hard put to it to escape. A great mistake has been to imagine that an ideology consists of a set of answers to neutral ques-tions; whereas in fact it consists in the questions.

II. THE LURE OF THE POSITIVE APPROACH

One way in which the liberal movement influences behavior is by suggesting that everyone has a duty to work for the improvement of human conditions. Now one might not think that such a duty would lie very heavily upon us. For in a very ordinary sense this is just what human beings, individually and collectively, spend much of their time doing. Each day they produce goods, construct buildings, work out new rules of behavior. But we have missed the point. For once improvement turns into a duty, preoccupations change. We become receptive to the liberal notion that we *ought* to be "improving" both society and ourselves. The effects of this harmless-looking doctrine have been so striking that it has acquired a name which, for want of a better, we shall adopt: Meliorism.

Meliorism is less a doctrine than an attitude which has fathered many doctrines. We have already encountered one of these doctrines in discussing moral experience, namely the view that the task of moral philosophy is to produce principles which may validly guide our conduct. "The reason why actions are in a peculiar way revelatory of moral principles," writes Mr. Hare, "is that the function of moral principles is to guide conduct."[3] *The* function? But as we have observed, everything can fit into many policies, that is, have many functions. And it is significant that this passage is almost immediately followed by: "Thus, in a world in which the problems of conduct become every day more complex and tormenting, there is a great need for an understanding of the language in which these problems are posed and answered." Given the intrusion of this kind of salesmanship into moral philosophy, it is not surprising that moral enquiry has virtually passed into the hands of novelists and literary critics, people who are less subject to meliorist pressures.

Or, again, we may find meliorism in the doctrine of social commitment, which asserts both that we *are* and that we *ought to be* "in society." The first proposition is supported by the unexceptionable statement that whatever we do or refrain from doing is likely to have social and political consequences. The second proposition suggests that if *we* (whoever is being appealed to; the doctrine is primarily aimed at artists and intellectuals) do not get in there and fight to improve society, then political leadership will pass by default to the less qualified, or the positively sinister. This is a fairly crude doctrine, an obvious hook for landing intellectual fish on the shore of some prefabricated cause. But it has had an interesting career in this century and, like most meliorist doctrines, its most important result has been to quieten scruples. The socially committed man will on occasions refrain from criticism in the higher interests of the cause.

3. R. M. Hare, *The Language of Morals*, Oxford, 1952, p. 1.

The doctrine of social commitment has two typical meliorist characteristics. It incorporates as an imperative the duty of improvement, and it is hostile to criticism. It is this second feature which reveals that meliorism is more than a temporary folly of the present time, but has important roots in perennial western attitudes. For one of the commonest ways of evading criticism is to suggest that the criticism does not help in the solution of some cognate practical problem; and this fallacy is connected with our hostile attitudes to what is "merely critical" in contrast with what is "constructive," or better still, "creative." The popular version of this attitude would be: "It's easy to criticize, but what we need are constructive proposals." In other words, if something is bad, one ought not to say it is bad unless one can do better. Like most doctrines, this one has a substratum of commonsense. There is such a thing as carping criticism, and we are often irritated by it. There are also, however, times when we simply do not wish to be criticized, and here meliorist attitudes are useful to push the criticism away. Literary criticism has suffered extensively from these attitudes, being often regarded as subordinate either to the artist or to the appreciation of the audience; it is allowed respectability only in performing some limited function, and is widely distrusted as parasitic and decadently self-conscious.

The loaded distinction between "positive" and "negative" is also used, especially in social theory, to make the same sort of point. Consider a discussion of the movement from Feudalism to Capitalism: "Where the former purpose had been the maintenance of an established order, and thus in these prescribed terms positive, the new purpose was at first negative: society existed to create conditions in which the free economic enterprise of individuals was not hampered." But there is no distinction between a "positive purpose" and a negative one; in both cases something is being done, and the distinction can only arise by paying attention, in a complex situation, to what is *not* done, rather than to what is being done. And this direction of attention inserts into the argument an unexamined assumption that something *ought* to be done.[4]

---

4. We have already noted the ideological device of negative definition. By a similar device, unwelcome situations can be tendentiously explained if we attribute what is unwelcome to the *lack* of some admired power or faculty. For example, a report in *The Times*, 9.4.62: "People in academic society seemed constitutionally incapable of grasping the fact that they were performing a kind of public service, said Mr. L. J. Barnes." On the contrary, academics reject this view not out of a "constitutional defect," but out of a well considered belief in the totalitarian implications of such "public service" ideology.

Meliorism is, then, a way of discriminating between activities according to how effectively they produce results in which we happen to be interested. The various doctrines to which it gives rise are really tangential to meliorism itself; and at the center lies the metaphor of building. For if we are to build something, we must first prepare the ground, and only then can we begin to construct. But generally we are uninterested in preparing the ground; our dominating preoccupation is the construction of the building. Locke, in a celebrated passage, described his work (i.e. that of philosophy) as "removing some of the rubbish that lies in the way to knowledge."[5] The metaphor allocates status to kinds of work. We have already seen criticism demoted by this kind of device; and other kinds of activity may suffer the same fate. Teaching suffers frequently from this device, in such sayings as "those who can, do; those who can't, teach." It is taken not as an independent but merely as an instrumental activity, something done in order to get the end-product—the skilled or cultivated man.

The construction of buildings is the melioristic metaphor *par excellence*. And clearly, our ranking of these various occupations depends upon our relation to what is being done. If we look forward to occupying the building then we shall regard clearing the rubble as a mere preliminary, but if we specialize in demolition, our interest will be different. Meliorism in this case takes what is indeed usually a majority point of view, and assumes that we all belong to that majority.

The conversion of a majority point of view into a monolithic one lies behind most versions of meliorism. But one man's improvement is another man's disaster. And again, what may be thought an improvement at one point of time may cease to be so as time passes. More commonly, we have mixed feelings when we contemplate some future change, and must work out whether "on balance" we prefer it, i.e. regard it as an improvement, or not. This preoccupation with comparison leads to the intrusion into social and political questions of the intellectually irrelevant question of whether we *like* the phenomenon in question or whether we don't, combined with a singular obscurity about the basis of comparison.[6]

---

5. In the Epistle to the Reader, which prefaces the *Essay concerning Human Understanding*.
6. For example, "Is it as evil for a State to order the explosion of a bomb, whose fall-out will ultimately, over several generations, cause the death of, say, a thousand people from

Meliorism is the assertion that political and social thinkers ought to concern themselves more with "practical affairs." It is a special development of the utilitarian view that everything gains its value from its usefulness. The value of intellectual activities will therefore be determined by their conduciveness to reform or improvement. Intellectual criticism of politics can only be justified as a preparation for "doing something about it." And the influence of meliorism is so strong that it will sometimes be explicitly disavowed and implicitly asserted in the same paragraph.[7]

Since meliorism is less an argument than an attitude, it is hardly something to be refuted. But we may at least state the objections which invalidate the doctrines it generates. First, we may point out that the activity of criticism and the activity of constructing political or ethical solutions are two different and clearly separable things. The same people may, of course, do both. But the one is philosophical and the other is at least part of the activity of being a politician. They demand different talents, and while, as I have said, these talents *may* be combined in one person, there is a good deal of evidence to suggest that such a combination is infrequent. Few politicians have had anything very interesting to say about political philosophy, and political philosophers have been undistinguished (where they have not been disastrous) in tasks of political responsibility. There is in fact no earthly reason why they should be yoked together in this way.

Secondly, in social life, the consequences of demolishing a situation (overthrowing a government, abolishing an institution, creating a new system, economic or political) do not become evident until after it has been done. This

---

harmful gene mutations, as it is for another State to order its police to shoot a thousand people personally in the back of the head? I do not think the answer is altogether obvious." C. H. Waddington, *The Ethical Animal*, London, 1960, p. 17. No, indeed, it's not obvious. But the point is that "evil" here has been vulgarized by the use of the comparative into a matter of preference.

7. "One does not demand, of course, that an ethical theory should propound solutions to all the problems of its day. . . . What is demanded of an ethical theory is primarily that it should be relevant, and applicable to a world in which the crucial actions of a thousand million people are predicated on the belief that scientific technology is good. The intellect will have failed to carry out the functions for which evolution designed it if it issues merely in the conclusion that it can suggest no criteria by which one could hope to decide whether this belief has either meaning or validity. We must cudgel our brains to be able to do better than that." Waddington, *op. cit.*, pp. 19–20.

point has been widely explored in postwar criticisms of liberal ideology when it took the form of central economic planning. In other words, reform is always to some degree blind. It cannot accurately calculate and control the consequences of its work. The "constructive" political thinker is in fact faced by a dilemma. If he provides a detailed scheme, then his details will necessarily be out of date by the time his scheme is applied; further, the only kind of person sensitive enough to adjust the details is not the philosopher but the politician.[8] On the other hand, if he confines himself to making clear the general principles on which change should take place, he quickly becomes virtually banal. In so far as the greatest happiness principle is intended as a practical guide for politicians, who can doubt but that it is completely useless? Statements of a generalized end or principle of government merely state the beginnings of political problems, or the conditions which may indicate that a solution has taken place. But they are no help to the politician.

Thirdly, political philosophy of the constructive sort falls into the idealists' trap—the belief that everyone will love one's ideals for the right reasons. A good example of this was the Prohibition Amendment in the United States. It will be remembered that repeal of the prohibition amendment was fought to the last ditch by a motley alliance of fervent moralists insisting that prohibition would work if only people gave it a chance, and on the other hand gangsters and bootleggers intent on making a fast buck. Society is in fact so complex that every proposal is likely to be welcomed in at least some circles that the liberal would regard as very sinister indeed. Marx recognized the force of the idealists' trap in refusing to become a reformist—to make constructive suggestions. To do so, he pointed out quite correctly, would be to play into the hands of the bourgeoisie.

The logical issue here is one we have already met—that of causal discontinuity. A political proposal only makes sense upon determinist assumptions which alone will allow the proposer to predict its effects. The proposer, on the other hand, assumes that he acts in a causal vacuum. He slips outside causality and social pressure; sitting on a lonely and timeless eminence, communing with reason, he ponders the question: "What ought we to do?" Then, his prin-

---

8. Cf. Hegel's ironic remark in the preface to the *Philosophy of Right and Law* that "Fichte could have omitted perfecting the passport police to the point of suggesting that not only the description of suspects be entered in their passports, but a picture."

ciples nicely enunciated, he steps back into reality. Many philosophers appear to have had some idea very like this of what they were doing. But there is no magic in the question: "What ought we to do?" which conducts a human being to another plane of reality. Nor do the walls of a study insulate the thinker from social influences. If human beings do act in a more or less regular and predictable manner (social life, social enquiry and political actions all assume that they do), then the philosopher himself must also be placed within this causal nexus. The question: "What ought we to do?" may then appear as one of the steps by which social causes issue in social effects. But for purposes of persuasion, it is often useful to insinuate the individualist phantom, the chooser without a criterion of choice, into the process. For everything within the causal nexus is tarred with the brush of special interest and partiality. Prescriptions are far more likely to be convincing if they come from a causal nowhere, a transcendental realm of absolute values.

The first step in understanding this situation correctly is to realize that every social proposal or plan can be used in a different way from that intended. Gangsters can use prohibition, scoundrels can use national assistance, capitalists can use techniques of social therapy, and vested interests can use political proposals, all in a different manner and with very different consequences from those originally intended. All social movements and institutions are intensely inventive and capable of improvisation; they are all accustomed to conflict, and to changing their shape as new threats emerge. Some do it more successfully than others. This is not to say that society cannot change; it is merely to say that it cannot often change exclusively in a desired direction. Further, the innocent idealist is misguided in thinking that his proposals are as abstractly good as he imagines; the forces operating within him are things he cannot, in the nature of things, fully understand. Nor does conscious realism help very much; it merely frees the political activist from some of the grosser errors. A Lenin busily engaged in creating parallel hierarchies of Soviet administration turns out to have been preparing the soil in which a Stalin can grow. Political proposals are in a profound sense made to be distorted, just as theories are expressed to be misunderstood—or better understood.

The welfarist energetically creating sequences of political changes designed to improve the society we live in suffers a double-pronged hazard. The first prong results from the fact that, like all individuals, he is complicated. Often

no one is more distressed than he at the growth of philistinism and anaes-
thetic popular culture—indeed, he often takes it far too seriously, distressed
at a world in which literacy simply means being able to read advertising slogans. Yet he is often the last to realize what he is doing to weaken social institutions that might better combat this philistinism. His right hand hates what
his left hand is doing. When all possible bases of independent social action in
the community have been levelled in the name of democratic government
control, our welfarist will be the first to start worrying about the stranglehold
of bureaucracy. In other words, apart from the axiomatic long-term unpre-
dictability of social action, the welfarist does not even examine the predictable
difficulties of the social ends he has set himself—often because he is bewitched
by a concept of "the people" as a set of counters in a political game.

The second prong of this hazard is that while the welfarist is concerned
with vague general ends, it is in fact the means which are crucial in society—
for the simple reason that the ends are never reached. Especially where the end
is vague and utopian, the politician will be particularly liable to misunder-
stand the actual implications of his work. How many visionaries have unwit-
tingly prepared a hell on earth because their gaze was stubbornly fixed on
heaven? And when hell comes—well, there is always some *ad hoc* theory of
sinister interests or Judas-like betrayal to extricate the theorist from his disaster. What his illusions have prevented him from understanding are the forces
he in fact served; and good intentions are quite beside the point. Stupidity is
a moral as well as an intellectual defect.[9]

9. Freud long ago observed that the human race indulged in a polite conspiracy to accept forgetfulness and slips of the tongue as insignificant accidents. The widespread acceptance of good intentions as a full justification of foolish acts is interestingly parallel. The issues involved can be seen if compared with the question of intelligence testing—itself a
good example of meliorist confusion. The strongest impulse towards the use of intelligence
tests was "practical"—in particular, the demand by the United States Army for a test which
would indicate those men who would make good officers. The tests produced around that
time yielded a high correlation between success in the tests and success in the military (and
later academic) fields. This kind of success was thought to be due to the *presence* of a mysterious faculty called intelligence. Some had it, some didn't. Psychologists have until recently devoted much of their energy to trying to work out what this thing could possibly
be. Was it one thing? Or a cluster of related talents? In any case, it was something you could
have more or less of. Now, returning to the question of moral stupidity, we have a logically
similar position: Is it due to the *absence* of a faculty (moral intelligence or perceptiveness,
perhaps) or is it alternatively due to the *presence* of strong and perhaps mostly unconscious

In its encouragement of the view that we can ultimately control the world, meliorism promotes this kind of stupidity. The view that it is the peculiar duty of philosophers and scientists to help improve the world is untenable.

It has a further interesting side-effect in that when the illusoriness of the dream of control dawns upon people, a feeling of impotence grows on them. The current vehicle of this feeling of impotence is a belief in the size and complexity of the modern world. These are thought to dwarf people. The individual, it comes to be said, doesn't matter today. All change is something for the big battalions. So we get what the French call *je m'en foutisme*. The hell with it! The political effect of this feeling is not hard to discover. It plays into the hands of experts and bureaucracies, of large organizations who are eager to arrange things for people. Yet the belief itself is a corrupt form of self-consciousness. The simple reply to the notion that people don't matter is that, in a sense, people never did. As for the emphasis on the complexity of the modern age—that is largely the result of self-pity. There are many respects in which the modern world is less complex than many which preceded it.

A full account of meliorism would necessarily lead into that marshy intellectual upcountry where the study of "the values of western civilization" is carried on. Such an account would consider the prestige of action and will in western cultures. The mind has traditionally been divided into three kinds of activity—thinking, feeling and doing. In spite of the prestige which at times has gone to the thought of the philosopher, the sensitivity of the artist, the agony of the saint, or the contemplation of the monk, reality has always seemed to reside in *doing* rather than "in merely experiencing." The western talent for technology arises from this passion for action, and in turn feeds it.

In modern thought, this characteristic operates to diminish the independence of feeling and thinking. The sensitivity of the artist may be admired, but ordinary men soon grow impatient if it does not issue in accessible works of beauty. Again, the function of thought is seen as a preparation for action.

---

motives towards misunderstanding (which, when discovered and rejected, are called illusions)? Are not those who act from ideas of political necessity or strong ideals of brotherhood (many Fabians, for example) sometimes fascinated by the social possibilities of bureaucratic order? There is no doubt that acts often prove disastrous because of totally unforeseen circumstances, and here it is the intention of the act (or the direction of the policy) which is conventionally taken as the basis of the moral judgment. But this form of moral justification can be extended too far.

There are, of course, recognized niches in the universities for those unfortunate people whose profession of philosophy has marooned them in the upper reaches of thought; but meliorism (and the curiously muddled dislike of "ivory towers") is always there to float them downstream into the center of European action and experience. Those who study classics, or devote themselves to philosophy, frequently feel impelled to defend the utility of their occupations by relating them to this fancied mainstream of activity: the study of Latin helps us to speak English better, and philosophy trains us to think more clearly. Both of these statements may be true; but they are irrelevant. Belief in action and control is so profound that intellectual argument barely touches it; all that we can do is plot its course and consider its consequences. A full explanation of the liberal movement would have to consider these characteristics of our civilization.

We have already remarked that liberalism, like all developed ideologies, has various devices for fending off criticism. In the case of needs, we found an obsessive feeling of obviousness which would simply go on reformulating the doctrine in the face of all criticism. Meliorism defends itself in a different manner—by regarding its critics as advocates of intellectual isolation, "ivory towers" and "art for art's sake." The critic of meliorism is faced by a false dilemma: Either you support social commitment, or you believe that philosophers and artists should retire to their own private worlds. But as the meliorist himself insists, there *are* no such private worlds. All thought belongs to the same social reality. And this reveals (what the meliorist formulation does not) that the question is not one of commitment or not, but of the *way* people commit themselves, and what they commit themselves to.

III. HOW TO MAKE TRENDS AND INFLUENCE PEOPLE

One of the guiding slogans of modern liberalism states that "we live in a changing world." It may be a cliché, but it has many uses in argument both offensive and defensive. Break it down, and it turns into a collection of trends, general descriptions of the way things are going.

Trends describe that unstable part of our environment which is likely to affect our hopes and fears. Simple prudence recommends that we should be alert to them. If we see a threat, then we are well advised to consider in advance how it may be averted. This alert posture is part of responsibility; and politicians in particular must always have a sharp nose for the way things are going. But, as we have noted, it is characteristic of liberalism to make politicians of us all; and in this case we find liberalism promoting alertness to trends among the population at large. Indeed, to be liberal *is* to accept an obligation to be concerned with matters beyond our direct responsibilities.

To every trend there must be a response. But this principle of a reforming liberalism runs into two important difficulties. The first is that people's reactions vary. It is not merely that one man's threat is another man's hope; it is also that people become bored, or change their reactions, or get used to living with a threat. Progress and improvement require a monolithic attitude towards any interesting trend, combined with a steady and persistent attempt to turn it to what, from the monolithic point of view, is an advantage. Propaganda must therefore seek to establish an absolute interpretation of trends, irrespective of the hopes and fears of any particular group.

The second difficulty is provided by the ostrich class, the large and decisive collection of people with votes who yet can seldom be enticed to take an interest in anything beyond their particular and local circumstances. Typically enough, these people are described negatively, as the apathetic or the complacent; in fact, they are simply those not emotionally engaged by the things which engage liberals. And here the solution must be to infect the apathetic with the same set of anxieties which already affect liberals.

The matter cannot be solved by the simple use of command, for there is no authority now left in political life whose instructions will automatically carry weight. It has been one of the achievements of liberalism to force authority to justify itself. And the only kind of justification available has been a utilitarian one. We must have authority in order that . . . something which we independently desire can be achieved. The kind of persuasion by which people may be induced to take an interest in the major trends of the world situation must therefore be teleological, and the persuader must cast around for some pressing hopes or fears which can be technically connected with the trend in question.

A trend is simply a statement of any series of events forming a pattern amidst the flux of life. When projected into the future (an operation people will often do for themselves) the trend becomes a prediction. There is an unlimited number of possible trends, but for purposes of persuasion, only a few are suitable for liberal use. The persuader must offer us both fulfilment and salvation, and the technique of trend persuasion soon turns into the construction of a certain kind of future, which is both enticing and menacing.

Time is very important in the intellectual world that results. There are the mistakes of the past, from which we may learn; there is the crisis in the present, which forces us to act; and there is the question of survival and fulfilment in the future, which we must face. The persuader thus appears as someone more prudent and more longsighted than we are, and since he is purporting to describe an objective situation, his vested interest is not at all obvious. Indeed, there seldom is anything which might vulgarly be considered a vested interest. In the elevated sphere we are describing, vested interests are usually emotional rather than material or financial.

This kind of persuader is generally an idealist. And he may move further away from the embarrassing logic of persuasion by seeing himself as a protagonist in a drama. Rather than a man with a policy to recommend, he may see himself in the role of a man of active virtue battling against the vice of complacency or apathy. If the persuader does take up this role, he may begin to outline a moral psychology in which the conception of will-power plays an important part. The mistakes of the past, he is likely to say, resulted from no one "finding the will" to put them right; people preferred to drift. But now things have reached a crisis point, and therefore our survival is at stake.

The pronoun "we" is an outstanding feature of trend persuasion. By means of it, the reader or listener is beguiled into an implicit alliance with the persuader, and there are many general theories which can be called on to substantiate this alliance. The theory of the common good has the effect of showing that no individual can retreat from his community. Or, to take a more extravagant example, the theory that "society is really the criminal" opens up many possibilities for the persuader (especially the more moralistic one) by asserting that crime cannot be eliminated until we "reform" ourselves. The effect of all such theories is to bring the widest possible audience into the persuader's net and infect them with a generalized sense of responsibility. The harassed citizen can no longer ward off these Ancient Mariners with an irritable: "It's none of my business." The eye of the persuader is not only hypnotic, it is righteous too.

Entrenched thus, the persuader can safely use his two key terms—"crisis" and "survival"—as absolutes affecting everybody. They are, so to speak, the ultimate persuaders. If one asks: "crisis for whom?" the instant reply is "for you." If one demands: "Whose survival is at stake?" then the answer is always "yours." Problems also acquire a spurious objectivity; they are presented as social problems, and they are everybody's business. In this way, the persuader has a moral claim upon the attention of everyone, and inattention has become a sin. He can now present his trends—the increase of world population, the growth of delinquency, the incursions of communism, the new brazenness of homosexuals, etc.—in the confidence of having a receptive audience.

The emotion which the persuader first hopes to arouse is that of urgency in the face of his problems. The ideal situation, in a sense, is therefore war, when such questions as survival are more compelling than in peacetime. When not using a problem-solution type of logic, the persuader is happiest when employing military metaphors. It is thus that we find ourselves now waging the cold war against communism, the war against want, the battle against crime, and even the persuader's battle *par excellence,* the fight against apathy. The contemporary importance of war has no doubt greatly affected the technique of trend-persuasion. War is habit-forming, and peace is confusing to many people who cannot deal with conflicting standards and feelings of guilt. Besides, war has demonstrated what immense things can be achieved "if we really set our minds to it." Thus the trend-persuader, with an ambitious policy to recommend, is offering us something far better than war which, even with its incidental advantages, is a nasty and destructive business: he is offering us a war substitute, a despotic goal in terms of which life can be organized.

The trend in question here is voluntaristic; it contrasts a picture of what we can achieve with another picture of what will happen if we do not rouse ourselves. This kind of trend is now dominant. There was a time when the deterministic trend, which sees the future as a wave in which we either swim or drown, was more striking, and threw up such classic instances of the *genre* as the *Communist Manifesto.* But the determinist trend has been weakened at all levels. Intellectually, it crumbled along with its close relation, Historicism. And as a vehicle of popular support, generating fanaticism, it was most successful when it was virtually without rivals. When the market-place was full of persuaders, peddling equally inevitable but rather different trends, the populace became bored and sceptical, and the determinist trend disappeared from the scene. It may return, but not for some time.

The result has been to make the voluntarist trend the more convincing. If things are not inevitable, then we can be roused to do something about them.

Persuaders using the voluntarist trend can co-operate in a way not open to those favoring determinism. They can join in attacking complacency. They can infiltrate the democratic conscience with a conception of the good citizen as a man who understands the Great Issues of Our Time, giving their own content to this promising slogan. This kind of thinking has lately become one of the main vehicles for the diffusion of liberalism. It draws people into the intellectual and emotional vortex of liberalism, whose symptoms are a feeling of guilt about complacency and strong moral feelings about the duty of responsibility to others. How do we explain this susceptibility?

The reader trained in the social sciences will already have observed that what has been outlined as a technique of persuasion is identical, if certain refinements are neglected, with the operative rules of much social science. It used to be thought desirable to create something called a "value-free social science" in which the trends would simply be identified, measured and related, whilst their "use" was left to "policy framers." The social scientists thought they were concerned only with *means* whilst others decided the ends. One main difficulty of this position was the sheer psychological impossibility of the separation. Trends won't lie down. They become predictions, or justifications, or refutations of something the moment they are detected. Great numbers of social scientists are, in any case, too confused to tell the difference between a practical problem and an intellectual one. Further, trend detection becomes as habit-forming as taking drugs. Just as the neurotic scrutinizes the faces of his associates for signs of hostility, so those who form the trend-habit cannot help scrutinizing everything they encounter for signs. The discovery of trends even grew into an art form: the sociological best-seller, in the tradition of Veblen, spread the habit. As Lionel Trilling has remarked, this form of social diagnosis has taken over some of the talent and much of the impetus which in other times has gone into the novel. This development flows along with an obsession with change and insecurity; such a world is paradise for anyone with an inclination towards the voluntarist trend (and most of us do have such an inclination).

All this might mean that we have all become alert, responsible, democratic citizens; or, alternatively, that we have all become rather hysterical babes in a wood, looking for a gleam of light. What it would certainly indicate is a connection between gullibility on the one hand and the orthodox theory of democracy on the other. Somewhere between those responsible for policy in a society, who live in a world of speculations about the future, and those who care for nothing except their immediate and local life, there is a large class whose interest in social and political problems lacks the anchorage of direct responsibility. They are eager to do the right thing, and have been taught that their duty is to take an interest in world affairs. Normally they lack experience of these matters, and often their education has not made them discriminating about the printed word. They are, indeed, a valuable section of the community and they are not the least effective of checks on government. Perhaps for this reason they often have an ingrained suspicion of politicians, yet their own political judgments are wildly erratic. They are decent, sympathetic and idealistic. They are at present the main bearers of liberalism.

Their main fault is that they are prey to intellectual fashions, and fashion is the main guide to the vicarious worries they take upon themselves. A decade ago, their primary worry was Communist aggression. More recently, it has been the prospect of total annihilation from Hydrogen Bomb warfare (with such allied worries as genetic effects). More recently still, the gap between arts and science, as related to perennial problems like food shortage and over-population, have come back into vogue. It may be true that each man's death diminisheth me, but this doctrine can easily be taken to the verge of hysteria. No one would deny that these are important questions opening up explosive political and social possibilities; but for most of the inhabitants of western countries they are vicarious ones. Short of disrupting his normal life (which he is not usually prepared to do), the average man can do very little about them. But feeling a compulsion to act, he chooses substitute acts—passing resolutions, going to meetings, writing letters to papers—and imagines that he is "doing something about it." This type of mind is found most prevalently, though by no means exclusively, in the political tradition of liberalism.

Trend-persuasion is, then, a modern and popularized version of the kind of calculations which politicians have always had to make, combined with an extraneous philanthropic moral theory. How should one estimate this development? One consequence is to keep democracies alert and flexible in a "changing world." Yet trend-persuasion is also subject to fashion, and therefore likely to distort social and political policies according to the (often misguided) emotions of the moment. A vicious circle operates: the more trends we discover, the more insecure we feel; and the more insecure we feel, the more we go on looking for trends. If the anxiety grows too much for us, we may become easy victims of the charlatan who offers us a panacea. Logically speaking, this road leads on to totalitarianism, the attempt to find a total solution for a bogus problem. But this would be to take trend-persuasion as itself a trend.

We have already seen how ideologies work by imposing a single point of view upon us. Our principle of criticism in these cases has been one of reversal: we took the means to be ends, or the ends to be means. In the case of trend-persuasion, the point of view arises from the logic of problems and solutions. Yet the fact that the problems are always new, whilst the solutions are old, must make us suspicious of these constructions. We imagine that experience presents us with problems, and *then* we start to seek solutions. Whatever the weaknesses of this belief, it yet determines the way in which the persuader presents his case. Historically, however, the solutions always come first. Seldom in the twentieth century have we lacked prophets telling us about the need for competitive industry, the duties of international philanthropy, better distribution of world production, the need for more science in education and the value of the lash as a deterrent. Such policies are part of the air we breathe, and as such, rather too familiar to rouse us very much. They are much more striking if they can be presented not as possible policies we might follow, but as *solutions* to problems. The persuader is thus not a man who must find solutions for problems, but one who must construct problems to fit pre-existing solutions.

It remains to consider the possible distortions which trend-persuasion might have on social life. If society be considered as a complex of activities and institutions—religious, artistic, industrial, commercial, academic, etc.—then the character of the society will emerge out of their relations. But these institutions not only cooperate; they also compete (financially, morally, intellectually, for example) and each tries to carve out a larger future for itself. Now if into this context of struggle one introduces ideas of the "great issues of our time," then it is clear that some institutions will be strengthened and some will be weakened. If the great issue of our time is how to prevent malnutrition among Asians and Africans, then the events of scholarship must seem very far from the battle. Who would elucidate a text of Chaucer when his duty lies out in the monsoon region? How futile experiments in painting technique must look when the survival of the species is in question! Artistic movements are implicitly reduced to the role of entertainment, and a Flaubert, torturing himself for a week over the structure of a sentence, can only seem absurd. Universities have traditionally followed the trail of truth; but truth is an irrelevance in a world crying out for "science in the service of man." Here is a menace more insidious to religious institutions than any debate about evolution. Industrialization, wrote one recent prophet,[10] is the only hope of the poor— words which have an evangelical ring, and seem to announce the discovery of a new religious truth.

This idealistic, persuasive movement might be compared to a wind sweeping across a landscape. Without the wind, the air grows fetid and stale. But if the wind blows too violently, and if the fixtures of the landscape lose their anchorage, then the wind becomes destructive. To talk of the "great issues of our time" as fashionable worries may sound cynical; yet it is exactly the element of fashion which reveals important facts about trend-persuasion.

IV. SCIENTIFIC MORALISM

The various supposedly scientific evasions of ethics and politics hold out a promise:

> Treated as principles beyond the necessity for argument [rules of sexual morality] have been established as categorical imperatives to be imposed with the help of social sanctions, and the result has only too often been to divorce theoretic assertion from practical acceptance. Only when they are seen as rationally conceived guides to happiness, or as conditions of happiness empirically determined, is this divorce ended. Then, for instance, the nearly universal rule against incest ceases to appear as an unexplained decree, and is seen as arising out of the requirement for preserving the stability of family life. Similarly rules against adultery, which show much greater variety, instead of being rested on authoritative dogmas can claim rational acceptance as being grounded in the need and desire for permanent marital relationship and the demonstrably damaging effects of its breach upon this. And "thou shalt not commit adultery" is transformed from a commandment, rested on fear and aimed at restraining "natural" desire, into a commonsense guide to behaviour, grounded in demonstrable psychological facts in the field of the causation of attitude and habit, and which by ra-

10. Sir Charles Snow, whose Rede lecture, *The two Cultures and the Scientific Revolution* (1959), has deservedly come to be recognized as a classic of the trend-persuasion *genre*.

tionally establishing the behavioural conditions of happiness tends to direct desires along channels leading to its achievement.[11]

Psychology, physiology and biology in close alliance are the props of this scientific moralism, and each is taken as a source of technical prescriptions: "the psychological is thus tending to replace the moral point of view, and there is little doubt that, in so far as the new approach proves *effective,* the process will continue."[12] These are statements appropriate to a liberal manifesto; what is the program they embody?

The program is clearly utilitarian: the maximization of happiness or satisfaction. It is a technology for getting the largest quantity of preferred things which the condition of the world will allow. Being a technology purportedly geared to our own desires and needs, it does not have to command or condemn; it is merely technical guidance. Indeed, the liberal objection to morality can be summed up in the formula: morality condemns, liberalism tries to understand. This is a scientific attitude which was powerfully codified in the operation of psychoanalysis, for no analysis could possibly overcome repressions if the analyst persistently interjected remarks like: "What a deplorable thing to think about your mother!" For condemnation separates people, whereas understanding brings them together.

This unobjectionable formula may with some justice be claimed as scientific; on its most obvious interpretation, we accept the world, including moral behavior, as evidence from which we may construct a theory of what the world is like. But the inroads of ideology here arise out of the ambiguity of the term "understanding." For while understanding might be simply an intellectual development, the comprehension of what was previously obscure, it might also include varying quantities of sympathy, as in the phrase: "Yes, I do understand." Given the intrusion of sympathy, much liberal understanding includes forgiveness, or, even, an implied renunciation of forgiveness on the grounds that forgiveness arrogantly assumes an unwarrantable superiority. Among liberals, understanding in this sympathetic manner became a duty, one of the stigmata of true tolerance. But understanding as a duty, like anything widely presented as a duty, undergoes considerable distortions. Given *tout comprendre: c'est tout pardonner* it is an easy step to *tout pardonner: c'est tout compren-*

11. Greaves, *op. cit.,* p. 124.
12. J. C. Flugel, *Man, Morals and Society,* London, p. 21 (my italics).

dre. If the only proof of "understanding" is the emotion of sympathy, it is rather tempting to take the shortcut of automatic sympathy and omit the hard work of actual comprehension.

Yet while scientific moralism never strays very far from its protector Science, it can still claim continuity with earlier moral doctrines by pointing to the fact that it very largely incorporates the same rules—doing unto others as we would have them do unto us, restraining selfish desires, looking before one takes the indulgent leap. But—and here the program makes its claims to superiority—whereas the earlier grounds offered for these moral rules were confused, dogmatic and subject to endless dispute, the new grounds are irresistibly rational and must appeal to all men. There is nothing very novel about this belief. Hobbes shared it; so did Bentham, and neither could conceal an arrogant contempt for his bungling predecessors.

The most obvious criticism of scientific moralism is in terms of the naturalistic fallacy—even though most scientific moralists are aware of the danger. Both moralist and critic are here on the same ground, and they are even united in the suspicion that if we shut the door on values, they'll come sneaking back through the window. Thus when the scientific moralist relates moral rules to terms like "health" or "adjustment," his more rigorous critic will quickly point out that these terms are value-loaded and may go off. The rigorous critic is simply one who will not move from the position that the only thing which can constitute a value is actual demandedness. If people insist that they do not want health or adjustment, then the scientific expert must be silent. Values are created by personal choice and can be created in no other way.

The scientific moralist is not necessarily reduced to silence by this kind of criticism. For his studies have taught him to look deeper into the mind in search of the *function* of certain kinds of preference. And this has led him to the conclusion that a man who does not want to be healthy, for example, is sick in a peculiar kind of way. He is a hypochondriac, who uses his illnesses as an escape from personal responsibility. Therefore one must set out to cure this defect. For all rational men will agree that health is preferable to illness. To deny this position, concludes the argument of scientific moralism, would be merely irrationalist.[13]

---

13. Flugel (*op. cit.*, pp. 17, 18) has an ingenious argument in general support of this position: "the distinction between means and ends," he remarks quaintly, "is *nearly always*

Scientific moralism depends, then, upon placing every act in a policy context and studying its efficiency. The trick is simply to isolate a function, demonstrate the inefficiency with which it is currently being pursued, and proceed to recommendations for maximizing efficiency. The crucially loaded value in this system is therefore not "health" or "adjustment" or "satisfaction" or any of the many other variations of this kind of idea, but rather the conception of generic man as a system of functions.

It is the concept of generic man, or humanity, which makes plausible the idea of human progress. For if we begin with a single abstract hero called man, emerging in the springtide of his infancy from the caves and hovels of prehistory, and attribute to this hero all the swirling dramas of history up to the present time, and if we also consider those things which we *now* think most important, then it will be difficult for us to resist the conclusion that he has "improved himself." He is cleaner, more knowledgeable, more comfortable, and each cell of the abstraction lives longer. If medical science, for example, is taken as the activity of discovering the character of human illnesses and the discovery of ways of removing them, then it makes very good sense to talk of progress in medicine. And if we invalidly take the utilitarian step of adding together into a single quantity all those things in which we detect progress, then the plausibility of attributing the progress-trend to "humanity" becomes

---

relative. There exists a whole hierarchy of values, each of which is a means to the value that stands just above it in the hierarchy" (my italics). This line of thought might have led him to a total rejection of teleological ethics; but its uses are too attractive to permit that. "Indeed," he goes on, "the distinction between means and ends, though often convenient for the consideration of some relatively narrow problem, is largely arbitrary. At best there can only be a few unquestionable intrinsic values at the top of the hierarchy, such as Truth, Goodness, Beauty; or, if we press the matter further (?), there should strictly speaking be one only, a *summum bonum* or supreme value, to which all the rest are means—and, as we know, moral philosophers are not yet in agreement as to what this supreme value is." The last sentence is a memorable understatement. Flugel is in the unhappy position of seeing that this hierarchy of values is an imposture, yet he cannot bear to abandon it. The reason is soon evident: "When it is objected that psychology can have no concern with values, it is of course meant that it is not in a position to state what are intrinsic values. But in view of the relative and fluctuating position of intrinsic and instrumental values it is hardly possible to say exactly at what point in the hierarchy of values its (psychology's) influence must cease." The splendid vagueness of this position simultaneously exiles moral philosophers to the vapid and airless heights of the ultimate, and underwrites anything at all that scientific moralists choose to assert.

nearly irresistible. All of this depends upon a theory of man as a purposive creature who will merely blunder ineffectually in the mire of his own ignorance and confusion unless he pursues goals clearly and rationally. In moods of complacency, for example, we find it easy to patronize rainmakers who were so palpably inefficient at producing their declared end. "Magic, divination, sacrifice and prayer may relieve our feelings and reduce our fears when we are ignorant and impotent, but as our knowledge and our power increase we tend to abandon these practices in favour of others which we can see to lead more surely and directly to our goal."[14] *Our* goal? But we have many, and some are incompatible with others. The great error of any doctrine of progress is to regard past behavior as incompetent and inefficient; whereas, if we are to continue talking in these functional terms, all incompetence and inefficiency result from conflict about the nature of what we are doing.

We have, thus, the possibility of regarding the people of history either as radically different from us, not least in that they wanted different things and suffered different torments; or alternatively, we may regard them as failed replicas of ourselves. If we take this latter view, we will prefer to attribute those elements of history on which we have improved to a lack of reason or understanding—certainly a *lack* of something—in historical people. If, however, we take the former view, then we will attribute the different conditions and different achievements of times past as the product of quite different interests and preoccupations. And this latter view involves the abandonment of functionalism.

But it is difficult to abandon functionalism, because it is so tempting to go on inventing new functions to explain what was inexplicable before. We may, for example, assume that businessmen are rational pursuers of profit; and wherever we find inefficiency, we may diagnose deficiency. If this simple scheme appears to be inadequate, then we may simply go on adding functions: ". . . both politics and economics are as much competitive games as they are instrumentalities for meeting recognized needs or satisfying wants."[15] Again, since William James particularly, war has often been interpreted in functional terms as an outlet for various competitive or aggressive impulses in human nature, an interpretation leading to the search for moral substitutes—getting

14. Flugel, *op. cit.*, p. 21.

15. Frank H. Knight, *Intelligence and Democratic Action*, Cambridge (Mass.), 1960, p. 129.

the kicks without spilling the blood. Both of these cases exemplify the intellectual device by which functionalism evades the moral character of the people engaged in these activities by splitting the situation up into generic man combined with some kind of policy.

Scientific moralism arises from the search for a single point of view which will ultimately harmonize human relations. The point of view requires the creation of a *system* in which everything can find a place. The meliorist concept of improvement means greater systematization, at the same time as meliorism demands active, improving behavior from people. The strategy of the system is determined by needs and similar functional concepts, and the tactics arise from a close attention to trends. In this system, everything finds a place, but only as a means to or function of some general abstract entity like happiness, satisfaction or equilibrium. Disinterested acts[16] must be reduced for they cannot be systematized. A sculptor, for example, cannot simply do a piece of sculpture; he must have reasons for his act, that is, it must be a means to something else. It is only in this way that the system can preserve its flexibility. And it is only by being flexible, by being susceptible to continuous adjustment and revaluation, that the promise of ultimate harmony can be sustained. The system constructed out of generic man provides a point of view by which traditional moral rules can be judged and reinterpreted. It is in this way that they turn into "rationally conceived guides to happiness."

But not all moral rules survive this transplantation to new grounds. Some must be discarded, and they are rejected because they are the functions of a corrupt human nature, in contrast to the fundamental human nature from which the moral principles of scientific moralism itself derive. On this principle, we encounter the interests argument.

The interests argument depends upon the assumption that everyone is maximizing happiness, and that for this reason people "promote their interests." The promotion of interests involves, furthermore, the assertion of moral and political opinions. Such opinions, however, are merely epiphenomena,

16. Disinterested acts are spontaneous; they are done for no purpose and have no function in a system. The fact that the very word "disinterested" is now commonly misused to mean "uninterested" may be a symptom of how thoroughly utilitarian assumptions are accepted where modern liberalism is strong. Gide's theory of the *acte gratuit* and many varieties of modern irrationalism may be seen as baffled attempts to escape from the incessant pressure to calculate behavior, constructing systems and being guided by them.

rationalizations of a pre-established interest. Why do white settlers in African territories believe that Africans will not be capable of governing themselves for centuries? Obviously, runs the interests argument, *because* they have an interest in remaining politically dominant. Why is it that rich people assert the sanctity of property? Obviously *because* they wish to safeguard political order in their possessions and privileges.

Logically speaking, the interests argument is a *petitio principi* if it is taken as a refutation of the moral and political opinions concerned. But the point of such a sophistical device is precisely to evade anything that might look like an invalid argument. The main successes of propaganda come not from invalid argument but from diversion of attention. Our concern is moved from the moral or political argument involved to items of economic or sociological information which "put the argument in perspective."

Intellectually, the objection to the interests argument is its crudity. An interest is something assumed to explain the motives of human action and belief; but the only interests we can examine are the *visible* ones—the economic interests. The theory of human behavior involved is that which has generated the model of economic man; a calculator who mechanically responds to changes in his possibilities of consumption. It is much more difficult even to discover, much less to systematize, the psychological undercurrent—the passion to be proved right, the sudden moral intuitions, the fanatical convictions—which develop independently of any visible interests. It has been observed[17] that one reason why Bentham preferred self-interest to sympathy among the moral concepts of the eighteenth century was the fact that self-interest is conceivably measurable; sympathy is not. The same consideration applies here. Visible or vested interests can be measured, and for that very reason they seem to be more real.

It is the theory of ideology which most elaborately justifies our acceptance of the interests argument. The difficulty is that the generalizations are false. It is not true that all industrialists are conservative, any more than it is true that all trade unionists are natural radicals. Both these beliefs are sound enough as political maxims in some circumstances; both have, on occasion, betrayed politicians. But when a cherished political maxim fails to fit the facts, it can be given a certain grandeur by the device of metaphysical elevation. The rich as

---

17. By Wilfrid Harrison, Introduction (p. lii) to the Blackwell Edition of Bentham's *A Fragment on Government*, etc., 1948.

such are conservative; or, in a sociological ideal model, conservatism is one of the attributes allocated to the rich, though the model may have to be modified if it is to be applied to reality. Our political maxim now leads an uneasy logical life, half-way between fact and definition, the kind of device by which the absurdities of Marxian or sociological class theory are propped up. The next move must be the construction of *ad hoc* hypotheses to explain to us why some rich are radical. Addenda of this kind might be a possible escape from this fantasy world, but even this escape is blocked off by the temptations of scientific moralism. For we might explain the fact that some rich are radical, or some white settlers espouse African majority governments, by the fact that these people are rational. They have seen a truth which their fellow members of the class have missed because of the distorting mists of interest. This kind of enlightenment solution is—as Marx pointed out—illogical if we are concerned with ideologies, and it leaves the interests argument with no higher status than that of a highly selective propaganda device. For the question remains: What are the *interests* which led to this espousal of Reason?

Paradoxically enough, the interests argument is a distant relation of a hallowed moral preoccupation—that of judging the disinterestedness of good acts. If certain political and moral policies, presented as the dictates of reason or experience, are seen as the product of economic or political interest, they are quite literally "demoralized." The plausibility of the ensuing disparagement rests upon a generalized suspicion of motives where interests are involved. The criterion of interests is one which everyone uses in practical affairs to a greater or less extent.

Doctrines, then, are epiphenomena, outgrowths of passion and interest. So too are political organizations. Both are the functions of something deeper. These liberal beliefs may seem to arise from a somewhat eclectic borrowing from Marxism; and for particular liberals Marx may be the source of such beliefs. But liberalism has its own tradition of thought leading to the same conclusions. British empirical psychology can perfectly well tamper with the autonomy of thought by its use of the doctrine that "reason is the slave of the passions." And liberal political thought has grown out of the social contract doctrine in its Lockian form, by which the State is an agency of something called Society. For in the monistic conception of society, modern liberalism has increasingly found its main criterion of political judgment. To this conception we must now turn.

CHAPTER FIVE

Society and Its Variations

I. SOCIETY AS AN ASPIRATION

I F WE ASK what it is that a Scottish crofter, a London stockbroker, a Welsh steelworker, and a Manchester journalist all have in common, then it is not difficult to give a political answer. They are all British citizens, can travel on British passports, pay taxes to the British State, and can vote in British elections. The political unity of the British State is clear and precise, and it includes all individuals equally. But what makes each of them a member of British "society"? Only the fact that they are members of the British State. There is virtually nothing else they have exclusively in common. Moral standards, linguistic usages, traditions, customs and prejudices will all vary. The State no doubt includes an enormous number of institutions, laws, "norms," "folkways," communities, associations, beliefs, etc. But none of these is precisely co-existent with the boundaries of any given State. They are all either parts of the State, or else spill across its boundaries and constitute international linkages.

Yet if the liberal distinction between State and society is to be sustained, there must be something held in common which is not the creation of the State. Still, the ambiguities of the term "society" allow a good deal of hedging on this point before it ever need be faced; and the hedging is facilitated by the fact that the liberal uses of "society" are seldom qualified by any adjective, especially any political designation of boundaries. Used alone, the term will absorb from the context sufficient in the way of connotations to be clear to any-one who is sympathetic. At its widest, "society" may be taken to "include all or any dealings of man with man, whether these be direct or indirect, orga-nized or unorganized, conscious or unconscious, co-operative or antagonis-tic."[1] This is the generic use of the term, and it is simply an organizing ab-straction which covers all possible instances of our more businesslike use of the adjective "social." This meaning of "society" will certainly absorb politics; it will absorb anything. But just because it is so hospitable, this meaning is of no use to liberalism.

But "society" may be distinguished, Professor Ginsberg tells us, "from *a* so-ciety." And a society in this more precise meaning is a much more promising candidate for liberal usages. "A society is a collection of individuals united by certain relations or modes of behaviour which mark them off from others who do not enter into those relations or who differ from them in behavior."[2] Now the members of any State will, in terms of this definition, also constitute *a* society; and if we also bear in mind the more extensive generic meaning of society, then we will easily be convinced that the members of any State consti-tute *a* society independently of their political association.

But how can the members of a State also constitute *a* society in this non-political manner? One obvious answer lies in discovering things upon which they all agree. This was the view taken by Locke. It is a moral view, for it is an agree-ment to approve of certain common acts and objects. Society, then, is constituted by our agreements, the State by our conflicts. Here we may observe a continuity between the liberal and the Marxist views, both linked to the nostalgic desire that the State might "wither away." This solution runs into the difficulty that there is nothing upon which all the members of a politically constituted class also hap-pen to agree. There will always be times when many of them act disagreeably to whatever is thought to be the consensus. They do not thereby cease to be mem-bers of the State, but in some sense they withdraw from "society."[3]

---

1. Morris Ginsberg, *Sociology,* Oxford, 1955, p. 40.

2. *Ibid.*

3. This might suggest that "society" is a more exclusive term than "state," and in this us-age, and in many sociological contexts, it is. In this liberal usage, it retains valuable over-tones of that earlier meaning by which "society" indicated only the respectable. But "soci-ety" may also become wider than the State, as in this rather baffling proposition from a letter to the *Listener:* "The enemies of the State are not necessarily the enemies of society."

Social and moral disagreement is something normally tolerated in free States. But there are certain circumstances, particularly that of modern war, when internal dissension and conflict are found to be disruptive. In such times the State is expected to take on a more cohesive unity which will promote a "high morale." The crofter and the stockbroker, whatever their variations, are expected to consider their membership of State and nation as the deepest and most important thing of all. The State seeks to monopolize the emotions and services of its citizens; it demands further that these things should be willingly given.

Even when there is no such crisis, the doctrine of nationalism may develop exactly the same demands. Such a doctrine naturally becomes an ethic. It insists on the goodness of national devotion, and places the sceptical or the recalcitrant in various undesirable categories. At its height, this kind of movement becomes an exaltation. "There is something terrible," said St. Just, "in the sacred love of the fatherland; it is so exclusive as to sacrifice everything to the public interest, without pity, without fear, without respect for humanity. . . . What produces the general good is always terrible."[4] The State generates a great range of powerful emotions, and directs them towards a metaphysical idea; it can hardly do anything else, for the particular actions of any existing government cannot in themselves justify such sentiments.

It might be imagined that here we have a fairly rigid distinction between liberal and totalitarian kinds of political thinking. Liberals insist that the State is simply a piece of machinery designed for the good of individuals whilst their totalitarian enemies make of the State a small god, and project violent emotions on to it. On this argument the distinction between the State and society is the whole crux of the liberal-democratic position. It places a limit on the activities of the State, making the latter responsive to the demands of its subjects. This is exactly the position of Locke, who kept the State on a short chain which could only be loosened for the good of the people, and then only in emergencies. Society, as Locke saw it, was rational and conservative, composed of a multitude of individuals, who needed political arrangements but were determined not to become enslaved by them. This theoretical position would seem to be amply confirmed by experience. Wherever a country has fallen into the hands of leaders claiming unlimited authority to regulate social

4. Quoted by Elie Kedourie in *Nationalism*, London, 1960, p. 18.

affairs, oppression, misery, and usually war have been the result. And in all these countries, the prevalent philosophy denied the distinction between the State and society.

This argument is one that deserves to be taken seriously. But it depends very much upon how "society" is conceived, and as we shall see, a good many changes have been imposed upon the original Lockian formulation. Society has in fact become a person. It features in a great variety of roles, not only in political propaganda, but also in sociology itself. Convicts are said to be "paying their debt to society." Race riots, visible prostitution, capital punishment and a whole set of things which the speaker dislikes are said to be "an affront to society." Or again: "The existence of race prejudice indicates a widespread social failure." But how can a complex of relationships "fail"? Society is, furthermore, something which can be tested: there is a social order which is only good if it satisfies social (or human) needs. We are the products of our society, yet we are also told that we must decide "what kind of society we want to live in." If we extend our search for such usages into the fields of sociology and political theory, we shall find the word "social" qualifying such terms as objective, purpose, order, system, needs, problems, etc. Now sometimes a "social purpose" simply will mean a purpose arising out of social relations, as it means sociologically. But more often we find a curious monistic use, by which these objectives, purposes, etc., are thought to qualify "society" as a *whole*. It is this monistic usage which is the basis of liberal propaganda.

Our problem, then, is to discover what it is that collects debts, suffers affronts, determines the behavior of people and is also determined by them (whichever is convenient), fails, moves in different directions, has purposes and problems, and so on. A reader trained in linguistic philosophy may at this point hasten to enter a demurrer: All of these usages, he will say, must be evaluated in their contexts and on their merits; to look for a single meaning in a collection of usages is the sort of basically misguided question which has created the metaphysical confusions of the past. To this objection, we may readily agree that we shall be unlikely to find a single real entity to which all these usages clearly or confusedly refer. But this kind of single entity is exactly what is necessary to make sense of the many liberal uses of the term.

Liberals emphatically reject the idea of obligatory nationalist or totalitarian participation in the State. They accord to each individual the right to go about his own business within the protection of the State, so long as he does not illegally interfere with others. For something like a century now, however, they have been evolving a new form of obligatory participation. This new form of participation can be stated in the form of a moral argument.

The first premise of this argument would be the assertion that Britain is a democracy. Most of us would give some sort of qualified approval to this proposition. Democracy may be a vague term, but it has a number of signs (freedom of political organization, a thriving opposition, extensive freedom from official censorship) which are certainly present in Great Britain. Still, it is always rather inaccurate to connect an actually existing, concrete, political organization existing over time, with an abstract system; such a connection will rapidly lead us to conclude that Britain is only imperfectly a democracy, and (since we are supporters of democracy) we find that our harmless political proposition has turned into a program of action under our very eyes. There are some writers who take this bull very firmly by the horns and declare that democracy is an "ideal" (that is, that it fits as an end into *someone's* policy) which we can approach but never quite fully attain. Ideals often get less tolerable as one gets closer to them. Our proposition can also generate all sorts of elegant intellectual difficulties: When did Britain become a democracy? For example—in 1688? 1832? 1867? 1884? 1920? 1928? 1945? Or, if Britain is still moving closer to the ideal, then our proposition is false, and Britain is not a democracy. The position here is similar to, say, "Britain is a Christian Community." The assertion is a strange mixture of fact and aspiration. It is, in other words, a device, fitting into the endless flux of propaganda and persuasion.

The argument develops by unmasking some fragments of a definition: Democracies are states in which all sane adults participate in making political decisions. We are all by now familiar with the picture of the democratic citizen as one who takes an intelligent interest in public affairs and, when election time comes round, votes for the party which he judges will be better for the country. This picture has been under fire during the last decades from some political scientists writing articles with titles like "In defense of apathy."[5] The line taken in these arguments is that apathy is usually evidence of a well-governed State in which the populace is content to go about its business, and

---

5. For example in an interesting article by Professor Morris Jones, in *Political Studies,* February 1954.

that it is frequently a preferable condition to the political hysteria which sometimes accompanies a protracted period of popular interest in political affairs. This account of political life has pretty clear conservative implications. The conclusion we may draw from this kind of dispute is that whether we are politically active, or inactive, we are going to please some people and displease others. More generally, what looks like a more or less academic question of defining the abstract term "democracy" is in fact a highly loaded ideological dispute. (How the political scientist, seeking to remain uncontaminated by "values," and to supply means to anybody's ends, gets off this hook is a fascinating question. Even if he merely reports usages—like a linguistic philosopher—he is still dealing with inflammatory materials.)

The general point about such definitions is that their content varies according to the political situation of the promoters of the abstraction. Those who are promoting an unestablished abstraction in hostile country (the champions of Moral Rearmament for example) are keen to define it in terms which will appeal to everyone—as being wholesome, idealistic, anti-communist and whatever else happens to be popular or support-gathering at any given time. On the other hand, those defining an established abstraction will write hortatory strictures with titles like "What is a Democrat (Communist, Nazi, Liberal, etc.)?" in which the emphasis is very much on how people must accommodate themselves to the movement. In the contemporary west, Democracy is such an established abstraction. Most people feel strongly attached to Democracy and are therefore likely to be receptive to all duties which can be presented to them as democratic.

We may now state the argument in the form of a rough syllogism:

> Britain is a democracy.
> A democracy is a State in which all sane adults participate in making political decisions.
> *Therefore* all sane British adults ought to participate in social and political affairs.

Strictly speaking, one needs a number of supplementary propositions to establish, for example, that one can only make intelligent decisions if one has first taken an interest in the matters to be decided, but these are refinements we may neglect. Also, we may note that the duty reported in the conclusion is another version of meliorism: the theorist who completes his "negative" and "destructive" analysis and then goes on to make "constructive" suggestions is simply conforming to this democratic duty of participation. Its political effect is, as we argued in discussing trend-persuasion, to bring within the range of political propaganda people formerly protected by apathy.

But the main point that concerns us here is to discover what is the relation between the democratic duty of participation on the one hand and the liberal conception of "society" on the other. The clue to this relationship is to be found in the conception of a "social problem." In strictly liberal terms, and indeed in all pre-liberal societies, there is no such thing as a "social problem." There are political problems, which States and other institutions have to solve, and there are individual problems which individuals must deal with as best they can—and this may, of course, include turning individual problems into political ones. Institutions also have their problems—trade unions used to face the danger of political suppression or civil lawsuit; churches face such problems as a declining membership, or a disposition among enemies to persecute them. Now, as we saw in our earlier analysis of a policy, there cannot be a problem unless it fits into someone's policy—unless, that is to say, it falls in principle to someone or some institution to solve it. If "society" is simply a complex descriptive abstraction, then it clearly cannot even have problems, much less solve them. In a purely formal sense we can say that the conception of a "social problem" is incoherent and impossible. Taken seriously, it yields a definition of "society" as "that for which the thing in question is a problem."

But that obviously does not dispose of the question. For the modern liberal conception of society has nibbled away at the State so successfully as to reduce the State to "society in its political aspect," an agency for making effective the wishes of the community. Here we are in the perilous territory of interacting abstractions, and some intricate untangling is required.

To say that the State is an agency of society is to indicate a causal direction. We are asserting, in fact, that society acts as a cause which determines (or, given the calculated ambiguity of these propositions, *ought* to determine) the acts of the State. This situation is very familiar to us, in which what starts off as a factual statement ("The State is an agency of society") abruptly turns into a criterion, that is, into a particular policy. To be properly understood, the proposition requires to be prefaced by: "In a fully liberal world . . ." or "In terms of the policy of liberal movement. . . ." If we remember to add such a preface, then we shall not be puzzled by this perfectly ordinary logical dualism. But what is objectionable about the statement is that the causal relationship is one-directional. In other words, society determines the State, but the State is not allowed to influence society. And this, of course, is absurd, whether it be taken as a factual or a normative statement. Liberal theorists would no doubt agree that an executive act, or a piece of legislation, can indeed influence social affairs, but they would wish to insist on some criterion by which the political act could be shown to have social origins. For the liberal idea of political evil is a governmental act which springs full grown from the brow of politicians, and which lacks the antecedent of social support.

Next we must turn to elucidate the significant word "aspect" which crops up in the definition of the State as "society in its political aspect." Here again we must analyze the matter in terms of policies. An aspect is something which interests us about an already determined whole. The dimness of this definition may be illuminated by an example. In wartime, the morale of the people is an "aspect" of the war effort; but to the people themselves it isn't an aspect of anything—it is simply how they feel. Or, to take another example, the general policy of understanding and investigating the world leads to the field of knowledge being carved up into a number of subjects or disciplines. A scholar who is concerned to explain rural settlements in the Highlands of Scotland might, in some contexts, be said to deal with an "aspect" of geography, but to the scholar himself his subject is not an aspect, but a whole in itself—one which will no doubt have its own aspects. As long as this is understood, there is nothing especially objectionable about seeing the world in terms of wholes and aspects, though when this becomes a metaphysical exercise, it rapidly turns into idealism and begins to undermine the independence of everything in the world. In idealist terms *everything* is simply an aspect of an all-inclusive whole which is usually referred to as the absolute.

How does this general point affect the definition of the State as "society in its political aspect"? Obviously the definition is positing society as a whole which includes and determines politics. But in that case, we will have some difficulty in discovering the nature (or the defining principle) of this peculiar whole. We observed at the beginning of this section that the *only* thing which equally united the citizens of Great Britain (or of any other country) was the political fact of citizenship. The borders of "societies" and their internal constitutions are all produced by the work of politicians—whether kings or statesmen. It is, of course, true that all manner of social, geographical, linguistic and historical circumstances went into the definition of any given modern community; but the work of creating States and maintaining them is political, and inescapably so.

The unity of that "society" which claims the State as its "political aspect" is thus itself a political unity. The State is not an aspect of society; it is the only unity that society can lay claim to. In digging a grave for this widely accepted formula, we are actually laying to rest the ghost of the social contract theories, which also (and for ideological reasons) wished to establish that society was logically prior to the State, and therefore ought to control it. But once we are free of this assumption, we are able to detect the bones of liberal ideology. The unity of society in the liberal sense thus emerges not as a fact but as an aspiration—which might become a fact if everyone followed out the democratic duty which emerged from the syllogism we discussed. Liberal social unity is that of obligatory social participation, and it gains its plausibility from confusion with the sociological definition of society as a "complex of relationships"—for everyone is involved in many sorts of social relationships.

The liberal who argues in this manner is now in a position which is very characteristic of all ideologies. He is able to say both that social unity exists (i.e. there is such a thing as society apart from its political unity), and that the fact that social unity does not exist, is a social problem. He can have things both ways, shifting from one position to the other according to whether he is arguing with ideological opponents or trying to affect the behavior of ideological supporters.

II. THE USES OF SOCIETY

We are now able to understand how the British liberal traditions could, more or less in defiance of the facts, remain consistently individualistic for so many centuries. We can understand also how misguided were those nineteenth-century German writers who despised the English as being selfish and grasping—those who thought that Bentham was actually describing real people. The answer is perfectly simple. It is that liberal theory managed to combine an atomistic account of the State with a monistic account of society. The liberal individualist always had this extra card up his sleeve, one which could always deal with the many dangling bits of social and political life left over by utilitarianism. Now while we may deplore this split intellectually, we are unlikely to do so politically. Intellectually, there is no distinction between State and society; life cannot be carved up in this convenient way. And if the attempt to do so is made, then the result will be bad social and political theory, that is, theory which constantly has recourse to mystery, ambiguity, evasion, and downright falsity, in order to give a coherent account of its material. Politically, the story is rather different. On the basis of distinction between the State and society, an ideology has developed to support the British political tradition whereby an autonomous set of institutions live together within a single and limited order, within which politics functions to adjust conflicts of interest. As we have already argued, the adjustment of interests conception is a limited and local view of politics, a view which is not even fully adequate to the small area which it does appear to cover. It omits the crunch of truncheon on skull which always lies just in the background of political life; it has no place for the shadow institutions which arise out of those inadequately characterized "interests."

So long as these autonomous institutions—churches, sects, business companies, social circles, universities, local communities—retain their vitality, then the notion of balance can remain the presiding theory of British (and indeed all) political life. But the vitality of these institutions has long been under attack from a variety of forces and circumstances. The main circumstances have been war and industrialism. The main force has been the socialist version of liberal ideology. But the curious and significant thing is that the attacks on these institutions have been made in the name of society.

Why has society been preferred to the State? One minor reason has been that States have earned a bad reputation. They have always had a pretty bad name, except in times of nationalist enthusiasm. Besides, conservative critics of socialist planning like to build up the State as a frightening bogey, pointing legitimately enough at totalitarian States. By now, society has a much nicer ring about it.

Society, in any case, is a usefully vague idea. It has become a great causal rag-bag and hold-all, accommodating without protest virtually anything arising out of the communal experience of mankind. It is therefore a suitable term in which to dress the vaguest sorts of fancy; those projects which it would be preposterous to advance in the name of the State may be plausibly attributed to "society." Thus wherever we come across statements suggesting that "society must act thus or decide thus," the only meaning that can be attached to them is a political meaning. They are exhortations that the State should act in a certain way. What limited plausibility the use of "society" has in these cases arises simply from the democratic assumption that the indispensable prelude to any governmental act must be the support of popular opinion. And this, of course, is by no means always true.

Most conservatives are ready to accept the State as *au fond* a coercive organization which holds social life together. It includes the severe impartiality of the law and the sometimes brutal machinery of police, army, prisons, punishment and execution. It presents individuals with the choice of obedience or punishment. We cannot realistically consider the State without including some of these unlovely facts about it; but liberals have tried very hard to do so. They describe the State in terms of competing claims, maximizing happiness, provision of welfare, eliminating suffering and injustice. The State—all States—do actually carry out programs of this kind, with considerable variations from State to State, and from time to time. In so far as States behave coercively, however, the conclusion of liberalism is usually that they have failed. By the assumption of ultimate unanimity, and by that of the externality of causes of evil, liberals are led to believe that the coercive role of the State is necessary only because the State is inadequately organized. Now given the inescapably coercive and brutal conduct of all States at various times, liberal doctrines begin to sound unrealistic if they claim to be concerned with the State. And therefore it is much more convenient to talk about society.

Not, indeed, that liberals cannot deliver a sharp rap over the knuckles when they talk about society. Here, for example, is a curiously petulant passage from L. T. Hobhouse: "On the other side, the individual owes more to the community than is always recognized. Under modern conditions he is too much inclined to take for granted what the State does for him and to use the personal security and liberty of speech which it affords him as a vantage ground from which he can in safety denounce its works and repudiate its authority. He assumes the right to be in or out of the social system as he chooses. He relies on the general law which protects him and emancipates himself from some particular law which he finds oppressive to his conscience. He forgets or does not take the trouble to reflect that, if everyone were to act as he does, the social machine would come to a stop. He certainly fails to make it clear how a society would subsist in which every man should claim the right of unrestricted disobedience to a law which he happens to think wrong. In fact, it is possible for an over-tender conscience to consort with an insufficient sense of social responsibility."[6]

In this remarkable passage, we have the other side of that spirit of liberalism which expresses itself in the abstract delineation of the compassionate spirit. Here we have "community," "society," "State," "social system," even the "social machine," all mixed up indiscriminately together. Here, in the figure of the rascally critic who steps in and out of "the social system," we have the liberal confusions about causation which we discussed on the issue of social commitment, which is both a fact and yet also an aspiration. And here also we have that curious moral criticism which is sometimes elevated into a moral philosophy: a concern with the consequences not of the act in question, but of the universalized act—the eternal complaint of angry headmasters crying: "What if everybody did it?" Which is, of course, not the point. For in the relevant situation, everybody is *not* doing it. And lastly, we have the mention of that sinisterly vague idea, a sense of social responsibility, which conjures up a future of sternly benevolent heads of organizations explaining to the errant subordinate the beautiful general ends of the particular system, which his deviations are selfishly threatening.

Thus our first conclusion about the uses of "society" must be that it is a way of avoiding talking about the State. Further, the reason why this transition takes place is the ordinary propaganda reason of confusing the implications of a political program. If political demands are advanced then they come from a determinate source and can be appropriately criticized. But the idea of a social problem appears to come from no particular location in society. It is a social incoherence arising out of an ideal; and this ideal can most persuasively be put in moral terms. For this reason, while it is absurd to talk of a "sick" or "healthy" or "decadent" State, we often find people applying holistic moral descriptions of this kind to society. Society as a propaganda term must therefore be conceived as an organism. The "real question," in liberal terms, is "whether the social order actually serves our needs."[7] We have already considered the use of needs propaganda. Here we have illustrated the use of "needs" as something mysteriously outside the social order and acting as a moral criterion of the "social order." But what is the "social order"? If "society" is

6. *Liberalism*, 1934, pp. 149–50.
7. Raymond Williams, *The Long Revolution*, London, 1961, p. 104.

simply the "complex of social relationships" then it is not a single manipulable order. In so far as there is a single order, then it is that imposed by the State and expressed in laws. Similarly, when we read that "the true nature of society" is that it is a "human organization for common needs,"[8] we can only observe that a complex of relationships is not an "organization" at all—only the State and the institutions it sanctions are "organizations" in that sense. But it is precisely the aim of liberalism to *make* society into a single, complex *organization*.

We cannot understand the force of the liberal conception of society unless we understand the impulse behind it. As Lady Wootton formulates it: "The contrast between man's amazing ability to manipulate his material environment and his pitiful incompetence in managing his own affairs is now as commonplace as it is tragic."[9] Well, contrasts depend upon our hopes and interests, but the point is clear enough. "Society" is man controlling his own affairs, consciously and deliberately. From the liberal uses of the concept a dream of controlled harmony begins to emerge. Such dreams have often been influential in human affairs.

In this dream, we find a single all-embracing organization in which each individual can find fulfilment and the completion of his own personality. We find a spontaneous moral harmony, without anything more in the way of dogmatic presupposition than is imposed by the guiding idea of harmony. This is particularly true in respect of sexual deviations; liberals are prepared to leave the question of homosexuality, for example, to one side, pending the advance of medical techniques. Science is expected to provide a progressive revelation by means of which we can construct such a harmony.

This ideal has no place for barriers between classes of people. It is hostile to social class, racial discrimination, and any kind of social differentiation, except in some cases a differentiation based on vocational ability. The pervasive emotion of the ideal is that of love, for love creates and is constructive, whilst hatred destroys and creates barriers. In some versions of the concept of society, loving seems to be an attribute of generic man. For hatred is taken to be an irrationality produced by mental illness and social circumstances; remove these and men will naturally love each other and behave considerately.

8. Raymond Williams, *op. cit.*, p. 112.
9. *Testament for Social Science,* London, 1950, p. 1.

Some of the details of this picture emerge from descriptions of the concept of "mental health."[10] Many such definitions include the notion of inner harmony within the personality; most also use the idea of adjustment (especially "positive, emotional, social and intellectual adjustment") to the individual's environment. The fact that this harmony would be a system comes out in the frequent reference to function and role which is found in these definitions; it comes out even more strikingly in the references to efficiency: ". . . the end result will be an integrated, harmonious personality, capable of attaining maximum efficiency, satisfaction and self-realization with the least expenditure of energy and the least strain from interfering and conflicting desires and habits, and maximally free from serious inner strife, maladjustment, or other evidence of mental discord." The conception of human beings functioning in a systematic organization is, of course, a mechanical one; and the careless inattentive reader of some definitions of mental health is likely to be brought up short by an eerie feeling that he is reading a disquisition on diesel engines. Particularly do we find this in the more extreme and optimistic views of mental health: "Industrial unrest to a large degree means bad mental hygiene, and is to be corrected by good mental hygiene. The various anti-social attitudes that lead to crime are problems for the mental hygienist. Dependency, in so far as it is social parasitism not due to mental or physical defect, belongs to mental hygiene. But mental hygiene has a message also for those who consider themselves quite normal, for, by its aims, the man who is fifty per cent efficient can make himself seventy per cent efficient."

It is clear that this particular area of the social sciences exemplifies scientific moralism; that is, a moral and political movement advancing its banners under the camouflage of science. But, as we have argued, the claim to be scientific is a bogus one. The movement includes the metaphysical idea of generic man; and it depends for its incursions into ethics on the rationalist teleology of ends and means: ". . . actually many of the apparent needs of everyday life are, in fact, means dressed up as ends as a matter of practical convenience; they are logically derived from some much more general principle, which for practical purposes it is assumed that they will

10. A useful set of definitions of mental health has been collected by Barbara Wootton in *Social Science and Social Pathology,* London, 1959, pp. 219–224, where they are also discussed and criticized. The examples quoted here are taken from this source.

promote."[11] We have already dealt with many of the objections to this kind of argument; the main point being that where something is taken as both an end and a means, there exist (as a matter of social fact) two policies which determine its dual role. The scientific procedure here would be to discover and investigate these policies. The liberal movement, however, dogmatically classifies whatever it can as being "in reality" a means. In other words, it espouses one policy uncritically and rejects the other, whilst simultaneously confusing the issue by its claim to science. What we confront is a metaphysics of the familiar appearance and reality type, proceeding under a heavy smokescreen. Science is concerned with issues of truth and falsity, the liberal movement with an imperfectly defined conception of improvement or reform; and there is *no* necessary relationship between the desirable and the true.

The function of these ends-means arguments is to make the system flexible. What is "normal" or healthy must be able to fit into it without strain. But there are some classes of people whose behavior cannot be universalized to fit into the system called "society." These people are called deviants or "social problems." And since the system is itself a moral conception, though it tries to avoid seeming so, then deviants must also be morally significant. We have already argued that the conception of a social problem is strictly speaking meaningless. But it is made plausible by its moral content.

III. EDUCATION AND SOCIETY

The liberal conception of society is, then, determined by the moral and political policies of modern liberalism. It has only a tenuous connection with sociological description (though sociologists themselves often adopt it). The ends of this policy are described, usually in the abstract singular, as "social purpose." The means or necessary conditions of the policy are "social needs," and the barriers to it are "social problems." It is an ambitious policy which aims at nothing less than the transformation of human life. So ambitious a project necessarily takes a great interest in education, for like all movements, it is eager to recruit the young. In liberal terms, education, like everything else,

---

11. Barbara Wootton, *Testament for Social Science,* p. 121. Cf. the note on Flugel above, p. 117.

is a means towards something else, and once this instrumental character has been established, then outside manipulation is not far away. For it is inevitable that "that of which it is an instrument" (*viz.* "society"[12]) will begin to apply its own criteria of efficient functioning. The only way in which we can expose this kind of attempt to reduce education to a socially dependent role is by making some remarks about education as an independent tradition.

Education depends upon what we may call, with a maximum of vagueness, the impulse towards understanding. Sometimes this impulse is said to be produced by curiosity; sometimes it is even elevated into an instinct or natural disposition of human nature. Men have exhibited this impulse under a great variety of circumstances, and in western civilization it has generated a tradition of immense complexity and significance. It is an impulse which may clearly be distinguished from the meliorist conception of a search for knowledge to promote the satisfaction of desires. For, however the impulse towards understanding may begin, it is capable of freeing itself from practical considerations.

The distinction between the academic and vocational pursuit of knowledge may be developed into an ethical argument. The pursuit of knowledge for its own sake has often been taken as a good; as something distinguished from other kinds of pursuit by the ethical quality of goodness. A man dominated by the mood of philosophical enquiry has been thought to be one who has stepped aside from the blinkered confusion of everyday life, and who alone is fully conscious of himself in the world. Those who pursue other kinds of desire necessarily limit themselves; they have eyes only for what is relevant to the object of their pursuit. They are liable to frustration, hope, fear, disappointment, even hysteria—all emotions capable of precipitating evil acts. The pursuit of most desires necessarily promotes illusions—sometimes facts must be

---

12. "Society" is sometimes used in conjunction with another logically similar term, "the economy." Thus John Vaizey (*Britain in the Sixties,* Penguin Special, 1962) has a chapter entitled "The New Society and the New Economy," which begins: "It is worth spending money on education because it assists the economy . . . in the last ten years Britain's national income has *risen less sharply* than those of other countries in Europe, and this *failure in growth* is associated with a profound shift in the country's international position" (my italics). This passage, with its propagandist transition from "risen less sharply" to "this failure of growth," is part of the heavy fall of Snow which has followed the Rede Lecture of 1959. It is an example of trend-persuasion as it affects education.

ignored or distorted, but always transient objects and satisfactions are allowed an importance which other moods will find disproportionate. The philosopher, this argument continues, is therefore the model of the good man, and the disinterested pursuit of truth is a good activity. This argument is Greek in origin; further it is one which does not involve exhortation. It does not lead to the command: Pursue knowledge. For as a matter of fact, men *will* pursue truth, though intermittently. Exhortation, or the command to pursue knowledge, would in fact defeat this purpose, for it would subject truth-seeking to a policy.

We may therefore adopt this conventional distinction between vocational and academic pursuit of knowledge, though we should be careful not to vulgarize it into a distinction between practice and theory. All societies make some provision for vocational training; but not all have strong and independent traditions of academic investigation of the world. And while it is rather pointless to struggle over the possession of a word, we may note that "education" has traditionally referred primarily to the academic pursuit of knowledge, and the preparations for it.

Arguments asserting the autonomy of freedom of enquiry have always had a prominent place in the liberal tradition. *Areopagitica* and the *Essay on Liberty* are both passionate defenses of the social tradition of enquiry; but they are both expressed in individualist terms, and in each there is a tendency to support freedom of enquiry because of the incidental utilities which accrue to a political system in which it is untrammelled. But defenses of free enquiry are only as strong as their weakest argument; and any defense which points to the outside interests which free enquiry may serve is a hostage to fortune: it may have to submit when the balance of utility turns against it. If philosophy is for the greater glory of God, there may come a time when those entrusted with the earthly affairs of the Deity decide that it no longer glorifies Him. At the present time, liberalism is weakened in its defense of free enquiry by the meliorist question: Knowledge for what?

Free enquiry, like any social activity, has to fight for its existence in a hostile environment. The most obvious hazard is orthodoxy. An orthodoxy which asserts geocentricity of the universe as a truth on the same level as that of transubstantiation is likely to be understandably flustered when men start building telescopes and toying with Copernican ideas; and one which asserts the inferiority of certain races will wish to keep a strong grip on its social scientists. These, of course, are merely the dramatic examples; what they dramatize is the constant and ceaseless pressure upon enquiry to arrive at required conclusions. The first antagonist of the educational tradition is dogma, which limits the free play of enquiry. People have been burned, shot, hanged, imprisoned and exiled for the questioning of politically established dogmas, those which are thought necessary to the stability of the régime. In a free society, the consequences of contesting any particular dogma are not fatal.

The tradition of free enquiry has developed institutions, and institutions very quickly develop their own momentum. In particular, questions of status, comfort and respectability begin to arise, and play a powerful role in the minds of those who are officially custodians of the tradition. We have noted as a general psychological principle that any act will be determined not by a single motive but by a cluster of motives, and the holding of an opinion is an act. The participants in controversies will often include among their motives not only that of understanding the issue, but also those of self-esteem, ambition, security, or fear of giving offence. All manner of ideological motives are likely to force their way into academic life. These dangers are often more insidious than the dramatic force of threatened persecution, and they are inevitably part of the milieu within which enquiry must operate. Where the tradition is strong, these motives will themselves be criticized and exposed; at other times they will encompass the slow strangulation of the tradition. When that happens, free enquiry may languish, or, alternatively, it may simply move outside the universities, as it did during the seventeenth century, when modern science and philosophy were most vigorously carried on by a network of communicating private individuals.

What has primarily burdened the tradition of education over the last century or so is the weight of hopes and expectations which have rested upon it. For the Enlightenment, education was the instrument which would bring us out of the darkness of superstition. Then, more significantly, in the nineteenth century, education became an indispensable instrument of industrial advance. It was the pressure of industrial demand which was the necessary and sufficient condition of the spread of literacy and instruction towards the end of that century. The very usefulness of universities meant from that period on that government and industry were ready to employ the products of their training. And very soon, universities began to receive public money. In earlier times, they had managed to subsist off private support, at the cost of only intermittent attempts to influence the content of what was taught and thought.

In the early stage of public support for universities, no question arose of universities meeting "national needs." The universities of Britain were dominated, and to a large extent still are dominated, by wily men who know perfectly well how to deal with ideological encroachments of that kind. In any case, given the political policies of the last half century—by which large private accumulations of wealth were systematically mopped up by the central Treasury—universities faced the alternative of public support or total collapse. But having been forced into this position, they were bound to face demagogic criticism framed in terms of: What are the taxpayers getting for their money?

But above the demagogic hustle more profound-sounding themes are persuasively broached. What is the true purpose of a university? What are the values of education? Where should it lead? Here the ideologist approaches on tiptoe, often himself unaware of his role. And here the only full response to such questions is a comprehensive understanding of social life. Otherwise the disputants flounder around looking for points which will clinch the argument. Some answers to these questions are readily rejected. Few people at the moment could be induced to believe that a university ought to produce unshakable patriots, men who will never accept the view that any act of their country is wrong. Nor would many people believe that a university exists simply to state the dogma of the one true religious belief. On the other hand, those who have not considered the matter closely (and some who have) might agree with any number of vague formulae: that universities exist to promote self-realization, to express the values of society, to play a vital social role, to educate the whole man, or to investigate the purpose of life. Exactly what meanings lurk in ambush behind these mellifluous phrases is difficult to detect. Sometimes they are as vapid as they sound; sometimes they are not. Frequently they are the innocuous source of a whole range of prescriptions demanding reform of curricula, different directions of university interest, or a more "committed" attitude on the part of academics. In other words, they are "criteria," or determining policies, which once established are to be used to adjudicate conflicts of interest within universities, or between universities on the one hand and the State or any other social institution on the other. For this reason, they cannot be ignored.

In beginning this section with some brief remarks on the tradition of enquiry and education, we have implicitly established one possible answer to these questions; namely, that universities were created and sustained by the activity of free enquiry. There is a sense in which free enquiry is their "purpose."

For various reasons which are only imperfectly understood, traditions and activities are liable to a decline, and sometimes this decline may take place even though the institutions remain powerful and perhaps even continue to exhibit a glittering and impressive appearance. Traditions can lose their flexibility and inventiveness and degenerate into dogmas. The French army, for example, spent vast resources upon elaborating the assumptions which it considered had brought success in the First World War. The motives lying behind this hardening would seem to have been fear resulting from the shock of that earlier victory. And it is possible that fear always lies behind the defensiveness that results in a tradition hardening into a set of dogma.

It is probably some realization of this kind which leads to the universities being criticized for resistance to innovation—with "not keeping up with the times." But here the complexity of ideological battles becomes very evident; for those who make the criticism are often seeking to impose their own demands, indeed their own kind of hardening, upon the institutions they criticize. And whilst fashion is a fatal influence on most activities it is peculiarly dangerous to artistic and academic traditions. It amounts to importing all the currently fashionable slogans into the work of free enquiry. If the latter is in a vigorous condition, it will proceed to criticize these slogans, to lay bare, in particular, the simplifications and illusions involved in modern thinking. Such criticism is likely to be as unwelcome to very strong interests in the State as was Socratic criticism to the Athenian orthodoxies.

The social pressure resisting criticism is very strong, but it must not be seen as an outside pressure working upon the universities, for the simple reason that it exists within. University teachers, in so far as they are involved in social life, are themselves resistant to criticism. The result is that the controversy over the "role" of universities is a highly confused struggle, in which some of the external criticisms are true. In the twentieth century, universities have gained greatly in self-importance, and the pronouncements of their members are attended to with gravity by the authorities of other institutions. In realizing this very condition, university teachers are liable to a peculiar feeling of self-consciousness; in particular, they are liable to be especially receptive to the ethic of social responsibility. If issues of great State importance depend upon them, they are forced into the role of being politicians. And when the discussion turns upon the question of responsibility, they are forced into working out just what they are responsible *to*. Is it the State? Is it to "morality"? Is it to universities as institutions? Is it to the spirit of free enquiry? And, as we argued earlier in discussing policies, there can be no determinate answer to questions of this kind. Each answer which is implicitly or explicitly given registers the social character of the people involved.

We have noted that problems arise in the context of policies. Now what is a problem in terms of one policy may not be a problem in terms of another. The problems of the balance of trade, for example, may be of little intellectual significance to economists; the theoretical elements can be laid bare. But the problem as it exists for the Treasury is of a different kind. The economist who accepts the Treasury view of the problem is doing something different from advancing economics. It is doubtful whether the problem of juvenile delinquency in the social sciences has a sufficient intellectual unity to mark it off from other forms of social behavior; the fact that it is a problem to police forces does not necessarily mean that it is the same sort of problem to social scientists. On the other hand, the problem of what causes cancer happens to be one of great importance for a number of policies. But here again, the intellectual problem of causation may well be solved whilst other difficulties prevent the establishment of a cure for the condition.

None of this, of course, is to argue that people ought not to work on so-called practical problems. People obviously will. But they will not necessarily be doing work of much intellectual significance. The point is indeed a rather obvious one, yet its importance for the social sciences is immense. What claims individuals may legitimately make upon governments is a question of very little intellectual significance. The answer does not allow us to understand politics any better; yet just this concern has immensely influenced politics over the last century and more—indeed is one of the reasons why political theory is generally so drearily unilluminating. Again, what mechanical adjustments to a constitution will make the country safe for democracy is intellectually a banal and irrelevant question, yet thinkers write many books upon it—books which are thus intellectually sterile and, because of their abstract generality, of no use to politicians.

The damage done by this—in fact meliorist—confusion does not lie simply in the diversion of attention. It lies partly in the fact that such preoccupations are capable of imposing "commonsense" upon the conceptualization of a subject. And, as we pointed out in discussing trend-persuasion, given that the investigators of a subject are saddled with a set of "practical" categories, the use of statistics and similar devices is now so extensive that results which are in some sense meaningful can be squeezed out of a barren subject for a very long time. Further damage is done to a subject by the fact that the defense of already unacademic procedures maneuvers its protagonists further away from the tradition of academic understanding. Such people are forced into elaborating the duties of the scholar to the State, the community, society, the well-being of mankind or various other vague conceptions.

The awareness of this question that does exist has often protected the universities from the cruder forms of outside pressure. Both governments and private foundations are often careful to insist that the money they donate shall be used for academic purposes and not devoted to the trivia of everyday life. The fault to a surprising extent lies within the universities themselves—in the empire-building of professors and the kind of research which is done. The most useful defense of academic immunity against outside pressures has been the argument that if scholars and scientists are allowed to carry on in their own way, they are likely to produce some useful by-products in the course of their academic work. Developments in science and mathematics are an excellent illustration that such things have happened. A constant flow of scientific wonders has so far kept the utilitarian pack of critics from baying too hard at ivory towers. A more serious threat comes from contemporary ideologists of national purpose, who would subject the universities to the changing demands of competitive nationalism.[13]

To defend education by pointing to its incidental utilities is unsound. Academic enquiry is not strictly useful to society, for, as we have argued, society in this sense is meaningless. But it is indispensable to the continuance of a number of civilized traditions which are still very strong, and which would be threatened by the wholesale barbarization implicit in the program of making universities practically useful. In these interests, the universities are likely to find a number of dependable allies in the immediate future.

---

13. "I think we are lacking, clearly, in effective leadership: I mean, a leadership in getting things done, a leadership in terms of a sense of national purpose"—Anthony Crosland, in a broadcast discussion, printed in *The Listener*, 5.7.62. And Professor McRae, in the same discussion, remarks: "I believe that if we are going to get out of our stagnation over the next generation, the heart of this lies with doing something about education—not with just adjusting the educational system but actually with thinking education out anew."

CHAPTER SIX

Freedom

I. FREEDOM AS A MANNER OF LIVING

FREEDOM AS A political slogan is an ideal, a goal to be pursued. But an ideal can only be something constructed out of what we have already experienced. In studying freedom, we may, on the one hand, consider it simply as a set of facts about social and political life; or, if our enquiry is ideological, we may seek those of its characteristics which are suitable for erection into criteria. What makes freedom difficult to study is that most investigations succumb at some point or another to its desirability; and an interest in what it is gives way to a concern with how it may be promoted.

Among the conspicuously free groups with which we are familiar are the citizens of Athens, and the enfranchised of Britain and America. In each case, these peoples, finding themselves in conflict and consequently attempting to define what they were and what their struggles sought to defend, discovered that they were free peoples. This discovery was attended by a considerable outpouring of rhetoric; and all of it was subject to the fallacies inevitable when a moral characteristic like freedom is confused with a concrete historical situation. But embedded in the rhetoric, and susceptible of extraction by enquiry, was a theory, not of how freedom might be attained but of what it was. Let us consider some of the characteristics of a free society, taking as our model one of its earliest formulations, the Periclean Funeral Oration.

Pericles was concerned not with the statement of an ideal but of those characteristics of Athens which Pericles considered to make her distinctive and great. These characteristics are not so much political as moral. Further, all of the characteristics interlock, one with another, so that the presence of one leads to the development of the others.

It was courage which Pericles identified, partly for topical reasons, as the first quality of Athenians. But it was courage of a very complex kind. For Aristotle, courage was a mean between rashness and cowardice, and for Plato it was the knowledge of what is not to be feared. The courage we are trying to identify is thus not the kind which is often evoked by the presence of an enemy; it contains no element of hysteria. It leads to a special kind of reaction to crises. In a national emergency, two extreme reactions may occur. On the one hand, the populace may fuse together to such an extent that they resemble an organism. They think and feel the same way, and their social fusion is generally capped by adoration of a leader. Tribal behavior is predominantly of this kind, and so was the totalitarian cohesion of Germany and of Japan during the Second World War. It has the advantage of simplifying matters, so that all problems seem technical problems related to an overriding objective. Alternatively, we may find that a national emergency evokes social dissolution; the State breaks up into institutions, families and individuals whose main concern is to cut their losses and survive. People distrust each other, and few are prepared to take the risks of political organization for fear of treachery by others. Something like this occurred in the French collapse of 1940.

These are both entirely different social reactions, and we are only tempted to see them as polarities because under most circumstances both reactions are likely to occur; some people will risk everything for the national effort, others will attempt to profit from the situation. Politicians have an understandable preference for the former kind of behavior which they describe as unselfish and heroic.

A free reaction to a national emergency is difficult to describe but clearly distinguishable. It consists in a kind of social cohesion which combines cooperation with the full maintenance of individuality. There is neither blind devotion to a national cause nor utter scepticism about it. All that happens as a result of the emergency is an unusual consensus of opinion about priorities, but there is no complete capitulation to an overriding goal. As a result, free societies do not drastically alter their structure and their customs as a result of the emergency, perhaps because they are in any case highly flexible. One celebrated instance of this would be the maintenance of civil liberties in Britain from 1939 to 1945. But that instance depended entirely upon the fact that unity already existed; had there been deep divisions the British government would, like any other, have had to use repression to deal with them. But then again, the behavior and policies of the government were an important cause of whether or not deep divisions might occur.

If we take it that free co-operation is a special and distinguishable social relationship, our problem is to discover why it occurs. Pericles, as we have seen, attributed it to courage; but for Plato it was a form of knowledge. It has at times been called rationality, in the sense of a refusal to succumb to passions like fear or the desire for security; but the distinction between reason and passion is moralistic and narrow. Certainly full co-operation depends upon a populace accustomed to facing new problems, and confident that it can deal with them successfully. Another way of describing it would be in terms of balance; political issues are extensively discussed, and this can only happen if some individuals resist the strong impulsions of panic that often cause people to accept any solution with a majority behind it. Small groups with unpopular policies need a good deal of courage to continue advocating their policy in circumstances where their enemies are liable to invoke charges of treason and disloyalty. In moral terms we discover courage on one side and a kind of tolerance on the other, and the whole picture is of a community involved in conflict, but deliberating, and capable of coming to a decision. If we can explain the elements of this situation, then we will have discovered much about freedom.

One crucial element of free co-operation is a respect for truth. Under all circumstances, the pressure of expediency causes considerable distortions of fact. In a crisis, this pressure increases. Further, if the national goal is taken to be an overriding criterion of action, then truth, like everything else, must take a subordinate position; always to some degree essential to the success of any operation but twisted for convenience in many particulars. This fact is most clearly seen in the case of totalitarian societies which feed on crises, and depend upon a set of dogmatic beliefs whose questioning would indicate a threat to the whole system.

Now a respect for truth is never the result simply of an act of will. It can only exist as part of a tradition which has continued for a considerable time. In particular, it must gain support from independent institutions in society, for whom truth is a concern overriding everything else: primarily, universities. In all our examples, a tradition of enquiry was sufficiently powerful to impose its standards in other areas of the life of the State: a truth-respecting integrity was part of the conception of honor prevalent in those States. Further, this kind of honor is irrational and imprudent, for there are many occasions both in political and personal life when there are advantages to be gained from suppressing the truth. The temptation to deceive becomes more pressing in times of crisis, and each side attempts to gain allies by distorting the ends of its policy and evading the unsavory facts about its own position. Too great a desire to persuade others is fatal to truth; it leads rapidly to the strident and rigid world of propaganda. In free States, then, there are always people who are irrationally attached to the truth, in the manner of Socrates and Zola, and who will not be turned aside from this by appeals to national interest or slogans like "national survival."

But this fact tells us even more about the character of a free society; for universities nurturing a tradition of free enquiry cannot exist in isolation as the only independent institutions of the community. There must be a wide variety of institutions independent of the government and capable of cultivating their own interest within a political framework. Freedom has often been associated with variety, and even eccentricity; it is certainly hostile to the notion of a single dogmatically held truth. The existence of such a variety of independent institutions is both politically and intellectually necessary for a tradition of truth. Politically, because universities cannot remain free whilst other institutions are carefully regulated by the government, for their independence would undermine the dependence of others. Intellectually, because the clash of ideologies which goes on between institutions—between churches, or the various organized interests of the economy—generates many of the theories with which investigation deals. For there are always some areas of life which are most thoroughly cultivated by some particular institution, and it will, for its own purposes, turn up problems and solutions which for scientists, philosophers and historians, have other meanings.

These institutional arrangements are closely linked with tolerant behavior, another moral characteristic which waxes and wanes in people. "We are free and tolerant in our private lives; but in public affairs we keep to the law," as Pericles expressed it. Now this condition only arises as a social custom; it is a manner of life rather than the product of a desire. It lies outside the control of individuals; governments may encourage or discourage fanaticism, but they can neither create the fanaticism they want, nor destroy the fanaticism they do not want. In a State which is radically divided by fanatically held opinions, a government has no option but to repress or be overthrown. But whilst fanaticism is not a calculable growth, some forms of political organization are more conducive to it than others; one which holds strongly to the distinction between a "public" and a "private" sphere is less likely to suffer from fanatics than one in which government regulation of everything is commonly accepted. It is difficult to define the private sphere in terms of natural rights or self-regarding actions; but if some such privacy is respected throughout the State, then governments cannot easily invade it.

These conditions are part of the lives of individuals. They describe the way people think and feel. In developing our account of freedom, we may employ a distinction commonly made between technical and deliberative thinking.

Technical thinking is the solution of problems within fixed limits, as in the discovery of means to ends.

Deliberative thinking, on the other hand, is the reaction to a situation made by something which is itself capable of changing. I am referring here to what is commonly called "free choice" or "man's freedom to choose." The objection to these terms is that they are individualistic, assuming a fixed (but mysterious) human identity which opts for one kind of principle or act rather than others. In deliberation, however, the crucial fact which determines the outcome is the character of the chooser, and that is not known until the choice is made; for choice is a determination of character, something which happens when we are making up our minds to "take a stand" on some issue. But it may also happen unconsciously, which suggests that the term "thinking" ought to be avoided. We may distinguish three possibilities in deliberation. In one, the kind which normally draws the attention of moral philosophers, a moral problem is posed and solved by means of an intellectual effort whose course (in terms of principles held or ends considered and rejected) can be plotted at each stage. Much more commonly, however, life poses for individuals a moral problem which they seem almost to solve by impulse. Without consciously thinking about it, they come to a decision, finding that the issues have become clarified in a manner analogous to the solving of intellectual problems in sleep. Finally, there are occasions when the problem is both posed and solved before the individual is even aware of it—often because he is strongly resisting.

This last fact about deliberation is significant; it indicates that deliberative problems are often painful, and therefore avoided. In fact, avoidance of these problems may become the solution. Such problems can produce anxiety, and a political solution to the problem posed by anxiety is the tribal social cohesion mentioned earlier. The effect of such a political development is to convert deliberative problems into technical problems: or, at least, so it seems to the members of the tribe.

Now in a free State, characterized as we have seen by a wide variety of independent institutions, individuals must constantly face deliberative problems about what they ought to do. They become highly skilled either in solving such problems or (which is also a solution) refusing to meet them. Children learn to behave in this way, partly because they are taught to, and partly because they have to. They are subject to a considerable bombardment of propaganda, and there is little in the way of an established intellectual orthodoxy on political or religious questions to serve as a protection. Given an education of this kind, people are less often tempted to succumb to the hysteria of indecision, which often leads to the desire to submit to a striking and dramatic orthodoxy.

In such varied social circumstances people cannot be generally judged in terms of their status and function, for there will be many sources of status— money, birth, place of education, intellectual distinction, celebrity, popularity and so on. This fact, too, is a source of confusion to people who are not accustomed to deliberation, and they may therefore prefer a single system in terms of which everyone can be conveniently assessed at a moment's notice. This dislike of different sources of status often gives rise to a virulent dislike of snobbery, leading to some single criterion of "true worth" which would clarify our judgments about people.

A free State is one in which there is a strong resistance to professionalization; it is marked by that "versatility" which Pericles claimed for Athens. The sort of personal behavior indicated by versatility is one in which people are ready to "try their hand" at anything they have to. It is for this reason that pioneering communities have many of the characteristics of free States; the more difficult question is how freedom exists in States with a stable social structure. The situations which most contrast with this kind of versatility are a caste system, a rigid form of feudal system, and a bureaucracy, for here each person has a fixed status which determines the kind of work he does, and usually the *only* kind of work he will do.

Individuals in a free society may be described as independent. This means, for one thing, that they will organize themselves, and resist attempts by other people to dominate them. But that is only possible if such people dislike not only domination by others, but also submission by others. Independent individuals have no desire to crush the independence of others, for independence is not simply a social relationship, but a characteristic which only exists by rejecting both domination and submission—a point which Plato made in arguing that the despot himself was a slave.

It is a mark of the interlocking signs of a free State that this immediately brings us back to truth. For in considering the circumstances in which free independence is possible, we must observe that it depends to a very large extent on an intellectual interest in how things are, in contrast to the desire to make things conform to a pre-established plan. A passion to control is the attempt to create dependence from a fixed position, as a father may attempt to control the development of his children not simply by insisting upon fixed standards of behavior, but by crushing any signs of independence or deviation. Truth is frequently a deviation from our explanatory categories and from our ideas of what the world must be like, and philosophy and science are therefore marked by a respect for the independence of facts, a characteristic which is likely to be carried over into other kinds of social activity.

Free individuals can modify themselves in a traditional manner in the face of the possibility of the breakdown of order. They are not "slaves of the passions." In social terms, men who are afraid will abandon their liberty to a protector. Men who are covetous and acquisitive will abandon their freedom to rulers who will leave them free to acquire wealth. Men dominated by gambling or drugs will not be able to see clearly enough to recognize threats to their liberty. Further, wilful men, hungry for fame and ambitious to command, will soon cease to respect the liberty of others.[1] Historical generalizations of this kind indicate the connection which the idealists have always seen between virtue and liberty, however difficult it may be to elucidate this connection.

One further fact about free societies may be noted: they will show a con-

---

1. It is difficult to describe free men without making them seem like paragons of virtue. Any of these virtues will no doubt make only an intermittent appearance in the lives of particular men. But in free States, these virtues are available to men in their public capacity, and they dominate the situation. Where this is not so, free political institutions will not long survive.

siderable degree of institutional creativity. One consequence of freedom, and one mark of its existence, is the proliferation of institutions and associations created by groups of people, often for *ad hoc* but also sometimes for permanent ends. States in which this happens will show what de Tocqueville[2] observed in Anglo-Saxon States—a craving for public affairs and a thirst for rights. The work of creating and maintaining social institutions is something which has to be learned; one cannot simply make up one's mind to do it, and then go ahead. Many traps lie in wait—from futility to dissension and on to the possibility that the institution may misconceive its social importance and enter into violent conflict with the authorities; further, in a despotic society, governments are likely to assume that all initiative on the part of citizens is subversive in character, or will quickly become so. Thus to state the social and political conditions under which citizens may be spontaneously associative is to outline once more the various marks of freedom which we have already described.

This account of freedom attempts to set out the materials from which an explanation of freedom might be constructed. Inevitably it raises a great number of questions, some of which can be summarily considered here. In particular, it requires us to distinguish between freedom as a moral character and a free society. Freedom is something spontaneous and unpredictable in human affairs, and is likely to be found anywhere. A free society, on the other hand, is a society in which institutions have developed which are peculiarly suited to conserving a tradition of free behavior. We will find in free societies, as in any other, all those kinds of behavior which are most antipathetic to freedom. Any historical society will be a mixture of kinds of behavior, a location of moral struggle. It is only in the propagandist circumstances of war that countries are thought to stand for abstractions like Liberty, Democracy, Aryanism, or the Homeland of the Proletariat.

It is a historical commonplace to find many groups and nations claiming that they fight for freedom. And in many cases, at the end of the struggle, they find that they have merely substituted one kind of oppression for another. It is common to believe, when this happens, that the revolution has been betrayed. Yet it is more often the case that the betrayal is simply the measure of

---

2. See the passages quoted by A. V. Dicey in *Law of the Constitution*, Ninth Edition, London, 1945, pp. 184–87.

the illusion that one can literally fight "for" freedom. When slaves rise against their masters, it is usually the particular domination they object to, not to domination itself. The revolution, in other words, is always betrayed not by the leaders but also by the character of the followers. When the English struggled against the Stuarts, they were not slaves rising at last against a tyrant; they were men already free striving to maintain that freedom against what they took to be a new threat to it. Again, when the American colonies rose against the British government, they fought not "for" freedom, for they were already free; but to establish circumstances in which their manner of life might expand unfettered. What made the politics of the French revolutionaries so ambiguous in this respect was that the forces of dependence were so strong that when men shouted *Liberté* they had, in many cases, only a dreamlike notion of what the term meant.

When men claim that they love freedom, they can mean many things. In part they are admiring the independence of freedom, the refusal to obey masters no matter what orders may be given. But they will often mean by freedom a fantasy in which all the frustrating restrictions under which they suffer have been removed. And they will also associate this, in most cases, with an upper-class status which they have coveted from afar. It is out of these latter elements that a new bondage may be constructed for them. Most modern freedom movements have been closely associated with nationalism, and while freedom may be the flag they carry, it is nationalism which is likely to win in the end.

For while men may love freedom, they also love dependence. Those who come new to individual responsibility are likely to fear its risks and burdens. They like to take refuge in a function, desiring to be told not only what to do but also what they *are*. It is only clear directives from outside which can resolve the stalemates in the personality resulting from barely conscious conflicts. Such conflicts are personal problems which men unaccustomed to freedom can only solve in a dogmatic way, by unquestioning adherence to an organization, a role, a principle, or a person. The reason why freedom generally succumbs to nationalism is that a free man is an abstraction; he does not know what he is or what he may do. But in the nation, a man can find an identity and a set of satisfying duties. If freedom can only be attained by a prolonged military struggle, then what is attained is unlikely to be freedom. Actual warfare often generates demands for loyalty and solidarity of a dependent kind; and whilst there will always be some voices raised against the plea of common interest, they may not carry much weight against an established leadership and organization. The classic modern situation of this kind occurred on the Republican side during the Spanish civil war. Under these circumstances—where those who claim to be fighting for freedom are an unstable alliance of groups, each with a precise and uncompromising vision of a future condition—a free condition does not exist, nor can a free State be attained.

This raises a question to which we can only afford to give a sidelong glance, and about which nothing very much is known. What are the circumstances under which freedom can develop in a society? Taking a hint from Wittfogel's study of oriental despotism,[3] we may observe that the free societies which we are considering originated out of a combination of feudal and commercial circumstances. A decentralized feudal situation, in which honor and birth were the dominant considerations, was weakened and forced to compromise with the growth of cities and commercial activity. Freedom in each case arose out of a compromise of a peculiar kind between an established feudal class and a vigorous commercial one. Once the character and institutions are established, however, they can prove flexible and strong, and be transmitted to later generations and colonial extensions.

If this account of freedom is correct, then it is an ideal only in that it is widely admired, and like anything widely admired it can sometimes guide our efforts. But there is no question of approximation to some unattainable condition. For freedom refers to a complex set of moral facts. What might we mean by saying, for example, "Britain is a free country"? This proposition might point to the existence of free institutions in Britain—freedom of speech, opposition parties, habeas corpus. Such is the liberal view of the matter, and as far as it goes it is perfectly correct. But we may then enquire: Under what circumstances are such institutions possible? When the people arise and throw off their chains? When the victims rise against their oppressors? Hardly, for that kind of insurgence seems uniquely to produce a new set of oppressors. It may be that the conditions permitting free institutions lie beyond our conscious control; we cannot have them merely because we want them. It is impossible to avoid the conclusion that the proposition "Britain is a free country" refers not merely to political institutions, but also to a type of behavior which is sufficiently widespread among all classes of

3. Karl Wittfogel, *Oriental Despotism*, Yale, 1957.

the population (but especially the political classes) to permit and maintain free institutions.

II. FREEDOM AND SPONTANEITY

We have described freedom as a set of interlocking moral characteristics. This accords both with the so-called positive view of freedom and also with ordinary experience. For there are many typologies suggesting that some men are not free even when nothing external impedes their actions. One example would be the type of sycophantic courtier, a man enslaved to the will of another because his behavior is dominated by an overriding fear of losing favor. Another would be the anxious parvenu, ill at ease among his social superiors for fear that his actions will betray his origins. And there is the modern type of the other-directed man whose dominant fear is that of losing the approval of his "peer-group." None of these people is free, yet none suffers from political oppression.

So far as many liberal discussions of freedom go, this is none of our business. The use that people make of freedom is thought to be their own affair. Liberals feel uneasy if the enquiry turns in this direction, for it seems to lead towards the Rousseauist paradox of "forcing people to be free." This uneasiness reveals that virtually all liberal argument about freedom rests upon the image of the slave—the man who waits for his chains to be struck off. The chains have grown increasingly insubstantial, but the continuance of the metaphor suggests the fundamental assumption that all men naturally want to be free. And since this flies in the face of the facts, it can be saved by the view that the voluntary slave is enchained by his environment or the traditions of his society.

We may regard these elaborate metaphysics as an evasion of the moral issues raised by the question of freedom. Political freedom is comparatively simple to describe. It refers to a system of political institutions which is constitutional and in some degree popularly responsive. In liberalism, this *is* freedom, and the moral issues only arise when we consider what *use* people make of freedom when they have it. Yet it is quite clear that one of the most popular uses of freedom is to subvert it, and the whole distinction between freedom and how it is used collapses into the unanswerable question: Does a free nation have the right to sell itself into slavery? This was Milton's problem as the

Restoration approached. It faced the Weimar Republic as the Nazi Party grew in strength. It has faced many countries becoming independent after a period of colonial rule. Intellectually and politically, it is evident that freedom is what we do, not what we may be allowed to do. Freedom is not a set of abstract things which we might do if we wished; it depends entirely on what we choose in action.

Thus in answering the question "under what circumstances are men free?" most people would agree that one of the circumstances is political. Thereafter, however, discussions of freedom can go in two very different directions. One direction leads us to the moral considerations which we have already discussed. Even in this field of moral preoccupations there is a good deal of disagreement. The modern idealist tradition is likely to put a great deal of emphasis upon rationality and harmony, without ever quite discovering what it is that is being rationalized or harmonized. But the point which must be stressed about the relation between political freedom and freedom as a moral characteristic is that the first depends directly on the second. Freedom depends on how men actually do behave, not upon how they are allowed to behave. It is a matter of character, not of foolproof constitutional devices. For fools are paramount in politics, and there is nothing which they are unable to destroy.

But these questions can be side-stepped if we proceed in a manner which seems on the face of it to be more scientific. We can search for the conditions of freedom. Such a search is partly a concern with those things which have always been associated with freedom; but this concern is shaded by an overriding interest in discovering what can make political freedom effective. Effective, that is, in promoting human happiness. Freedom at this point becomes a means, and political freedom is seen as a necessary but not sufficient condition of happiness. For no man, it may be suggested, can be free if he is deprived of leisure, and must grind out his life in toil. To such a man, political rights are a mockery. Again, those who have been free in the past have enjoyed a certain prosperity. If we would make men free, prosperity must be our object; if we wish to make all men free, then we must also be careful to distribute this prosperity widely. For such is a condition of freedom.

Now it would merely confuse our discussion not to recognize that freedom, as it appears in this argument, is something quite different from the manner of behavior on which we have so far concentrated. It is here an abstract potentiality, a generalized kind of "being able" which in equity must be *provided* for all citizens. Freedom, as we have discussed it, has the peculiarity of providing the materials for its own continuance; that is to say, a tradition of free behavior creates habits and institutions which themselves require and encourage free behavior. On the view we are now considering, however, freedom is simply a power to do things, without respect to what things. Now we may say of such a power that it is entirely unreal; what people will actually do with such a power depends on what kind of people they are, and how they got the power. Freedom conceived in this way is quantitative; there can be more or less of it. But freedom as a manner of behavior is something which, at a given moment and in a particular situation, either exists or doesn't. The situation is constantly changing; there are always some things we can do and some we can't, but it is illogical to try to add up these abstract possibilities and quantify them. Money and power, on the other hand, are things which do allow of quantification; and, when freedom is quantified, we may well suspect that it is not merely being associated with money and power; it is being taken to *mean* these things.

The liberal preoccupation with the conditions of freedom can lead to another, equally fallacious, conclusion. The initial assumption, we have noted, is that no man is free without—say—bread and parliaments. This is a possibly defensible proposition, but its converse is not. For the converse would assert that all men who have bread and parliaments *are* free. Now this is to mistake a necessary for a sufficient condition, and serves the propagandist purpose of inclining supporters of freedom towards support for other social policies. "And it cannot be too strongly emphasized," wrote Professor Laski, "that those who seek the new social order are in this hour soldiers in the army of freedom."[4]

The most interesting assumption of this kind of argument is that freedom can be an object of political pursuit, and that such things as prosperity, industry, or certain constitutional arrangements, are means to the attaining of the end. One cannot organize a work of art; nor write poetry to rule. The man who sets out quite deliberately to maximize his own happiness is likely to fail. Whilst one may, perhaps, be able to create vast pools of technicians at will, one cannot create political stability or a nation of mystics. There are many things

---

4. Laski, *Liberty in the Modern State* (Pelican Edition), 1937, p. 40.

in the world which we cannot attain simply because we want them; and some are beyond our grasp precisely because we want them too much.

Here, we are forced to face one of the many paradoxes of freedom, namely that a political policy which aims at attaining any of the supposed conditions of freedom is likely to destroy free behavior. The French nation-in-arms of the 1790s, marching with libertarian slogans headlong into the Napoleonic dictatorship, would be the classic instance of this paradox. In such cases as this, and as I would argue in all cases, the political pursuit of freedom is always the pursuit of something else. There are no means which serve the precise end of freedom, for freedom, like happiness, is not an end that can be pursued.

Most ideologies which concern themselves with freedom deny this point explicitly, since they tell us what we must do either to attain freedom or to "increase" the amount of it. And a good deal of current political speculation denies it implicitly—notably the exponents of "thaw and freeze" analysis of the Soviet Union who are always hopefully looking for the moment when, a relaxed prosperity having been attained by the régime, freedom will evolve out of the primeval slime of despotism. It is certainly true that instances of free behavior will be found in the Soviet Union; but it is illusory to believe that some day the popular will to peace can alone bring an end to the cold war.

For if we are seeking the conditions of freedom, we must look not to those circumstances which happen to accompany it, but to the manner in which it has been attained. And we will find that it has always been attained because of a spontaneous growth of interest in truth, science, or inventiveness; a spontaneous growth of moral principles appropriate to freedom; a spontaneous construction of the political arrangements which permit of free constitutional government. Spontaneity indicates that free behavior has arisen directly out of the character of the people concerned, and that it is neither a mechanical process, nor a "natural" reaction to an environment, nor a means to the attainment of some end. Free behavior, in other words, is its own end. It may indeed be that "necessity" set the problem; that political antagonists in Britain had to work out some balanced form of constitution since none was strong enough to subdue the rest; but, once established, this element of balance was something desired for its own sake by people who criticized and rejected any recourse to absolute sovereignty.

It follows from this that free behavior cannot be understood in a context of ends and means, for it only begins at the moment when we forget about ends and begin to act for no other reason than an absorption in what we are doing. And this implies that an important element in free behavior is that we are prepared to accept the consequences of our actions, rather than adjust and modify our behavior in accordance with something external to us.

This explanation of freedom necessarily excludes those rationalist and utilitarian views of human behavior by which *everything* we do is a means to some further end, leading always—efficiently or inefficiently—towards some such goal as happiness. Rational behavior is the product of a judicious choice both of ends and of the means to them. It is certainly true that we do make calculations of this kind, though in fact most people consciously do so comparatively rarely. The moral significance of these doctrines is that they recommend calculation as a pre-eminently ethical manner of behaving. In utilitarian terms, prudence or caution is the highest virtue. In terms of our account of freedom, it is, on the other hand, unfree. This contradiction is not, however, as direct as it might seem, for prudence is an ambiguous virtue. It may be a servile concern to placate and serve others, the reference of every act before it is done to a criterion of self-interest, and this is what it often looks like in utilitarianism. This is prudence as it is found in our earlier examples of courtier, parvenu, and other-directed man.[5] But prudence may, on the other hand, be a recognition of the preoccupations of others and of the extent to which we can accommodate our preoccupations to theirs; and in this sense, prudence is essential to a free State.

III. PUBLIC PROVISION AND MORAL PROTECTION

Liberalism advocates the elimination of poverty and illiteracy by the provision of welfare; and it is most recognizably liberal when it recommends these policies as ingredients of, or means to, freedom.

We may observe immediately that in this respect, modern liberalism may be sharply distinguished from classical liberalism. Classical liberalism advocated a system of government which permitted the maximum room for self-provision; each family was expected to make its own arrangements; economic success was a carrot to encourage people to work, poverty was an indispens-

---

5. I refer, of course, to typologies; any particular courtier or parvenu may well behave very differently.

able spur. It is one of the ideological triumphs of modern liberalism that this classical version seems to us nothing more than a crude veil over the naked operations of the capitalist system, for we have become accustomed to estimating political doctrines in terms of the interests they appear to serve. What we must remember, however, is that the classical doctrine of self-provision was explicitly a moral doctrine, and one which must be discussed on its own moral ground.

The classical doctrine of self-provision was partly based on a sound distrust of political interference. It took government as no more than an instrument for keeping order; anything else was meddling. This point of view no doubt benefited the interests of some rather than others, just as the doctrine of State regulation similarly benefits some rather than others. But it was also based upon a strong dislike of the State setting itself up as a father. The classic rejection of this pretention occurs not in discussions of political economy but in *Areopagitica,* where Milton opposes any claim by the State to be the sole supplier of truths. Such a claim would condemn grown men to a "perpetual childhood of prescription." Milton's objection is a moral one: "Assuredly we bring not innocence into the world, we bring impurity much rather: that which purifies us is trial, and trial is by what is contrary."[6]

Milton was here attacking the doctrine which suggests that children are born innocent and learn corruption, and therefore asserts that each State has a duty to suppress heretical, blasphemous, obscene and untrue doctrines. Women, children, slaves, household servants, workers, soldiers,[7] must all be protected from such material. The Roman Catholic Church operates upon this protective principle, and so have most States, claiming that they are not merely the custodians of order, but of morality as well. The State, on this view, is a paternal institution which guides and cares for its subjects in exchange for their devoted obedience. It is further true that governments holding such views are often more solicitous of the welfare of the poor than their classical liberal opponents—the government of Charles I was, at least in its aspirations, a case in point. Such a doctrine fitted well into a patriarchal milieu—by which the landowner cared for the tenant, the officer saw to his men and his horses

6. *Selected Prose of John Milton,* Oxford, 1949, p. 290.
7. A selection of the kinds of people on behalf of whose tender minds censors have at various times claimed to operate.

before seeing to himself, and all of society was to be wrapped in mutual solicitude.

It is thus clear that modern liberalism, by virtue of its morality of public provision, has, with modifications, taken over some of the principles which in other centuries we would describe as conservative. The issue may be expressed in the formula State-provision versus self-provision, and the espousal of State-provision is perhaps the most important change that has taken place in the development of modern liberalism.

State-provision is supported partly by arguments from justice and partly by arguments—as we have noted—from freedom. Yet, if our interpretation of freedom is correct, the freedom argument is a mistake. Provision by the State of welfare and education does not necessarily promote freedom, and it may be positively inimical to it. Yet while the confident assertions of ideologies are often mistaken, there is usually a reason for their mistakes. And the reason why welfare is mistakenly assumed to be a means to freedom is that welfare is something *independently* supported. In other words, liberals would seek to promote welfare whether it conduced to freedom or not.

Modern liberalism, then, supports welfare irrespective of its bearing upon freedom. One reason for this emerges out of what we have called the suffering situation. Liberals seek to relieve generalized kinds of suffering, and it is plausible to argue that those who suffer are not free.

But we can find a more interesting reason why modern liberalism supports welfare if we extend the ends-means chain a little further. We have seen that, in liberal argument, welfare is a means to freedom. But what is a means to welfare? The classical liberal would immediately reply: "Self-help." His modern successor would shake his head and point to the handicaps which the poor endure. Hence he would advocate State provision, something which requires the development of new administrative and political techniques. And this extension of State regulation and provision can be presented as a necessity, for there is indeed no other way in which welfare can be provided in a modern State.

A clear grasp of this point not only bears directly upon the question of freedom; it also explains what we may call the paradox of simultaneous omnipotence and impotence of the people. It was the fashion not so long ago to talk of the "century of the common man." Democracy is now something almost universally supported because it allows the people, rather than the privileged few, to determine what governments should do. Yet, at the same time, each individual appears to be more and more impotent in the face of governmental control. What has happened is that whereas before many problems were things to be solved by some group of people organizing themselves, now all problems, having become social problems, can only be solved by putting pressure on the government to do something about them.

The significance of this situation is much clearer if we turn to those countries of the world which, in the jargon of liberal ideology, are called "underdeveloped." These countries have, even more strongly than others, the liberal conviction that the present time is "transitional." Once they had a stable past; sometime in the future they will again arrive at a stable industrialized point, but for the moment the most real thing about them is simply movement. This is, of course, pure illusion, and the expectation of some point of rest in the future merely utopian. Nevertheless, this conviction has imposed on these countries what we may call the politics of the gap. It provides a single overriding aim—that of industrialization—which has become a moral and national purpose. The condition of freedom in these countries is thought to be the closing of this gap.

The frenetic and impatient industrialization which has resulted is no doubt a matter of necessity; for where some western techniques have been introduced, they have created problems which can only be solved by further importation. Population increase due to medical advance is an obvious example. The solving of these problems requires enormous energy; there is the difficulty of understanding things which had previously been of no interest, and that of organizing and co-ordinating a national effort. What makes the difficulties even greater is a nationalist impatience to do everything quickly; the pace must be forced in the hope that the effort can then be relaxed. Now all of this is too much for individuals or for voluntary organizations. Each individual is weak and fallible. All agree that the gap must be closed, but there are many countervailing considerations—wanting to consume immediately, personal enmities, traditional rights, building up family or clan influence, simple laziness, and so on. Here in fact is the kind of situation which was uniquely rationalized by Rousseau's general will. In this situation individuals are perfectly prepared to be forced to be free, for they have, so to speak, invested their moral capital in the government as the only organizing center of the national effort. Once that is done, there quite genuinely need be no nonsense about democratic liberties or the counting of heads at elections.

The results are twofold. The first is bureaucratization, for it is only by means of an efficient hierarchy that difficult things can be regularly done. Judge and hangman, general and private, inquisitor and torturer—in all these cases, an unpleasant policy has been split into two or more operations. One person makes the decision, another merely obeys without having to take responsibility for the acts. There are, no doubt, a few enthusiasts who like to combine both jobs—monarchs who have carried out their own executions—but such enthusiasm cannot be relied upon as an institution. It is difficult not to describe this bureaucratic principle in ironic terms; but it must also be observed that without it any kind of administration would be impossible, and with it almost anything can be done unless the bureaucracy runs up against some kind of conscientious objection. The despotic implications of dividing the responsibility from the act are, of course, quite evident, which is the reason why the defense of superior orders is rejected in British courts as a defense against criminal charges.

A further difficulty of this device is that those who give the orders in a bureaucratic system are likely to live in a rarefied atmosphere. Especially if they are politicians, they are likely to succumb to dreams of national status and to live far from the life around them. They are, like most politicians, interested in the product, not the producing. They look at the industrial statistics and they set norms; they are unconcerned with the quality of life lived by the people, and the only happiness they are equipped to discern is a visible thing, measurable by acclaim or by some material result. They are like small new countries, where Philistines are perpetually trying to turn each artist, novelist or poet whom foreigners can be induced to admire into a national icon. The eternal symbol of such leaders must now be Mussolini, who swaggered around dreaming dreams of imperial prestige, misrepresenting the general will, and failing even to provide proper equipment for his soldiery.

Secondly, the politics of the national gap invests an enormous moral force in the State, an inappropriate and risky organ for such investment. Deposits are easily managed, withdrawals are almost impossible. For Locke, in describing governments as trusts, was being hopeful rather than descriptive. It may be true that the populace regards the government as an agent of its interests; but from the government's point of view, the people are agents of *its* interests. From a government's point of view, particularly in international affairs, regimentation and industrialization are very distinctly means to other ends; freedom is nice, but national strength and discipline are even nicer. Further, in any purposeful organization of the State, however temporary, new interests—both financial and emotional—arise in the land; they will not be easily dispossessed once the moment of fruition has come. Indeed, these interests will be among the forces making perfectly sure that it never does come, moving the future always a little further away. We may support this view by referring once more to Wittfogel's study of the development of technological bureaucracies into political despotisms.

The evidence on this subject and its ramifications are by now considerable. Among the more dramatic items is the manner in which purged communists, overawed precisely by this kind of moral authority claimed by the Soviet State, proceeded to accuse themselves and vilify an imaginary past. Yet even so, it is clear that this moral investment in the State is by no means a guileless submission to necessity. It is found among those modern liberals who seem positively nostalgic for some kind of national purpose, and who seem to imagine that unless we are all pulling together in some philanthropic national effort, then we must be given over to selfishness and apathy. It is found also among the young looking for moral causes, who are as ready to have the State supply them as any other agency.

The bearing of this on freedom is perfectly clear. A populace which hands its moral initiative over to a government, no matter how impeccable its reasons, becomes dependent and slavish. If the national tradition is in any case one of political dependence, then this will simply perpetuate the tradition. But even in countries which have a long tradition of individual enterprise and voluntary initiative, dependence is likely to increase; and just this charge has been made against the effects of the welfare State in Britain. It is certainly true that British migrants have, in some countries, a reputation for sitting passively around in reception centers until someone arranges a house and a job for them. A topical example of this kind of dependence would be the case of London's homeless—people ejected from dwellings after the Rent Act. As a political issue this was presented as one of victimization, and the only solution widely canvassed was that the authorities should hasten to provide houses for the homeless. Now it is at least possible that these people might, by co-operation, get credit facilities and build houses for themselves, something which has often been done in other countries. There would obviously be difficulties to surmount, but it is by now an almost automatic response that every problem is one to be solved by authorities; and it is liberalism which seeks, by a steady equalization of the circumstances of each individual, to make certain that no one except governments *can* initiate voluntary organizations; *all* political initiative must be that of the pressure group.

The changes in human behavior which we have been considering are not to be attributed solely or even primarily to modern liberalism. Yet it is preeminently liberalism which has accepted without much questioning the "necessities" on which those changes are based. Indeed, quite apart from ideology, there exists a genuine dilemma which has considerable bearing upon the future of free behavior. The politics of national purpose always poses the alternative of governmental organizations with the corollary of dependence and servitude, or on the other hand, allowing people to develop at their own pace and in their own direction, which for good or bad reasons is often found to be too slow. There is no evading this dilemma; and it is foolish to pretend that it does not exist. Modern liberalism, to the extent to which it recognizes the dilemma, attempts to evade it by aspiration. We must try, it would say, to keep governments democratically under our control and subservient to our interests. But the question of freedom, as we have considered it, is not at all a matter of interests. It is a question, not of what is done, but of how it is done and of who does it. And it will not be answered by cant about democratic vigilance. For people whose only recourse is to put pressure on the government will, when seriously frustrated, respond by pointless turbulence.

CHAPTER SEVEN

Conclusion

I. THE MORAL CHARACTER OF LIBERALISM

To MANY OF ITS CRITICS, liberalism is a thin and bloodless rationalism. The list of such critics is extremely varied. It includes many theologians, continental idealists, and artists like D. H. Lawrence whose battle cry is "Life!" In sophisticated conservative circles, it has been criticized as substituting the anonymous and antiseptic new town or suburban development for the warm, natural cohesion of the slums. And these charges have all been compounded by the fact that liberalism has attracted its full share of humorless prigs, people who love humanity, as the charge goes, but cannot stand their neighbors.

It is possible, especially with the help of the interests argument, to regard this line of criticism as no more than sentimental romanticism. Liberals can point to suffering as the reality of the slums, and ask pertinently whether such conditions are not an excessive price to pay in order that rich and jaded palates may enjoy the variety of the world.

We may begin to disentangle the issues arising from such an exchange of sentiments by considering the uses of a term which is an interesting example of the tactical realignments undergone by certain ideas. "Materialism" in philosophy indicates a metaphysical doctrine holding that the single ultimate constituent of reality is matter. One of the implications of this doctrine—though one which may also be held by people who are not materialists—is that at death, both body and soul (if such a thing is admitted) are dissolved. This implication, however supported, is clearly anti-Christian. Materialism has in the last few centuries been one of the main targets of attack by all the Christian Churches.

But materialism has also, in a manner typical of such philosophical words, gained a weaker meaning unrelated to metaphysics. It has come to describe a life devoted to the pursuit of material objects and advantages. The main use of this meaning has been to criticize those forms of capitalist behavior summed up in the concept of economic man. The Christian Churches have attacked this kind of materialism on two grounds: partly that it is ruthless and uncharitable, a selfish trampling over the interests of the powerless; and partly on the ground that it is a way of life which refuses to take seriously the religious mystery of the universe. Among the clearest examples of such criticism will be found in the two Papal Encyclicals devoted to the question of social justice, *De Rerum Novarum* and *Quadrigesimo Anno*.

Liberalism has on most occasions paid little attention to this kind of attack. It has done so for several reasons. For one thing the attack on materialism and what the Encyclicals refer to as "individualism" is largely directed at liberalism itself. The anti-materialist generally opposed natural rights and government by popular consent. The liberal response was to regard this attack as a manifestation of entrenched hostility and to reject the anti-materialist argument on grounds which were best stated by Marx: that anti-materialism is utopian rather than scientific. It appeals to employer and employee to get together in a friendly and Christian spirit to work out the practices of a just order. But this leaves the unjust order itself untouched; it relies upon fallible human goodwill: and eventually it came to be associated with the Fascist practices of the corporate State. For most liberals, then, the attack on materialism looked like nothing so much as a thin camouflage by which the privileged castigated demands for reform as "merely envious."

In recent decades, this situation has been changed by the extensive introduction of socialist measures in the working of most capitalist States. The consequence of these measures has been to bring many proletarians within the range of a more acquisitive way of life. The heroic, victimized proletarian has turned into the television viewer in the council house, and his enthusiasm for the class struggle has waned accordingly. A similar development has taken place in the Soviet Union, where the pursuit of material things has developed to a point where it threatens the working of the Soviet régime. The ironic consequence of this new situation is that Mr. Khrushchev, modern liberals, and the Christian Churches, are all aligned in calling for a more spiritual and dedicated attitude to life and work, and an end to materialist apathy.

We may make two observations about this chain of events, one intellectual, one political. The intellectual point is that the doctrine of materialism, as we find it in this propagandist use, is misconceived. The point cannot be that materialists are pursuing actual material objects as material objects and nothing else. The whole point about "keeping up with the Joneses," the acquisition of refrigerators and central heating, and the yearning to join the ranks of the two-car family is that these things are spiritual endeavors; each material object stands for something. We may not like what the objects stand for; we may reject this spirit and talk of empty lives devoted to nothing more than the maintenance of respectable appearances. But that is another matter.

The political significance of the attack on materialism lies in its attempt to stabilize a weakening internal situation. The message of the Encyclicals, and indeed of the Churches generally, is to accept the present status-structure of the community, turn away from a preoccupation with changing relative status, and concentrate on making the system work. What Mr. Khrushchev wants is a Russian populace which accepts the system and whose effort is turned "outward," concentrating upon the building of a Socialist future. The great political advantage of a single national objective such as war or industrialization is that it achieves exactly this effect. When such an objective either does not exist or loses its force, then exhortation, a poor substitute, is the only thing left.

The presence of modern liberals in this alignment is on the face of it not susceptible of the same explanation. For while Mr. Khrushchev and most Churches are to be found defending an established political order, modern liberals are not similarly committed. Yet their position is in fact exactly the same; for they belong to a movement which will collapse if the spirit of compassion should desert it. The sin of apathy is a version of selfishness; the apathetic lose their taste for reform, and become increasingly preoccupied with the advancement of themselves or their families.

If we observe that this passion for personal status is a kind of ambition, we shall recognize that materialism has always been a manner of life on which those in authority have wished to keep a tight rein. For it is their task to guide their followers away from the competitive preoccupations of status towards "getting on with the job." A faculty of professors will do little research if they are constantly struggling for position; and officers in an army are unlikely to achieve victory if their *predominant* interest is in competing with each other for promotion. Ambition has always been regarded as morally ambiguous; if it refers to the eagerness of those in the lower ranks then it has been thought to contribute to progress and widely encouraged. But if it is merely a thirst to enjoy the rights of the higher office, then it has been feared as destructive.

The impression that liberalism is a thin and narrow doctrine cannot therefore be attributed to materialism; partly because materialism itself is a confused description of an acquisitive way of life, and partly because modern liberals themselves are among its most relentless opponents.

We may, perhaps, come closer to explaining this impression if we distinguish, following T. E. Hulme,[1] between the classical and romantic views of life. This is a distinction capable of bearing very little weight, and we are concerned less with its usefulness than with its currency. For Hulme, the classicist was a man who believed that the capacities of man were limited, and that human development was the product of careful nurture by social and political institutions. It followed that, if we wish to maintain and advance civilization, we must treat established institutions with great care, and in particular control our own passionate impulses so that they do not weaken the social and political bonds which alone prevent a relapse into barbarism. The classicist believes that the institution of marriage, for example, must take precedence over the romantic involvements of particular married individuals. The consequences of this doctrine are conservatism in politics, and absolutism in ethics. Society is seen to be based upon a fairly rigid kind of differentiation. The sexes, for example, are functionally differentiated and must therefore expect to live different kinds of life. But each society also contains different classes of people, and for each class, a different range of experiences is appropriate.

In contrast, the romantic might be described, since Rousseau, as one who believes in the rights of feeling. Romanticism includes the belief that the capacities of men are unlimited—comparable, in Hulme's image, to a well rather than a bucket—and that they must be unchained from the bonds of social institution in order that each man may be truly himself—exactly what the classicist is afraid of. The romantic doctrine is appropriate to the young, and

1. T. E. Hulme, *Speculations,* London, 1924, p. 111.

169

to those extraordinary individuals who run away from home, endure poverty, collect a mistress or two, get married, make fortunes, and travel extensively—those who lead, as the saying is, a full, rich life.

The most likely political consequence of romanticism is liberalism; Hulme believed this, and, within the wide limits defining the two sets of ideas, he was largely right. For, as we have already observed, liberalism is implacably hostile to any notion of permanent natural differentiation between individuals. Women may be different from men, but, being equal, they must have as much access to the same experience as possible. Individuals may differ in skin color or racial membership, but must be allowed to live a decent (i.e. approved) life as soon as possible. And there can, of course, be no question of significant differences of life experience between aristocrat and laborer. All of this is simply another way of expanding the sentence "All men are born free" and elucidating the program implicit in "but everywhere they are in chains."

We may thus see one development of the rights of man doctrine in a new light. As first formulated, it was defended as a statement of those social conditions without which men would be unable to live the sort of life they wished. How exactly they *did* wish to live was not, short of criminality, of great concern to anyone. The doctrine was all rights and no consequences.

But, given the growth of a romantic view of experience, these rights might be seen as the necessary conditions of living "a full life"; and then, indeed, they would almost certainly seem deficient. For all of the victim classes, by definition, were being prevented from living this kind of life.

And if the romantic doctrine of a full life were to be brought into politics, then it would have to be standardized. Its specifications and general limits would have to be described. The experiences of individualists, and in general of the rich who supplied individualists in the largest numbers, must be abstracted so that they might be advanced as political demands. Nor could this ambitious project stop short at describing floorspace areas and the nutritional minima of the full life. It must also standardize spiritual experiences, like love, marriage, intellectual cultivation, and friendship. The vocabulary required for this set of specifications was to hand, in utilitarian doctrine. Friends satisfied social needs, marriage partners satisfied sexual and procreational needs, schools satisfied educational needs—which were the necessary conditions of many further installments of the rich, full life.

The romantic view of experience thus provides us with a generalized standard of the kind of life which ought to be lived by every human being upon the planet. It is a kind of life which is, in fact, lived by a minority of people mostly situated in the western world. Further, it is a kind of life which was not originally developed by those people in the pursuit of a general end, but which grew up out of the kind of people they were and the kinds of activity in which they happened to be interested. They happened to become interested, quite spontaneously, in science, logic, philosophy, technology and religion in such a manner as to produce western civilization.

The standardization of the notion of a full life cannot but result in a concern with comparative status. The individual is described, as it were, in the answers given on a form: What rights does he have? What kind of consumption does he enjoy? Which of his needs are satisfied? What experiences has he had? One can tick off the answers to these questions, and the blank responses supply a program. But any action taken in response to this kind of analysis is something which will be done for the wrong reasons; it will be done as a means to the end, which is the filling out of the form of the full life. This is a procedure which has both intellectual and practical defects.

We may take the practical defects first. The result of thinking and acting in this way is very frequently disappointment. Foreign travel, when undertaken as a status exercise, is no adventure and brings none of the promised "broadening of the mind"; it turns merely into a sterile exercise in tourism, endured at the time as an investment to be expended in conversation and boasting at a later date. Sexual experiences similarly undergo an instrumental transformation which renders them joyless; they are merely the materials of prestige. But these romantics do not merely seek prestige in the eyes of their neighbors. They suffer from a deep suspicion that they "haven't really lived." They want to feel the earth move, like Hemingway's heroine in *For Whom the Bell Tolls*. But meanwhile, as the various required experiences are undergone without quite yielding up their promise, they nourish the hope of possession by an ultimate experience. It may be anything from an *acte gratuit* to a religious conversion; from a sentimental love affair to a political passion in the midst of a crowd. What happens to actual individuals of course varies enormously, and some abandon, temporarily or permanently, this pursuit of spiritual status because they become genuinely involved in something else. But for many there remains a continual nagging anxiety, which is the only certain result of the conscious pursuit of prestige.

The intellectual defects result from the fact that human life is misdescribed if it is seen in terms of function, end, satisfaction, rights, and the rest of the rationalist vocabulary. The impression that a life seen in these terms is thin is therefore a sound apprehension that this account of human behavior is simply false. It is not true, for example, that a friendship between two people is fully described as a relationship in which each fulfills some need or needs of the other. In trying to understand this there is a strong temptation to become almost mystical; to point out that the whole is more than the sum of the parts, and that in listing the various functions fulfilled mutually by people is not to exhaust the subject matter. This at least makes us more aware of the subtleties of the question, but does not greatly advance our understanding. The mistake lies in subsuming all human relationships under the proprietorship of generic man, so that *all* human intercourse looks external.

A further consequence of self-consciousness about comparative status is the emotion of self-pity. Like all terms which rest upon the conception of "self," this emotion is difficult to define and its moral characteristics have seldom been deeply explored. The "self" involved in self-pity may concern an individual, his family, or, in any sense, his people—those for whom he weeps. Self-pity concentrates the mind upon those elements of the comparison which show the self at a disadvantage, and the cause of this disadvantage must in some way be externalized. Each supposed cause is praised or blamed; irrelevant moral characterization runs wild. The result may even be animism: rainstorms or other natural phenomena become "just the sort of thing that would happen to me." Self-pity is sentimental and passive, and it necessarily distorts our understanding of our own nature and that of our environment. It is an extremely common emotion, and in popular folklore is thought to be healed if one follows the injunction to "count your blessings."

Self-pity is clearly an important emotion in modern political life, for few groups are entirely prepared to accept and make the best of their current situation. It will be found in colonial peoples blaming their troubles on the colonial power. It will be found in any of the victim classes of the suffering situation—though its presence, of course, is not inevitable, but is the result of acceptance of certain moral and political views. It is also to be found currently among adolescents blaming their parents for their troubles; and among middle classes who feel their status threatened because manual workers are paid more or domestic servants hard to come by. It results in a persistent, dogged clinging to some conception of the status rights of the group, and in a considerable lack of realism in understanding social and political affairs.

In a world which is loud with the cries and arguments produced by self-pity, those who are receptive to the arguments will undergo the related emotion of self-reproach. And it is self-reproach which is an important determinant of many liberal points of view. For one thing, just as the self involved in self-pity may be a collective self, so also may the self in self-reproach. Thus one may reproach oneself not only for acts which one chose oneself to commit, but also for acts which were done in one's name by more or less representative political bodies; or for acts done by people long dead.

An example of the latter case would be the European anti-colonialist who reproaches himself for the entire colonial policy of his country, a man fruitlessly concerned to reproach himself with what "we" once did to "them." The result of this kind of feeling is the creation of a curious intellectual entity which we may call category guilt. Thus, as a political pamphlet put it, the concern of British policy (towards Jamaica, in this instance) should be "to repay the debt we owe them for long years of exploitation by now helping to develop the economies of their countries, and make possible a decent life for them there." There may indeed be good reasons for following such a policy, but they are not to be found in conceptions of moral credit and moral debt.

A similar kind of self-reproach arises out of the various classes to which British liberals consider themselves as belonging. Examples of such classes are the white race, Britain as a political entity, the Commonwealth, the North Atlantic Treaty Organization, and the Free World. Each of these classes includes political authorities or social groups which act in an illiberal manner. Whites in South Africa maintain apartheid; American money supports Chiang Kai-Shek and similar Asian régimes; NATO toys with the idea of admitting Franco's Spain and provokes Russian hostility; Britain engages in the Suez operation. All of these political acts invite liberals to feelings of self-reproach. They belong to these groupings, and they wish to dissociate themselves from them. They are the innocent part of these guilty entities.

The development of this particular complex moral sensibility appears now to have coalesced into a distinguishable political movement in Great Britain, a movement which we may describe as moral nationalism. This movement gains most mass support from the program that Britain should abandon her independent nuclear strength in order to give a moral lead to other nations; it is found in the political views of Sir Charles Snow, and has been summed up in the conviction that "our country's role is to be exemplary rather than powerful."[2] Like many moral movements, this one involves a withdrawal into inner moral certainties, with a consequent refusal to take external events seriously. As a political policy, for example, moral nationalism assumes that politicians in other countries will be moved to imitate the example which has been given; if this factual assumption were to be proved wrong, however, moral nationalists would not hesitate. They would still be concerned to do the right thing anyway. Moral nationalism is thus one more maneuver in the long tradition of devices which are thought to do away with politics, seen as the selfish exercise of power.

Moral nationalism extends far beyond the emotions of self-reproach in which it is grounded. But both self-reproach and moral nationalism arise out of a desire for a kind of purification—a repaying of moral debts and the wiping clean of a very dirty slate. It is the desire to begin anew, and in a world loaded with vengeful passions and bitter, unreasonable conflicts of interest, the only way to begin anew is to make concessions.[3] One thing especially is important: the principle that one must not act except for motives which are both pure and known to be pure. Now, as far as actual political life is concerned, this is a quite impossible principle, one which, if taken seriously, would lead first to total inhibition of political action and very quickly to the dismemberment of the inhibited State. It is simply not a possible way of carrying on in the world. We can find the effect of influences of this kind in the British attitude towards Nazi Germany during the thirties, when many were strongly disposed to justify Hitler's policy as the legitimate response to the victimization of Versailles. Similar emotions arose in connection with Nasser over the nationalization of the Suez Canal, and they still arise in liberal attitudes towards the Soviet Union—moving from a legitimate attempt to discover what the Russians think and why, to a remorseless determination to accept blame for the situation and thus exculpate others. This may perhaps be regarded as a generous moral attitude; but it is the product of a moral fantasy which from many points of view is politically dangerous. For it constitutes the use of

2. Christopher Martin in a talk in *The Listener*, 5 April 1962.
3. Cf. Freud's analysis of the Jewish superego in *Moses and Monotheism*.

moral terms as a device to evade certain facts; an attempt to cloud the significance of what *has* happened by attending to whether or not it *ought to have* happened.

We arrive, then, at something which looks like a contradiction. For we have argued that liberalism constitutes an evasion of moral understanding; and yet in moral nationalism we find that liberals have constructed a world which is fastidiously moral in the sense that everything in it is subject to the rigorous application of praise or blame. The way out of this contradiction lies in the notion of the suffering situation. Liberals have discarded moral judgment and substituted technical thinking when they consider the victim classes; but on "us" they have concentrated the full battery of moral examination. It is, indeed, a false and misleading kind of moral understanding, but it is undeniably moral.

II. THE BALANCE OF LIBERALISM

A concern with truth has long been a characteristic of western civilization. Liberalism arose when this passion for truth took on a new intensity and many new directions. Truth has no gaps, and a concern with it is likely to make us disputatious and quarrelsome. There is no more liberal figure than the muckraker, the man who dredges up facts that everyone else—and especially the powerful—would much rather forget. Liberal political argument has always defended passionately the work of those individuals who from the beginning of the modern era challenged the mistakes of orthodoxy. Not, indeed, that such individuals cared very much for truth in the abstract. Nor were they very much different from other men in the ordinary conduct of their lives. But in a number of fields, in religion, in science, in exploration, they were capable of pursuing the urge to find out with enormous persistence and ingenuity. And they were enterprising *as individuals*, alone or organizing themselves into groups for the pursuit of profit or the salvation of their souls, creating new political forms even within the framework of established authority.

Yet liberalism is subject to a number of illusions. In spite of its deep involvement with truth, it is, like any other ideology, prone to subject its view of the way things are to a hopeful picture of the way it would be nice for things to be. We have examined a number of these illusions: the belief in a rational harmony, the illusion of ultimate agreement, and, perhaps most central of all, the idea that will and desire can ultimately be sovereign in human affairs, that things will eventually pan out the way we want them to. The issue that arises within liberalism is often one between truth on the one hand and improvement or utility on the other. This is simply to restate the persistent dichotomy which we have already detected in the liberal mind.

How can we explain this dichotomy? Only by recognizing clearly that a passion for truth, carried beyond convenience, is likely to provoke the most violent social opposition and political repression. For truth assaults consciences, disrupts vested interests, outmodes profitable practices and undermines the myths and illusions which sustain powerful institutions and corporations. Those who, in any field, are driven on to discover what is the case, who wish to conduct experiments or sail unknown seas, must therefore make their way in a largely hostile world. They can only do so by offering bargains and making alliances—offering vastly greater convenience in the future as an incentive to accept inconvenience in the present. The men of enterprise could offer the by-products of their work: the silver of the Indies for three ships with convict crews; immunity from Papal regulations for the opportunity to assert unorthodox religious truth; inventions and riches in return for the opportunities of enterprise.

More generally, to encourage others and to give themselves courage, the new men could offer the vision of a new world, never more than a couple of generations away, in which life would be richer, more comfortable and more rational. The fear of change and instability could be allayed by the promise of a point of rest some time in the future; and meanwhile installments of improvement were steadily provided.

This kind of utopianism arose out of the belief that setting forth on a voyage of discovery in search of truth was a finite enterprise; and truth was a finite collection of facts. If so, it was not entirely foolish to imagine that one day the search would come to an end. It was, in any case, explicitly limited to the things of this world. The advance of science depended on lulling the custodians of religion into the belief that the scientific spirit could be limited, and propagandists of the movement—most notably Bacon and Locke—were keen to insist upon the limits of natural reason. They did so with perfect sincerity, for their belief in reason implied both the possibilities and the limits of knowledge. From their day to this, we have seldom been free of the belief that the moment of imminent fruition is upon us; that all the important or relevant knowledge has been garnered, and that only the job of application to improving the world remains.

To a large extent, the preoccupation with utopia was the result of fear. In times of high self-confidence, when the exhilaration of truth-seeking was upon men, and when improvement was perceptible, men could even contemplate the indefinite continuance of this process; out of this self-confidence came the doctrine of progress. But the kind of social condition in which criticism and truth-seeking are regularly prosecuted can also induce the fear that things have gotten out of control—a fear which evangelists are especially prone to encourage. All this, it is said, comes of man trying to ape God. There is no one so repentant as a sorcerer's apprentice who suddenly realizes his experiments in sorcery may be the death of him.

From the alternation of these two clusters of emotions emerge what we have called the salvationist and the libertarian strands of liberalism. When fear is in the ascendant, we may expect an overriding concern with security, harmony, equality;[4] exhilaration will lead to a stress on freedom, enterprise and competition.

The shifting balance of liberalism is also affected by the fact that it has always encouraged the entry of outsiders into its benefits. These outsiders stand some distance outside the community. They are victims in the suffering situation. They are the people described in the inscription on the Statue of Liberty. They are a non-possessing class, though what it is they do not possess depends upon the terms of current political controversy. And they have been given a moral dimension by the use of the Marxist concept of alienation. Liberal politicians have always called on their support as foot-soldiers in a steady assault upon the entrenched positions of "reaction." These outsiders are of two kinds. In liberal countries, they are largely those classes who, for many centuries after the development and fruition of liberalism, continued to live in a thoroughly traditional manner, and who were only driven from their shelters by the ferocious inroads of industrial development. They are the European working classes. In the twentieth century, a larger and even more significant group of outsiders has appeared upon the scene—the entire populations of non-European countries, who are enthusiastic about the products

---

4. A policy of radical equalization only makes sense if we think we have reached the end of the road, when rewards need have no relation to contribution. One cannot cut the cake until it is baked. One may also suspect that a wide distribution of benefits morally involves everyone in the economic and social system; it distributes not only the gilt, but also the guilt.

of the European world, but who have a very hazy notion of the moral characteristics on which that world is based. But to talk in these terms necessarily gives a crude result, for we find in all the classes of outsiders many individuals with a liberal moral character, just as we find among European liberals of long pedigree many in whom fear of change is the dominant emotion.

What is at stake in the shifting balance between fear and exhilaration, between truth and utility, is the fate of truth itself. For improvement will be cultivated under any circumstances, but the moral character of truth-seeking is one which did not always play a prominent part in the world's affairs, and could return to obscurity. Whenever men have, in recent history, attempted to snatch at political salvation, it is truth which has always been the first casualty, since, of all the causes of human turmoil, facts are the most obvious, and therefore the first to be suppressed. The more we dream of utopia, the less we can bear to face our imperfections.

The psychological relations between truth and improvement, between the way things are and the way we would like them to be, between fact and value, are no doubt extremely complicated. They differ from one individual to another. One man may be stimulated by the hope of improvement into an extremely vigorous rapport with reality, whilst another may be drawn further and further into fantasy. There will certainly be many occasions when a deep involvement with our own hopes and desires will lead us to miscalculate; and this is particularly true in moral and political affairs, where other people know well how they may play upon our hopes and fears.[5]

Again, a concern with the truth about our own character and desires—a concern with moral truth—very considerably affects the things we value. We are, as individuals, liable to get caught up in pretenses whose charm vanishes at the touch of reality. Whole nations may be similarly deluded: Mussolini's armies awoke from their dreams of imperial grandeur in the Western Desert.

---

5. Modern totalitarian States, for example, have perfected a technique of playing on the hopes of democratic peoples at precisely those moments when they are being most aggressive, e.g. "We are stretching out a hand of friendship to the people and Government of the United States. We should like to pool our efforts with the United States Government and with other governments to solve all ripe international problems, to safeguard peace on earth." This from a Russian statement at precisely the moment of a large Russian arms build-up in Cuba. (*Times*, 12.9.62.)

But even while the pretense lasts, those involved will suffer the anxieties of imperfect imitation.

We may at any given time measure the vitality of liberalism by looking to the balance between truth and improvement; by looking to see if we find a tough-minded recognition of the facts, and a consequent rejection of the comforting, the face-saving, the prestigious, the boastful, and the unrealistically hopeful: looking, in fact, at the strength of political and moral fantasy. We shall always find some hope of release from the inevitable ferment which truth creates. In this kind of salvationism, we shall recognize a radical misunderstanding both of politics and of truth-seeking: the belief that politics will put an end to the necessity for politics, and that the acquisition of knowledge will put an end to the search for truth. And if salvationism is strong, we may well suspect that the balance of liberalism is in danger.

There are, currently, a number of indications of this kind. One is a widespread preoccupation with national prestige. Another is a nostalgia for great causes, often part of the moral débris left by great wars. But perhaps the most interesting of these indications and the one which nourishes the greatest hope of salvation is the idea that the final task before us is the rapid improvement of the "underdeveloped" countries. Certainly this is the most widespread source of modern political fantasy. The whole concept of "underdevelopment" is, of course, one which must be treated with great wariness. It lumps together a most heterogeneous collection of peoples and States, in a manner which tempts us to treat this similarity as the most crucial fact about them. It not only describes these States; it suggests a policy for them. And, to justify this moral imperative, liberals have attributed to the underdeveloped countries a curious kind of moral innocence. The under-nourished are set up as judges of our behavior.

Liberals at the present time find themselves poised between hope and fear. The hope arises from man's increasing command over nature, and is nourished by the realization that the domestic opponents of liberalism have either been extinguished or converted. The fear is symbolized by the possibility that before we quite enter into the comfortable kingdom of universal self-realization, we shall all be blown up. But both the hope and the fear are salvationist emotions; both are alien to the passion for truth which has long infused the liberal mind. It is salvationism which lies behind the target-setting and loin-girding of contemporary political discussion; and the habit of exhortation is so strong that we seem to imagine that every problem can be solved by resolving to do better. But the case of truth is like that of freedom and that of happiness: we cannot will ourselves to love it. We will not affect the fate of truth by making resolutions to face the facts and exhorting others to do likewise; but we may affect its fate by trying to understand why such resolutions fail.

INDEX

Index

Milton, John, 66, 155; *Areopagitica*, 139, 160
Moderation, 25
Modern liberalism, 96–97, 159–60
Moore, Dudley, viii
Moore, Thomas, 63
Moral character, 68
Moral disagreement, 75
Moral experience, 61–70
Moral identity, 48
Moral knowledge, 69, 74
Moral life, 65–70; legislative view of, 67; teleological view, 66–67
Moral nationalism, 173–75
Moral philosophy: imperative element in, 64–65; kinds of, 64–65; modern, 74
Moral principles, 75; utilitarian treatment of, 62–63
Moral problem, 68
Moral stupidity, 106–7
Muckraker, 175
Mussolini, Benito, 163, 178
Mysticism, vii

Nasser, Gamel Abdel, 174
National disorientation, xii
National emergency, free reaction to, 146–47
Nationalism, 59, 125; and freedom, 153–58
National prestige, preoccupation with, 179
Naturalistic fallacy, 117
Natural religion, 93
Natural rights, 2, 77
Nazism, 156
Needs, doctrine of, 41–42, 46, 91–99, 134; and children, 95; and conception of generic man, 99; needs as imperative form of desire, 41; permitting of substitutes, 97; propaganda function of, 98; vs. desire, 91–92; as way of discriminating between conflicting desires, 95
Negative definition, 94, 101
Neustics, 64

"New liberalism," vii
Nihilism, 59
Nixon, Richard M., 71
Nostalgia, 179
Nowell-Smith, P. H., 63–64

Oakeshott, Michael Joseph, 27
Oath, 26–27
Obedience, 54, 55
Object, of desire, 35–36
Oppressors, 8
Orthodoxy, 139–40, 150
Ostrich class, 109
Outsiders, 177–78

Pacifism, 9
Paine, Thomas, 34, 37
Pantheism, 48
Papal Encyclicals, 167, 168
Paradox of freedom, 11–12
Pascal, Blaise, 35
Peace, 24, 25
Péguy, Charles, vii
Periclean Funeral Oration, 145–46
Pericles, 150
Phrastics, 64
Plato: on cooperation, 147; on courage, 146; discussion of justice, 52; doctrine of goodness of philosophical life, 67; on independence, 151; on justice, 64; reason and, 22; treatment of democracy, 29
Policies, logic of, 21–22, 23
Policy of self-preservation, 26
Political discourse, 87
Political freedom, 155–56
Political maxims, 121–22
Political philosophy, and nature of man, 19–20
Political stability, 3
Political technology, 5, 62, 79–90
Politicians: as calculators, 86; responsibilities of, 82–85

185

This book is set in Minion, a typeface designed by Robert Slimbach specifically for digital typesetting. Released by Adobe in 1989, it is a versatile neohumanist face that shows the influence of Slimbach's own calligraphy.

This book is printed on paper that is acid-free and meets the requirements of the American National Standard for Permanence of Paper for Printed Library Materials, z39.48-1992.♾

Book design by Louise OFarrell,
Gainesville, Florida

Typography by Graphic Composition, Inc.,
Athens, Georgia

Printed and bound by Worzalla Publishing Co.,
Stevens Point, Wisconsin